ANDREA PALLADIO
And the Winged Device

ANDREAS PALLADIVS VICENTINVS.

PORTRAIT BY PAOLO VERONESE.

ANDREA PALLADIO

And the Winged Device

A PANORAMA PAINTED IN PROSE AND
PICTURES SETTING FORTH THE FAR-FLUNG
INFLUENCE OF ANDREA PALLADIO,
ARCHITECT OF VICENZA, ITALY, 1518-1580,
ON ARCHITECTURE ALL OVER THE WORLD,
FROM HIS OWN ERA TO THE PRESENT DAY

by James Reynolds

ILLUSTRATED WITH DRAWINGS BY THE
AUTHOR AND WITH PHOTOGRAPHS

CREATIVE AGE PRESS, INC., NEW YORK

55

To

R U S S B O R O U G H

Blessington

County Wicklow

Ireland

THE FIRST HOUSE IN THE PALLADIAN STYLE TO
CAPTURE MY IMAGINATION. ALL THE YEARS OF MY
LIFE IT HAS HELD FIRST PLACE IN MY INTEREST.

To build a shelter against the elements was man's first concern. After the cave came four walls and a roof. Down the centuries followed various enrichment; the simple basic forms, however, remain.

Andrea Palladio

PREFACE

It has always seemed to me a strange, almost incredible, state of affairs that so little is known about the life of Andrea Palladio. So few clear glimpses have we of the daily round in the life of this extraordinarily talented architect, whose life span encompassed the years 1518–1580, that we must look to churches, buildings, houses, and bridges to form a mental picture of this man as he must have walked, talked, and had his being.

Certainly no man was ever more articulate in giving forth his talent to posterity. Each building speaks, whether in the manner of the magnificently sweeping Villa Trissino at Meledo, acknowledged the world over as one of the grandest architectural conceptions of all time, or the engagingly simple, symmetrical Villa Pisani at Montagnana. This Villa, of which only the central block with its pleasantly cool cut-under room beneath the Doric portico was ever finished, has been the nucleus for half the pillared and porticoed houses south of the Mason–Dixon line in America.

About the country houses designed by Andrea Palladio there hovers an air of tranquillity, of lightness and grace, a mark of great style and dignity. One of their most signal advantages is the fact that houses in the Palladian taste seem to settle comfortably into the landscape of any

countryside, no matter on what continent. This fact has been proven countless times, for every civilized country in the world is graced by buildings
or houses either direct copies of, or influenced by, the designs of Andrea
Palladio.

When one considers the vast amount of work turned out by the
master himself and by the legion apprentices who surrounded him like a
school of cadets in the last few years of his life, as ill health and partial
blindness plagued him to the point of madness, it is odd to find that no
contemporary chronicler felt the urge to record the life journey of this
brilliant man. According to letters in the archives of the Pisani family of
Venice, he was an intensely interesting conversationalist and a mathemati-
cian of great knowledge. In the era that knew Palladio's conversations, the
power to prove mathematical problems was regarded as wholly admirable,
even smacked a bit of miraculous powers and a kinship with the divine
inhabitants of Olympus.

So much of Palladio's life is obscured by the mist of time that
many tales have formed about his name which we must take only as con-
jecture. Believe them or believe them not, as we wish.

It has been said by divers historians, and deduced from allusions
in letters written by Palladio to friends and patrons in later life, that he
shipped on a small sailing vessel bound from Venice to Athens when he
was not yet twenty years old. One point, which may be only coincidence
but assumed major proportions later, is that the sailing vessel on which
Andrea Palladio was said to have worked his way to the Pireas was loaded
with fantastically formed shells from the shores of the Adriatic Sea. These
were consigned to a rich merchant whose country house was being completed near Delphi. The shells were to be used to adorn the walls of a
grotto in a style then much in favor. A *designa fantastico* for a *grotto di
Nettuno*. Later in his life Palladio used the shell motif in many strange
and beautiful forms, as well as the heroic figure of Neptune crowned with
sea flowers and branched coral, trident in hand. Often he used the God
of Ocean to top the apex of a pediment, as in the fabulous galaxy of gods
and demigods ornamenting the glorious façade of the Villa Giovanelli, a
seventeenth century villa using portico and statues from an earlier Palladian house. It is within the realm of possibility that the young enthusiastic and impressionable artist from dusty Vicenza saw the grotto with its
shell-garlanded walls and forever after remembered his youthful reaction

fold over

to its quality as a striking piece of design. In his splendid chapter on ornament in Vitruvius, Palladio says, "The undulations of the lip of a sea shell may carry out the curve of an arch or intensify the apex of a pediment to fine effect; the bowl of the shell may cradle the head of a ram, an ape, a Bacchus, or any grotesque or monster used as relief."

We know conclusively, of course, that Palladio journeyed to Rome and was so entranced by the soaring pillars and pediments of the ruins of the Caesars that he borrowed measuring gear and spent many hot, steaming weeks through a Roman summer taking exact measurements of these marble monuments to Victory and the pagan deities. Palladio is said to have been sixteen at this time. Assuming his journey to Athens and the shell-encrusted grotto to be true, this interlude among the ruins of classic Greece would be after he had been deeply influenced by Vitruvian Rome. One has no idea how long he remained in Greece or how widely he may have traveled while he was there.

The detail most used by Palladio in all manner of buildings he called his "winged device." Actually this reference is to the window that has become synonymous with the name of Palladio down the years. As time went on, however, this immensely versatile man found many more ways of expressing the quality of "lift" and airiness that he so much admired. Keystones over windows became winged. Arched doorways sprang into being, full winged as the Victory of Samothrace. Colonnades threw crescent-shaped arms in a gesture of welcome from either side of the main bulk of the house. Drawings for pillared porticos, as in the Villa Giovanelli, were altered from the usual straight line and given wings, imparting an indescribable quality of grace to the whole frontage.

There have been detractors of even an architect as universally admired as Andrea Palladio has been for the five centuries since he gave a rare and distinctive style to the world. No artist who ever lived and distinguished himself in any field escapes the forked tongue, the tongue that differs. Some say Palladio designed "warehouses," vast barracks in which rich collectors stored rare furniture and whatever treasures of art they could glean from the world, by fair means or foul. In some cases I agree, or at least I see their point. I happen to like big houses with huge, high rooms. I look for considered wall spaces wherein tall, wide windows let onto sweeping views of wooded countryside, mountain ranges, grass-floored valleys or the ever changing sea. Living in houses is a state of mind. A quality in a given house may be perfection to one person, that same quality anathema to another. Very often I visit a house and immediately the sense creeps upon me that my hosts are *in* but not *of* the house they inhabit. For any kinship with the rooms they or a decorator have built around their hearthstone, they might as well live in the middle of Pennsylvania Station. The coldness of a house does not stem from mitered stone staircases, resounding corridors, or the many-windowed frontages built by Palladio or his admirers, Inigo Jones, William and Robert Adam, William Kent, Sir John Vanbrugh, Colin Campbell, Richard Castle, Thomas Jefferson, and others. A great architect builds a house in a given style for clients who profess to react so pleasantly to that style that they yearn to establish themselves within its walls. From then on it is up to them to create such beauty and comfort that the architectural features of the house are enhanced tenfold.

It is this fusion of warmth of personality and taste of the owner that makes the famous houses all over the world. Recall the legion times you have heard enthusiasms the like of, "I saw the most wonderful old house in Dublin, such mantelpieces and Georgian plaster ceilings." Or perhaps, "I stayed at a small Palladian house near Bath this summer. The view from the colonnaded terrace across the town toward Royal Crescent is superb. And the high cube-shaped rooms are hung with red, green, and yellow brocade. I've never seen handsomer." Pilgrimages are continuously on the march visiting the houses designed by Thomas Jefferson, "after Palladio," in Virginia. My favorite is Poplar Forest, designed and built by Jefferson in a forest a few miles from Charlottesville, as "a retreat from my too eager friends, where I may find the solitude and peace denied me at my second White House, Monticello." In this pavilion Jefferson captured the perfection of Villa Capra, in miniature.

Almost without exception in the finished buildings that remain standing, in whatever state of preservation, as well as the published designs for houses and churches marked "not executed," the winged device is traceable in curving colonnades, arched recesses across the front of the central mass, or series of wings diminishing in scale. Frequently the effect is of a crescent or three-quarters circle. All this gives tremendous lift, a pleasing sense of lightness and perfect balance to the frontage, no matter how large or formal the completed façade may be.

In 1570, Palladio finished compiling a vast treatise on his views on architecture. This veritable *magnum opus* had taken thirty years to polish to the remarkable state of clarity of observation which is the most distinguishing feature of the book. *I Quattro Libri dell' Architettura* was first printed in Venice. Reissued many times, the book has found its way into all civilized parts of the world.

To Vicenza is accorded the honor of being the birthplace of Andrea Palladio, and it is in Vicenza that his finest buildings rise. On a gaunt, lonely, wind-swept hill a few miles outside of the town looms one of the first—some say *the* first—of the large country villas designed in the grand style by Palladio. Villa Capra, usually referred to as Villa Rotonda, has been used as a model for many world famous buildings. Inigo Jones copied it almost exactly in England as a countryseat in the classic taste for the Honorable John Fane. Mereworth Castle, the house is called, and is, today, in a beautiful state of preservation. Again Villa Capra rears its handsome head in the Administration Building at the University of Virginia. Thomas Jefferson, who designed this building, called it The Rotonda. The name remains to designate one of the most beautifully articulated buildings in America today.

Ireland, England, Scotland, and America all share outstanding examples of houses and buildings in Palladio's style. Of the countries on the continent of Europe, Sweden, Poland, and Hungary derive town palaces and country houses, built by noble landowners, straight from Palladio's Italian villas. In Austria the general ground plan and arrangement of a central mass and wings is wholly or nearly obliterated by encrustations of baroque and rococo embellishment. Swags of silk belling from the grasp of chubby cupids, wreaths and garlands of flowers and fruit and curlicues, and foliations galore. All this detracts from the considered proportions wherein wide windows, a grandly executed pediment, and beautifully grouped soaring columns complete the Palladian picture at its best.

Saxony and Bavaria enjoyed a veritable orgy building sylvan palaces for electors and grand dukes during the years from 1695 to 1760. Very often these ornate pavilions were one and one-half stories in height. However intricate in carved and gilded detail the interiors of these bijoux might be—and faïence and mirrored ornamentation reached bewildering heights in some of them like the Amalienburg Schloss—the general Palladian plan of central mass with curved wings often embacing ornamental fountains and reflecting lagoons, was carefully adhered to.

In designing country houses, it is often said, Palladio began with Villa Capra and ended with Villa Maser. Elevations for over ninety important projects are recorded between the completion of these two houses. About sixty are known to have been partly or entirely finished according to plan.

Giacomo Leoni compiled a book on the architecture of Andrea Palladio with notes by Inigo Jones. In this volume Leoni says: "Albeit humbly born, this star, in consideration of the honors he did his native city, Vicenza, was made free of same and received into the body of the nobility."

His friend and patron, Giangiorgio Trissino, describes Palladio in this manner: "Face dark. Eyes fiery. Dress rich. His appearance that of a genius."

It is sometimes said of a singularly gifted man that he is for the ages. It may be very rightly said of Andrea Palladio of Vicenza; it is true to an amazing degree. There is no school of architecture but has reflected his personality in some manner.

Never have I been one to try to inflict my taste, in any of the many branches of the arts that I admire, on the consciousness of another. It never works out. Recriminations follow, nine times out of ten. If a person asks my opinion on painting, sculpture, furniture, architecture, I give it to him. My taste is considered drastic and my advice on these matters difficult to fulfill. My views on houses and the manner in which to live in them startles the majority. Mine is the European viewpoint, for I have lived most of my life in various countries, Italy, Austria, and Ireland. America possesses many startlingly beautiful old houses. Practically every state in the Union cherishes a distinctive style of architecture: the Georgian, a derivation of Georgian known as American Colonial, and the Greek Revival. Another rather stark classic gesture is called Federal. In each of these derivations the salient feature is some version of the pediment and the portico and even into houses known as Victorian, Hudson River Bracketed, and McKinley, creeps the Palladian window.

STARTED
VICENZA, ITALY
APRIL 12, 1946

FINISHED
CASTLE DAVAN
COUNTY DONEGAL
OCTOBER 20, 1947

CONTENTS

CONTENTS

LIST OF PHOTOGRAPHS

BOOK I.

VICENZA

VILLA·BORONINI

VICENZA

A light breeze stirred the *pilo* trees along the river Rerone, winding its amber shallows around the foot of steep, assertive Monte Berico. A league or more away the tawny walls of Vicenza rose sharply from the undulating plain that stretched away from this small city on all sides. If not precisely a city of the plain, Vicenza looked off and away across roughly plowed fields and small copses of olive trees and stunted hazelnut trees to imperious Venice, rising like gleaming, creamy alabaster forty kilometers to the west. In all the rich province of Vicenza in the area known as Venetia no more prosperous city had its being, except only Venice itself.

On this day in April, 1518, all was hurry and the sharp ringing cries of an early market within the walls of Vicenza. For it was a very particular day in the lives of the townsmen and the rapidly assembling *contadini* who, dressed in their bright and shining best clothes, were frantically trying to catch the eyes of buyers. All produce, cattle, pigs, and fowl, had to be disposed of before the procession of the Madonna of the Salute started out from the cathedral on the annual pilgrimage up the craggy cart track leading to the portals of the church of Madonna del Monte, on Monte Berico. This procession was a gift of the Venetian Doge. Each year in the month of April, a party of sixteen Venetian youths arrived in Vicenza with an escort and an effigy of the bejeweled ivory Madonna of the Salute. After mass had been said in the cathedral, the procession started on its long arduous walk up the mountain. Borne on a litter, draped with stiff vermilion brocade, the Madonna of the Salute seemed to float on her fiery cloud above the shoulders of her litter-bearers.

Three persons, who in the ordinary way would never have missed this spectacle, were absent today. This eagerly awaited day, when the wondrously blue and silver Madonna del Monte received the patron Madonna of Venice under her shadowed portals, made drowsy and fragrant by latticed spirals of incense.

Three persons who, at the very moment the procession wended its way across the hot piazza accompanied by the metallic clamor of cathedral bells, were breathing sighs of relief. One perhaps more deeply than the other two. This was Emilia Magini, who had just given birth to a fine man-child. To the clearly heard music of cathedral bells. Wild and a shade discordant, perhaps, but somehow, Emilia felt, a benediction and a portent of future good fortune. Emilia smiled sleepily into the sun-bronzed face of her husband, Pietro, as he bent over her. He smiled too, a proud and rather boastful smile, and told her to go to sleep; he and the old midwife Giulia would tend the boy. Had Emilia Magini, wife to Pietro the stonemason, known to what eternal renown her small son would someday rise as one of the greatest architects of all time, perhaps she would have slept even more soundly. Dreaming of high Roman columns, shimmering pediments and peristyles and ascending terraces whereon the great nobles of Venice, yea

4

the entire world, walked in sunlight. Dreaming, she would have seen long shadows cast by the setting sun, and murmurous starlit nights, when a full moon rose above sea or mountain to turn the sweeping proportions of Palladian palaces to the quality of white jade.

This architect "in embryo" was christened Andrea, because the day of his birth was the festival of a most popular saint, Andrea, as well as the day chosen for the procession to Monte Berico. It is recorded that the full name given to the boy was Giovanni Andrea Magini. Just when Giovanni Andrea adopted the name of Palladio is not known. Some historians say that the surname Palladio was first spelled Paladio, which he took from one of the many names held by his lifelong friend and patron, Giangiorgio Trissino.

The fact remains that when Andrea set out for Venice and Rome in his fifteenth year he was signing himself Andrea Palladio, ignoring his given name Giovanni, which he never used. It would seem by this that the man Trissino, who was to become so fine an influence in Andrea's life in the role of inspiring friend, entered the picture early on.

There is a story, told to me in Rome, which illustrates in an entertaining manner how early in life Andrea became absorbed in balance, scale, and proportion, always outstanding qualities in his chosen field of architecture. Primarily, Andrea was a creator. He designed buildings to suit his own ideas, and carried those ideas to brilliant conclusion. Frequently we hear of his being affronted by an object which he considered bulky, unwieldy, and ill-designed. In his own mind, at least, he would always put this error right. Hence the story of the pompous judge traveling from Venice to his country villa beyond Vicenza.

The day was midsummer, it had been an arid season in the Venetia, the flies were brutal, and life seemed a dull affair to young Andrea as he lounged about the piazza in his native Vicenza. More than anything else, he wanted to find a shaded patch where he might curl up and take a nap. He loped about the edges of the piazza and snorted in anger; each place he coveted was occupied by a snoring sleeper. As he turned away toward the portals of the cathedral, his temper was ragged. He seemed to have lost the desire to sleep. He would spend the afternoon in the shade of the cathedral porch, carving out of poplar wood the small houses that seemed to occupy his mind eternally. Suddenly he heard the sharp ringing of the shod hoofs of horses, lots of horses, on the cobbles of the

Via Monte Berico. Advancing at a swift pace, a richly caparisoned entourage swung into the piazza. Instantly the siesta calm of a small Italian city was shattered by the immediate wants of a Venetian patrician. At least ten outriders pulled to a halt in front of the chemist's shop. An officer, in what was once a vivid magenta uniform, now powdered white with summer dust, demanded a physic for *il guidice*.

Andrea was one of the first of a group of boys to gather about this splendid turnout. A big painted traveling chariot and six rusty-red and white dappled Spanish Barbs. *Una carrozza a sei cavalli.* Only a noble of highest rank was allowed six horses. A judge and a Venetian noble. It was all very grand, sighed Andrea. One day he would go to Venice and buy himself just such a coach with six horses.

Looking more closely at the painted, canopied, boxlike body of the coach, Andrea realized that it was a monument to bad proportion. The color and painting were garish, and the way the contraption was slung on its massive leather straps threw the weight of the occupants all off balance. No wonder *il guidice* needed a physic.

Andrea stood for a moment, his dark eyes darting at every detail of the cumbersome old vehicle. He found the whole conception of design crude and needlessly lumbering. One may very well assume that in the first quarter of the sixteenth century in Italy, a boy, son to a stonemason of extremely moderate means, would not know much about the niceties of coach building. Certainly the boy had seen a few coaches, for there was constant activity along the road leading through Vicenza to Venice and aristocratic Padova. And Andrea Magini or Palladio, whichever name he was known by at this stage of his temperamental journey, never missed a trick. What he saw he remembered; that is, if it engaged his interest. No, Andrea thought to himself, this old rattletrap coach will not do. I will show his excellency the judge what is wrong with it.

The boy looked eagerly about him for a stray piece of *carbone*. There were sure to be a few slivers about, dropped from the straw-tied bundles of charred wood that were delivered every morning to the housewives of Vicenza. Spying a chunk of *carbone* being rapidly reduced to black powder by the hoof of one of the Barbs, Andrea swooped upon it. He turned to the pale yellow stucco wall of the house behind him and rapidly sketched his idea of a well-constructed coach. This sketching of any design that entered his head, at any moment and on any flat surface

A Traveling Coach or "Chariot" of 15th Century Italy.

presenting itself, willy-nilly, became one of Andrea's outstanding characteristics. Before he became famous, this uninhibited freedom of expression on other people's property often got him into trouble.

At first, as Andrea worked at his sketch on the wall of the house next to the chemist shop, no one paid any attention to him. All eyes in the jostling group around the coach were intent on seeing just how brave a learned Venetian judge would be while gulping the draught of doubtless bitter brew he was lifting to his lips. But, alas, a footman drew one of the wine-colored damask curtains across this medical scene, so attention reverted to the large drawing of a truly wondrous coach taking shape on the wall. Under Andrea's sure hand strong black lines built up a large but graceful vehicle with style and beauty. Wheels, not too large, were spaced well apart. The body of the coach, instead of being as big and top-heavy as the Ark, sprang lightly from iron springs in the form of tripods. From these supports the light, well-balanced coach body swung. It is very probable that the owner of the yellow stuccoed house was not nearly as charmed by this minor masterpiece in *chiaroscuro* as the crowd of watchers or the tall boy who had fashioned it.

The art of drawing sharply contrasted black and white, with secondary planes of shaded black, is as old as linear drawing itself. Few draftsmen down the centuries have mastered the strength and subtlety imperative in this form of artistic expression. Many men try it. Nine out of every ten fail. Four great painters and one renowned architect are conceded by authorities on the subject to have brought this method of penetrating light into shadow, producing a three dimensional effect, to the very heights. Leonardo da Vinci was the leader in developing *chiaroscuro*. Correggio excelled in this, his favorite means of expression. Pietro Longhi filled countless portfolios with masterly, witty commentaries on the profligate society of his day: the *palazzo*, the *balletto*, and the eternal *ballo di maschera*. It is the Dutch school of painters who, *en masse*, hold conspicuous place in this art. Rembrandt occupies the chair of supreme exponent. Andrea Palladio was never as versatile in subject as the painters mentioned. For pure power and sweeping beauty of line in his architectural drawings he holds high place. When Giacomo Leoni, a Venetian, published his book on Andrea Palladio, it caused a veritable sensation that surged like the angry waves of the ocean to the shores of Britain. Here it was given an English translation in a magnificently produced book financed by Lord Burlington, a patron of Leoni. In this edition Leoni speaks at length and in singularly glowing terms of Palladio's vitality and imagination as a draftsman. Particularly of his triumph over the difficulties of *chiaroscuro*.

That Palladio had great fun practicing this medium is manifest in many of his annotations on the margins of elevations that he submitted to various persons who wished him to design a house for them.

A case in point is the set of large drawings which were sent to Conte Emo at Fanzolo setting forth in the most handsome manner Palladio's idea for a large country villa. The house is in the Vitruvian style. A central block, elevated on a high basement, which is actually divided into cellars and entresol. A long flight of wide shallow-tread steps ascend to the *piano nobile*, which in nearly all classic houses occupies the second floor. On this floor are generally a series of reception rooms, opening one into the other to form a vista.

At Villa Emo a gracefully proportioned portico and pediment decorated with crossed sheaves of corn rises above the steps. Long colonnaded wings, each twice the width of the central block, flank the portico at right angles, not in the demilune curve so often seen in houses designed by Palladio. A cube-shaped tower, probably a *colombaio* for the brown pigeons of the locality, surmounts the end of each wing.

While Palladio sketched fragments of detail, it is likely that one of his apprentices brought him his midday meal. In the ellipse that finishes the circumference of a Doric column is lightly sketched, in *chiaroscuro*, a tree, foliage suggesting a garden or meadow, a loaf, and the inevitable bottle of wine, without which no Italian, then or now, would consider touching food. (See sketch on page 10.)

This lighthearted touch frequently appears in the margins of Palladio's most severe Vitruvian elevations. Sometimes it will be a procession of huntsmen bearing aloft the antlered carcass of a stag. Again a fiercely warlike band of bravos waylaying the traveling chariot of a Spanish grandee, whose terrified mouth hangs agape while his arms are flung heavenward imploring the saints to succor him. A Spanish coach can always be instantly discerned by the cross that surmounts the peaked roof. Everything Spanish was the butt for ridicule to Italians in the fifteenth century, and the idea that no grandee could move a foot either in or out of Spain, unless his mode of transit resembled the altar of a cathedral, amused the Italian mind no end, be it ever so religious.

One of the most entrancing of Palladio's drawings for a country villa is now framed and hung in the foyer of the Teatro Olimpico in Vicenza. It presents two versions of an idea for a proposed *ritirata campagna*, one of the many designs for "a gentleman's retreat for a protracted sojourn in the country," the kind of house foremost in the architect's mind. He sometimes sketched in lightly a banner fluttering around an Ionic column, suggesting alternatives, as shown on page 11. He then presented his two versions of the *ritirata* in the manner illustrated on page 3.

Number one is in Palladio's most sweeping, grandiose manner. The style of the magnificent Villa—actually a palace, of purest ray serene—Trissino at Meledo. More than one hundred and fifty years later, two of the most sumptuous gestures in architecture, still standing today, were built in England by the architect–dramatist Sir John Vanbrugh in the ultimate Vitruvian style of the Trissino house at Meledo. Blenheim Palace, as it has always been called, flaunts a superbly proportioned but belligerent, not to say embattled, façade among the leafy acres of Woodstock Chase. The other house is Castle Howard. Its cold formality and rather overwhelming scale by day changes miraculously to a very dream palace of breathtaking contours and rich *chiaroscuro* detail by moonlight.

Both of these houses have been called monuments to man's ego. Perhaps Blenheim was built not so much for the ego of Marlborough, who was to spend many turbulent years within the grandeur of its walls, politically and maritally, but more to satisfy the ego of a nation that dotes upon erecting monuments to national heroes.

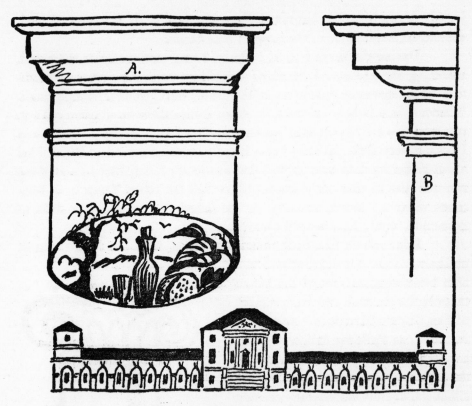

Elevation, Villa Emo at Fanzolo.

Castle Howard is another matter. Swollen ego and intense pride of name draped the rather portly form of Lord Carlisle like a gallant's cloak. No man alive ever enjoyed watching the erection of his fairy-tale castle, and later living in it as befitted its spacious grandeur, more than Carlisle. He had wisely given Vanbrugh (who said, "One may find a great deal of Pleasure in building a Palace for another; when one should find very little in living in't ones Self") a free hand with which to delve into what amounted to a bottomless purse.

It seems apparent to me that Palladio always enjoyed sketching his dreams in *carbone*, the forerunner of the charcoal sticks used today in sketching large cartoons for murals, and by students learning to draw from the antique. If not, though he was so prolific, he would never have spent valuable time, even in an unhurried age, ornamenting quite casual preliminary sketches with cartouches, the grinning masks of satyrs, a

10

loosely drawn hound, a farmyard. Very often the motif of a heavy-lidded, debauched Bacchus occurs to support a keystone.

During the years I lived in Italy, I was continually on the prowl, searching for whatever Palladiana I could unearth. All sorts and conditions of palaces were grist to my mill. And my mill grinds exceeding small. Whenever one is bent on tracking down information on a given subject, two qualities are imperative: patience and curiosity. In the ordinary way I possess very little patience but a large portion of curiosity. When I set about gathering data on a subject that warms my heart, I try to pool these two qualities so that one does not overweigh the other. There have been times when too much curiosity, or the brand of patience that sinks to desuetude, would have ruined everything.

Information, like little tongues of flame, licks out from the most unlikely places. A gondolier poling a slim black gondola around the island that cradles the rose and ivory church of San Giorgio Maggiore—*chiesa formidabile*, as Palladio called it—once gave me a banner of information about the statues of saints and apostles that silhouette against the intense cerulean of the Venetian sky. These figures, modeled with lovely free movement of draperies, appear to tread lightly along the cornice of the pediment, and those that inhabit the niches in the two winged screens flanking the portico draw back as if seeking a moment's shade. It seems that when the church was finished the pediment and niches were empty of statuary. This often occurs, even today. Perhaps there had been a delay in choosing the sculptor; perhaps sufficient funds could not be found. At San Giorgio Maggiore a feud caused the lack of statuary. Barbaro *versus* Mocenigo. Each family

wanted to present the statues. Time dragged on. The church had been finished for two years, but the question of the sculpture had not been settled. Niches and the cornices of the pediment showed blank. Finally, Venetians awoke one summer morning, and chancing to look toward San Giorgio, they rubbed their eyes, for lo! seven marble statues blazed like white fire in the sun. But they were not marble. Nor did they remain long in place. A member of the Barbaro, a cadet with penetrating eyes, examined the figures closely. The Mocenigo had pulled a hoax. The statues were papier-mâché treated with a high white glaze.

That night all who were abroad in Venice received a shock. "Fuoco! Fuoco a Maggiore," the cry rose, swelled in volume. "Incendio!" reverberated across San Marco and the Guidecca. But San Giorgio Maggiore was not burning. The inflammable cardboard saints were. After a time the excited cries of horrified Venetians died away. Charred remnants of San Giorgio and Santa Vittoria in Pace fell into the dark waters of the Canal della Guidecca. Soon after this incident the Barbaro presented the true marble statues one sees today. Or so one is told.

Palladio is said to have enjoyed this little skirmish between two of the great Venetian families for whom he built palaces. It is told that soon after the burning in effigy he sent a large packing case to the sacristan at San Giorgio. When it was unpacked, a splendid statue of his patron Saint Andrea was disclosed. One foot of Saint Andrea treads upon a scroll, which, unwinding, presents the carven words MARMOREO IN VERITAS.

Another chance bit of lore, which came to me quite by accident, had to do with the early boyhood of Palladio. I had walked out of Vicenza a mile or more to see a small farmhouse, which, I was told by Signore Foggi, custodian of the Museo Valmarana, was purported to have been the house of Pietro Magini. It was here that he had carried on his trade of stonemason. As I approached the low rusty-pink farmhouse, I noticed particularly the lovely color and softly luminous quality of the ancient tiles that covered the shallow peaked roof. Just a long mellow line of warm fawn-colored tiles, each shaped like a cabbage leaf, or *cavolo* as they are called in the Venetia. The patina of centuries glazed these rippling tiles with a rime of moss green. Nothing more beautiful can be imagined. Oddly, I had the feeling that I had been there before. Certainly I had seen that long line of simple white columns that formed a kind of loggia all across the front of the building. All the farm sheds and barns were at the back, screened by tall hazel trees. No other buildings detracted from the long pink and white flow of line. Well, I decided, I had never seen this farm before; it must just be that I am colonnade conscious.

I sought out the owner, who was intelligent, friendly, and pleased at my interest in his house. Yes, this was one of the houses in the environs of Vicenza where the family of Magini had lived in the fifteenth century. A number of houses in the city itself were shown to visitors as having been lived in by Andrea Palladio. He did not believe all he heard. Did I? I replied I listened to everything on many subjects up and down the highways of the world. Then I salted the information away for further reference. When the time ripened for the use of this data, I tried my best to substantiate all I found useful. A trickle here, a sliver of light on a murky subject there. That is the way narrative is built. Yes, he agreed, that was the way to do it. He had more than a trickle to offer me, however. A story he had told few people.

The man asked me to follow him. At the back of the barn where the lone farm horse was kept—a big handsome cream-colored fellow from one of the stock farms in the Udine—was a small square building, one story in height. A door pierced one wall, there was no window. Stooping to pass into the room which was no more than ten feet square, I noticed, even before the farmer pointed it out to me, a huge iron ring held to one wall by a rusted cleat.

The man nodded and said, "Come out and stand in the doorway and I will tell you why that ring is in the wall."

I waited, wondering how an old iron ring could have any bearing on information concerning Andrea Palladio.

The man continued, "That ring was used to chain young Palladio, to keep him from running off to Rome or Venice before he was old enough to have any idea of the world and its ways. It has come down, mostly by word of mouth, that the boy had big ideas. His father wanted Andrea to join him in the carving of stone. But the boy would always run away. At last his father's patience was tried to the limit. He is said to have chained the boy to this wall. Oh, he fed him well and gave him bedding. Left his hands free, of course. Somehow Andrea got hold of a knife and blocks of wood. This room was stacked to the ceiling with the little wooden houses he was forever carving. This very house I live in was just a long plain Venetian farmhouse when it was built. Then after Andrea had endured

13

his imprisonment, he showed his father one of his wooden models with a colonnade across the front. If you follow Palladio's drawings, you will see it is an idea he used many times. The Villa Piovene for one. There are pictures of that house in the museum."

Like a burst of light, I had it. That was where I had come upon this colonnaded farmhouse before today. The long wings that flank the main block of that most lovely and warm of all farmhouses, Villa Piovene at Lonedo, the fertile Val d'Lonedo, were exactly like these. Height, length of line, and mood. My memories of visiting Villa Piovene, first in 1929, rank high among the pleasures of my life. Because I believe this house is one of the most gracious dwellings on earth, from every standpoint, I am devoting a later chapter of this book to it.

The farmer asked me to sit with him and his wife under an arbor of almond trees, whose tops had been bent, when saplings, to form a canopy against the penetrating Venetian sun. White wine from the farmer's own vineyards was set before me, wine harboring a delicious aftertaste of slight mustiness, not cold but cool, to refresh me before my walk back to town. Just as I rose to leave, the eldest son of the farmer came in from grinding maize. A tall sturdy fellow, he looked like one of the statues of countrymen so often used by Palladio on the pediments of his country houses. More than ever because of the heavy coating of maize dust, which gave him the look of animated plaster. I told him he had only to leap upon the roof of his father's house and all passersby would think the *famiglia Borolini* had struck it rich. He laughed and told me a story about Andrea Palladio that had always interested him as a boy.

It seems there was once a huge black stallion—stallions in stories are invariably black, I find—with curious white markings. An eight-pointed star on both sides of his rump. He was sent by one of the sons of the Querini family of Vicenza to live out his old age as a respected pensioner at one of the *podere* or country manors belonging to this powerful family of the Venetia. Roderigo Querini was known as a *cavalleria prudente* at the court of the Marquess of Mantua. This slightly satirical title was bestowed on the household guard of Italian ducal courts. It meant, literally, that all was for show. A *cavalleria prudente* need not fight unless the castle itself was attacked.

It appears that Palladio, with a passion for symmetry and the grand scale in all things, was much taken with the old charger when first he saw him being led through the streets of Vicenza on his last journey to the feeding grounds of the Querini *podere*. Instantly calculating in mathematical, even architectural terms, he made known his desire to take the measurements of this animal whose conformation was impressive, old age or not. Apparently Andrea was granted permission to do as he wished. The story is that it was a mighty humorous sight. The tall gangling boy, armed with plumb line and ruler and surely the inevitable stick of *carbone*, climbed under, over, and around the drowsy old warhorse. The horse meanwhile ruminated on past glories, on the days when he bore the flower of the House of Querini in jousting tournaments. He probably thought the eager and intent Andrea some class of big gadfly. However, Palladio later used painted decorations of big-built horses to enliven the walls and ceilings of many of the houses he designed. In the margins of sheets from his portfolios he draws horses in the manner of the *facciata* or *posteriore* of a contemplated villa. Almost without exception these medieval horses are drawn with small graceful heads, enormous muscular quarters, bulbous fetlocks, and luxuriant manes and tails, as illustrated on page 16.

Now we approach the young manhood of Andrea Palladio. The mists rise and the picture is obscured. It always seems strange to me that when mists do enshroud the life of a person from the world, from interested posterity, those mists are well-nigh impenetrable. Certainly with Palladio they are a veritable wall of rock. One time in Rome I asked a man who is a famous authority on the life of Palladio if he knew anything about the days Andrea spent in Rome. How he lived, and where? Whom he consorted with, and why? The little, seemingly unimportant things, which, when added together, slip into place and a vivid portrait of the person stands before one's eyes. The man shook his head, thrust out his underlip, and muttered, "Oscuro—molto oscuro."

We know that Andrea Palladio had a wry sense of humor. If in no other way the little gesture of sending the statue labeled *Marmoreo in Veritas* to the sacristan of San Giorgio Maggiore proves this point. We know that all through his growing-up period he had a passion for designing and building houses. Although he built some of the most glorious churches in the world today, and palaces for the Italian nobility, it was the big, simple, comfortable country house that actually won his deepest interest. By the same token, to my mind, his three loveliest houses are Villa Piovene, Villa Caldogno with its unique frescoed façade and extraordinary sweep of wings, and Villa Pisani at Montagnana. The first two are "great" country houses because they are part of the landscape and broadly spacious as well. They have tremendous character. Without that saving grace, any house may as well be built of sheets of corrugated iron. Villa Pisani is a townhouse of an elegant simplicity that captures one's heart immediately.

During years spent in Rome, I occupied myself searching out whatever facts I could run down concerning the warp and woof of life as lived by all classes of people during the middle ages, that is, from the fourteenth until the end of the sixteenth centuries. Rome was then a papal city, with an imperial past. Life was lived at fever pitch. In the space of one day a man might reach the heights of honor, and taste the agony of the torture chamber. Papal intrigue set the tune. Direst poverty and squalor dragged at the richly brocaded hems of the most magnificent princes in Europe.

To a youth who was approaching his twenty-first year and whose

The Big-Rumped Horse of the Udine.

imagination was forever on a hair trigger, Rome would have seemed a most bewildering place. Daily he would range through quarters packed with plague-ridden humanity, from which Rome was never free. In other quarters, vast deserted palaces showed gaping windows to prowling bands of *bravazzone,* the cutthroats that lurked like wild beasts in the rotting caves along the Tiber. Rome was an unpredictable city of incredible vice and piety in the years that Palladio is supposed to have lived there, roughly 1528 to 1530. Apprehension rode the Apulian wind. Great Roman families, whose *stemma di famiglia* was a full-grown tree before the advent of the Caesars, would suddenly run afoul of whatever papal faction was in power. Within a few hours the male members were either murdered in cold blood or thrown into the reeking Castello Saint Angelo, which was as dire as any fate one could imagine. A young man eager to see the sights as Andrea would have been, might easily have passed and admired a great Renaissance palace, perhaps for its very newness. Many of the grandest Roman palaces were still in the long process of building in 1528. Indeed, Antonio da Sangallo the younger wrote in his famous notes commemorating his collaboration with Donato Bramante: "Ten years have passed and the Palazzo Farnese has risen only to the roof. We have no cornice. Nor have we a design for any such." Later Michelangelo designed the superb cornice that is one of the true wonders in existing architecture.

We may evoke young Palladio, *carbone* and the thin sheets of white gesso-covered wood in hand, hurrying through the hot noisy markets of the city, out along the Strada Giulia to make sketches of the high square palace he had gazed at so long a few days ago. The tall embrasured windows had impaled his interest. He must draw them. Carefully. But what has happened here? The great bronze-studded doors in the Porta di Cavalli hung slack on bent and shrieking hinges. Only two days ago he had stood across the piazza watching, fascinated by the life, the movement, and color that made the great house alive and humming. Horsemen had ridden out the Porta and a young woman with yellow hair had looked out of a balconied window, smiled at him, and jerked a crimson curtain across the window to shut out the sun. Now—a strange desolation hovered over the place. Gone, the family of Rovere. Where? Exile, if they were lucky. Saint Angelo if they were not.

This is the Rome Palladio knew. An ever changing city on girdled hills; and through the centuries, old Tiber, bearded in green waterweeds, shrugs his hoary and embattled shoulders in the sun, and murmurs, "Men never cease to marvel at my quality. It is illusive. It is Rome. There is no other."

Well and truly may Andrea Palladio have marveled at the picture of rapacity, filth, and beauty, so cunningly intermingled, which he saw daily. To a young country boy from the quiet of sleepy Vicenza and the undulating farmlands spread about its walls, Rome must have been a whirlpool. But he kept afloat, and as his writings many years later show, he not only enjoyed every minute of his Roman days but profited to an amazing extent. To the extent, in fact, of almost losing his identity in his complete surrender to the glory of the Vitruvian ideal in architecture. It is said that later Palladio made numerous visits to Rome, but surely none could have been so completely spellbinding as his first. It was his initiation to the wonders of rhythm, the calm beauty of undecorated spaces surrounding towering doors and windows, the veritable music in the lift of pillar and pediment that one can evoke in architecture.

It has always seemed to me a great pity that Palladio never saw Giovanni Bernini's immortal gesture in stone, the elliptical colonnade that embraces the piazza in front of Saint Peter's in Rome. I wager no other architectural conception, brought to such stirring completion, would have moved Palladio so deeply. The composition of the arranged columns, four rows deep, is not only Bernini's masterpiece but surely one of the wonders of the world.

Palladio writes in his *I Quattro Libri dell' Architettura:* "In Rome I drank deeply at the fountains of knowledge offered me on every hand. Inspiration and a challenge to create beauty rode the very air." He would have drunk himself to a standstill at the sight of Bernini's enfolding colonnades. The great bronze *baldacchino,* which Bernini designed and cast in bronze taken from the Pantheon, he hung under the central dome, ninety-five feet above the high altar. This canopy alone would have caused Palladio and his ever faithful *carbone* to work long hours as he gazed searchingly into the violet mist hovering from myriad candles and swaying thuribles of incense. Alas, all these wonders came into being many years after Andrea Palladio had been buried in the crypt of the church of San Corona in Vicenza. An octagonal urn of moss-green quartz from the Dolomites served as a sarcophagus.

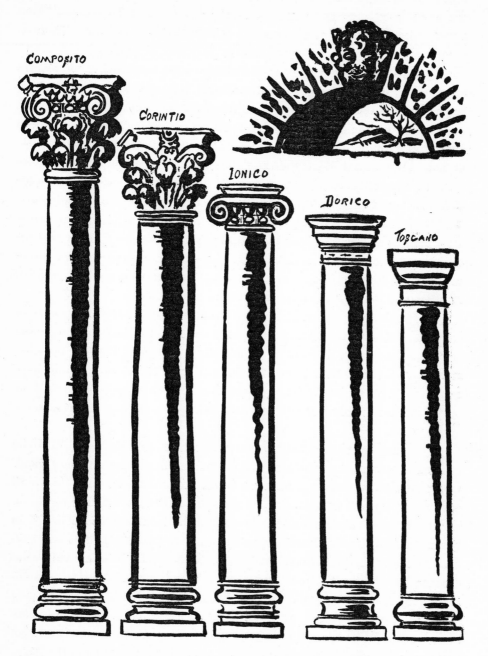

The Five Orders of Architecture Decreed by Palladio.

During the years when Palladio was designing and building one villa after another along the suddenly fashionable Brenta Canal—indeed, he writes his friend Conte Giovanni Batista dell' Torre at Verona that he was "engaged to the point of exhaustion, overseeing the erection of four villas at one time"—he wrote a small book, a kind of brochure, describing the results of measuring the ruins of pagan temples and triumphal arches, the palaces and churches of Rome. Some of this informal dissertation appears in the second book of his *Architettura*, wherein he states that his favorite church in Rome is Sant' Andrea della Valle. Whether this is because of the identification with his name saint or not, one does not know. Certainly the façade presented by this church today, while pleasing enough, is no great architectural piece. His favorite house is the fortress-palace of the Colonnas. It interested Andrea that this immensely ancient and powerful family derived its name from the Latin *colonna*, one of his favorite forms in architecture. He speaks of this in his writings of the Five Orders: *Toscano, Dorico, Ionico, Corintio, Composito.*

When Andrea Palladio again emerges from the mist that so irkingly clouds his activities from time to time, he is in his thirty-third year. In many ways he is at the height of his powers, his "first stage." From now on we can swing into stride with this prolific man and enjoy, as he most surely did, the transforming of his native Vicenza from a charming, but back-country, walled medieval town, hardly larger than a village, into a marvelously well laid out city of wide streets, spacious piazzas, colonnades and palaces fashioned in *rustico*, and the most beautiful exterior plasterwork in Europe.

Vicenza is a proud city today, as it was when Andrea Palladio lived there and spent years of his life fashioning from brick, stone, and marble the architectural masterpieces that have kept his name alive over four hundred years.

When the Venetian architect Giacomo Leoni wrote his book on Palladio, he alluded to the first, second, and third phases in the creative life of the supreme arbiter of Vitruvius. Roughly those periods may be divided thus: the first is after Palladio's return from Rome when he was occupied in enriching the city of Vicenza with public buildings and private palaces; the second is the Brenta period when he fashioned villas in both the grand and simple styles; and the third is his Venetian period

PALLADIO'S OWN ELEVATIONS FOR VILLA ROTONDA, VICENZA.
CROSS SECTION.

VILLA ROTONDA. PALLADIO'S ELEVATION, NORTH PORTICO.

when it was to the building of churches that he turned his mind. His last years he spent building farm villas for his friends.

According to Palladio, it was the second or Brenta period he enjoyed most in all his active life. He was physically very fit. He ate and drank sparingly, took long walks, and was poled up and down the twenty-odd miles of canal in barges of his own design. One barge is extremely original and certainly personal to its owner. This was his *barca osservare*, for on the deck was built a studio with benches and drawing paraphernalia to accommodate ten or twelve apprentices and one or two secretaries or assistants. As the *barca* was drawn over the waters of the canal by a team of big Fiume geldings, Palladio would recline under an awning of yellow and black striped linen and discourse on the merits of engaged columns *versus* widely spaced pillars. The latter, he always contended, if they were too widely spaced, weakened the look of a colonnade or portico wherein the cornice must appear well and strongly supported. Then he might branch away from discussing architectural motifs and deliver a learned solution to some problem in mathematics—no doubt rather baffling to the young apprentices. The main reason for these "water picnics," as he called them, was to keep an eye on the progress of the villas rising from his elevations along the pleasant waterway. It is fairly safe to venture that Palladio had his labor troubles in 1550. Laborers worked under a more rigid system in the days of the Renaissance, penalties for disobedience were more severe. But work was slow, and materials of all kinds needed in construction were made or prepared for use by hand, as against machine-made construction units of today. It would seem, from what one can gather, that Palladio kept a weather eye on all workmen under him, that he was universally popular and vastly admired by all whom he dealt with.

Although the third period—about 1565 through 1580—of Palladio's life was primarily devoted to erecting churches, he designed and brought to completion four of his finest villas, as well as beginning Teatro Olimpico. The observation that Palladio began with Villa Capra and ended with Villa Barbaro at Maser, or, as it is more widely known, Villa Maser, is substantially true.

As we approach the Vicenza picture, we will take first the splendid Palazzo Chiericati, one of the most graceful architectural structures ever

Stables Near Vicenza.

to be compiled in stone. If ever a façade was winged, this one is. The airy placing of cut-under rooms, rather like loggia, at either end of the long frontage, lend to the imposing scale of the house a delicacy I have never seen equaled. Only remotely comparable to this exquisite palazzo is the Hermitage in Russia which was constructed early in the nineteenth century from the original pavilion hunting-lodge of Catherine II.

The events that led to the first commission for an important building ever to be given Palladio are interesting, and a pleasant star to place beside that blotted page called "human nature." Soon after Trissino is said to have discovered Andrea Palladio, he showed some of the sketches the architect had brought back from Rome to an aristocratic and, it appears, autocratic man, Nobile Andrea Chiericati of Vicenza. Immediately interested, Chiericati invited Palladio to visit him at his country villa a few miles out of Vicenza. Andrea donned his best suit and presented himself to Chiericati. What was in his host's mind was the proposal that he, not Trissino, should become the patron of young Andrea, who, under his protection, should go to Venice to study architecture. Having already enjoyed Trissino's friendship and interest for years, Palladio could not see it that way. The upshot was that host and guest parted in anger. It would seem, on the face of it, that this was a bad beginning for a young man with no particular background and his way to make in the world.

However, it all turned out in the best possible manner. A few days after Andrea's unfortunate leave-taking from the house of Chiericati he was summoned to visit his friend Trissino. There he found another guest, Chiericati, who, it turned out, admired loyalty. Forthwith he handed Palladio a commission to design a country house for him near the one he was now living in, and later a palazzo in the town. The country villa which was called Rocca Rosa is now part of a flour mill, and any traces of Palladio's building are obliterated. But the town palazzo still remains a most lovely monument to loyalty.

There are many unusually interesting features in this building to reward one's study. Chief among them is the use of columns of the Doric order for the first floor tier. Those of the second are of the Ionic order. The effect of carrying a delicately designed balustrade across the entire front of the building above the richly ornamented cornice of the first floor lends great style to the frontage, giving the effect of wings. Actually there are no wings, but continuously lovely line. The only ornamentation on the entire façade—except the classic bull's skull and rosette motif of the cornice—are beautifully sculptured nymphs that recline in pairs atop each window pediment in the only wall space that is not an open-fronted loggia.

Palladio, while not caring at all for city life, realized the necessity for a gentleman of position to be appropriately housed for his sojourn in town. He writes in his "brochure":

> As certainly it is highly creditable and convenient for a gentleman to have a house in the city, where he is obliged sometimes to reside for the management of his private affairs or to keep a social state befitting his rank; so perhaps he may receive no less pleasure and advantage from a house in the country where he passes the rest of his time in improving his possessions. Here in quiet and in health he exercises himself in walking about his acres or on horseback. Here he luxuriates in sowing and harvesting the fruits of the earth, enjoying his table piled high with the bounty therefrom. Here he enjoys Vistas, Pleasure Houses, and Flowery Gardens. Diversions multiply. The only drawback is the unheralded advent of hordes of unavoidable relations and too virtuous friends.

This, I should say, covers everything. And he was just the man to supply both kinds of houses.

Vicenza has been called the cradle of Palladio, which may mean both his birthplace and the cradle of his finest works. But as much as he loved Vicenza and showered upon her the wealth of his genius, he frequently called himself a Venetian. Of course the countryside extending for many miles on all sides of Vicenza was termed Venetia. Palladio was always singularly happy in Venice, however little he liked cities, but then as now, Venice was like no other city on earth. As old Tiber, affectionately called *Tibero Antico* by Romans, muttered into the matted seaweed of his beard, "It is illusive. It is Rome," just so Venice has the quality that is only Venice. For centuries the coast of Istria, even cities in the foothills of the Alps, had withdrawn from any unnecessary contact with Venice. Suddenly a new light broke on the consciousness of these cities. Padua, Verona, Mestre came directly, and in a mood of rejoicing, under the spreading wings of Palladio and his followers. In all of these cities we find today well-nigh perfect examples of Palladian design. Palladio built the superbly original Villa Sarego at Santa Sofia not far outside the Verona gates. In this design we are introduced to columns the like of which Palladio used in no other building I have ever seen. The capital is of Ionic order. The shaft of the column is serrated in wide bands, and the serrations are deeply cut but not evenly spaced, a version of the rustico extensively used by early Roman architects. This is very likely what Vitruvius means when in his formidable ten-volume treatise on architecture he speaks of foundations and arched loggias being *intaglio profondo.*

Vignola used massive uncut rock for the basement walls of incomparable Caprarola near Viterbo. These were once obscured by the waters of the moat. Now that the moat is dry and filled with fitfully waving oleanders and tubbed orange trees, the magnificence of the carefully chosen rustico can be properly seen.

One of the most exciting pieces of design, purely as design, is Palladio's floor plan for Villa Sarego. Three colonnaded courtyards open one into the other. For sheer drama of vista within a house, I cannot remember its equal.

Although the first impression one gets of Vicenza is of a spacious town with plenty of light and air, on second sight and when one starts looking for the townhouses designed by Palladio, the illusion fades. For many of his finest palaces are placed on the side of a narrow street, making it impossible to view them with any satisfaction.

This is glaringly true of the Palazzo Thiene, which is certainly one of the most impressive buildings of the Palladian taste in Europe. There is a simple, rather gigantic grandeur about this house that defies description. Every detail is huge. Yet none seems overpowering. All fall into their proper place in the magnificently conceived scheme. It is in this palazzo with its great cube rooms and vaulted corridors, rather than the dark narrow rooms in the Palazzo del Tè in Mantua, that I should like to see one of the most entertaining frescos ever painted: that glorious absurdity, the *Sala dei Giganti*. In the painting all is action and ringing color. Giants of classic mold, sorrel and golden bearded, are engaged in pulling down a wall of the room in which one stands. It is a triumph for that misdemeanor of British law known as "breaking and entering."

To give a slight idea of the massive scale of Palazzo Thiene, the height from cobbled street to the *piano nobile* is thirty feet. The entire lower story is rusticated stone of a particularly handsome design that looks almost as if huge sea shells had been pressed into yielding plaster. But this is not so, for the six-foot blocks of stone have been elaborately worked over by stonemasons. It is within the realm of possibility that one of these masons was Pietro Magini.

Some critics contend that in the Palazzo Thiene Palladio was more influenced by Vignola than by Vitruvius. The reason for this view is probably the fact that Thiene does very much suggest the massive mood of Caprarola, though I believe it is doubtful that at this time Palladio had seen the palazzo of the Farnese.

Most of the houses built in Vicenza by Palladio were of brick faced with a thick coating of stucco, which has often fallen away from the brick background, adding a mellow patina to the structure. In some cases this revealing of the rose or tawny underbrick tends to soften the severity of outline. In others it seems to cheapen the façade.

Palladio has been blamed—in his country villas particularly—for using cheap materials and cheap inexperienced labor. Sometimes this is true. But the blame should fall on the client, for very often it appears in Palladio's accounts that his client tightened his purse strings when the house was half built, or divulged, when it was too late to remedy it, that his resources had dwindled—probably they never had been what he represented them to be—and economies must follow, a state of affairs not infrequently met by architects today.

We should rejoice that Palladio was such a master of invention

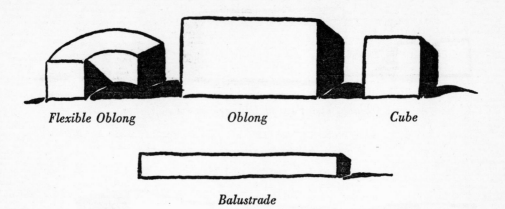

Flexible Oblong   *Oblong*   *Cube*

Balustrade

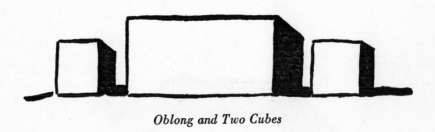

Oblong and Two Cubes

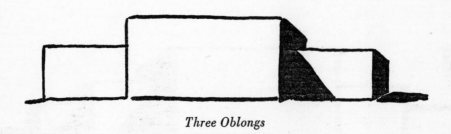

Three Oblongs

THE FOUR BASIC FORMS USED BY ANDREA PALLADIO IN DESIGNING HIS BUILDINGS.

Oblong, Two Flexible Oblongs, and Two Cubes.

Three Oblongs to Form Crescent.

Crescent Floor Plan.

Formation of Graduated Wings Using Five Oblongs.

Three Oblongs and Two Cubes.

Two Flexible Oblongs and Two Oblongs.

Floor Plan. Two Balustrades Added.

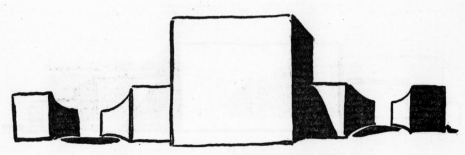

Plan for Townhouse and Stables. Four Flexible Oblongs, One Cube.

The Long Façade.

Oblong, Two Flexible Oblongs, Two Balustrades, Two Cubes.

Bradenstown House, the Long Façade.

One Cube, Two Oblongs, Two Flexible Oblongs.

Two Oblongs, Two Flexible Oblongs, One Cube Used in an
Entirely Different Manner.

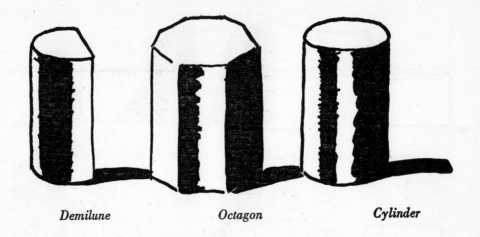

Demilune   *Octagon*   *Cylinder*

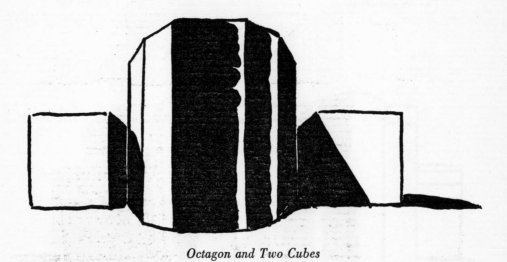

Octagon and Two Cubes

SECONDARY FORMS USED BY PALLADIO IN ARCHITECTURE.

Three Oblongs and One Demilune. This Arrangement Is Used at Caledon.

The Rather Unusual Use of Three Oblongs Up-Ended and Two Cubes.

Raynham, Norfolk.

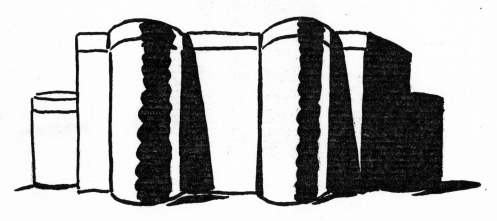

Massing One Oblong and Four Demilunes. Gynly Court, Carmarthan, Wales.

that he was able to produce splendid results with so many obstacles to overcome.

In the Palazzo Barbarano (or Palazzo Porto Barbaran), Palladio was fortunate to have his "grand design" carried out to the letter. So perfect in proportion and detail is it that Horace Walpole wrote: "There is great glory in this palazzo; the detail and all embellishments fill the eye with harmony." The first floor is of rusticated stone, incised to great depth. The half-columns are of the Ionic order. The upper floor is in Palladio's richest manner, ornate but so well composed that the effect is of enormously patterned lace laid over soft velvet. The texture of the wall spaces between the tall windows is rich beyond belief. In no other house has Palladio been so successful with his incrustations.

The nine windows across the front of the building have architraves and consoles supporting pediments, alternating triangular, and segmental. On these pediments recline nude nymphs of the forest bearing leafy branches. Boldly modeled balustrades front each window. As if to offset the wealth of detail, to form a restful contrast, the ten-foot attic is plain, unrelieved except by square windows. This unadorned band crowns the whole structure. Columnar lines carry up from the cornice at intervals supporting statues of Leda, Aphrodite, Mars, Mercury, Apollo, and others.

The interior is superb. In my opinion, nowhere in Italy are finer ceilings to be found. Carved, gilded, and the arabesques, circular, oval, and square, are painted in classic scenes in deep glowing colors. In one room the walls are silver-gilt oxhide with lunettes painted in scenes of the chase. The plasterwork throughout is in amazingly high relief. The frieze in the *salone grande* gains in vitality by having life-size figures of armored and plumed warriors so richly sculptured that they seem to be stepping out of the wall into the room.

There are two palazzi in Vicenza called Porto. One is only an unfinished fragment, known today as Palazzo Telegrafo, for it houses the local telegraph office. The other Porto is a very different story. Usually it is called the Palazzo Porto Grande. This large building faces on two streets, which are wide enough so that in walking along either of them one gets a good view of the house. The entrance from each street leads through columned halls to a great central octagonal courtyard, open to the sky. This is surrounded by a colonnade of Doric columns that rises two stories. Behind this colonnade is a corridor, a sort of covered passage on each floor, which serves as communication between the front and back portions of the house.

The long frontage of this house is extremely fine, resembling rather the façade of the Palazzo Thiene. The power of huge rusticated stones is complemented in the fine entablature around the square windows. Each window is set in a circular relieving arch, supporting keystones. It is in these extravagantly modeled keystones that the terrific style of the house strikes its highest note. Each one is different. A slavering monster, a grinning satyr, a satellite of Neptune shell crowned, a vulpine mask, and the inevitable Bacchus. These masks support the *piano nobile*.

The second story is of absorbing beauty. Seven windows pierce the front of the building. The windows at the extreme right and the extreme left and the center one are ornamented by carved figures on pediments and swags of loosely carved fruit and flowers that form plastrons and scarves on either side of the windows. The effect of the plain architraves against the enriched ones is indeed lovely. Between each window an Ionic column supports a simply modeled cornice. An attic extends across the frontage. Above the capital of each column caryatids, male alternating with female, support the roof. The attic is pierced by a square window after each caryatid.

The unfinished "fragment" of a palazzo is only thirty feet wide and consists of two stories and a half-attic. The first story is undistinguished. Three Corinthian columns support the handsomely modeled cornice, which is enriched by corbels in the form of lion heads. There are two pedimented windows with balustrades in front. The distinguishing feature of the whole design is, however, the wonderfully modeled garlands of wheat, fruit, and vegetables loosely wrapped with ribbons, which seem to sway between the Corinthian capitals. It is said that Palladio designed this house for his mother, Emilia, who died before it was finished. The original brown ink and wash drawing of the elevation facing the Piazza Publico is preserved under the name Palazzo Porto Bregance. This rendering shows five windows across the front with a superb winged window in the middle of the *piano nobile*.

A small, but immensely distinguished house, hardly a palazzo although it rejoices in the name Loggia Palazzo Danaro, is situated near the noisy jostling Merceria, and is therefore open to view. The lower floor has extremely interesting rustico treatment, with winged keystones, deeply pitted to mimic water-corroded stone. These stones spring from the arched entrance door and the square-topped windows. The entire building is no more than fifty feet in width and has only three windows across the front. The second floor is in beautifully proportioned stucco of pale watery green color. Three very tall windows support pediments of the pointed order. Four columns display Corinthian capitals that are partly shadowed by the richly molded cornice. These leaf and scroll capitals were at one time gilded. The small building has a dignified charm and completely dominates, in poise, the mountains of artichokes, melons, tomatoes, and onions of the morning market surging in pungent waves to its very portals.

A notoriously grand house is Palazzo Loschi Zilferi dal Verme, built by Palladio in his last year with the help of his most brilliant apprentice, Pollini. The façade is soaring in scale, but rather light and weak in composition, and sparse, even pinching, in detail, to my mind. I would say there is much more of Jacopo Pollini evidenced in this building than Palladio. One cannot judge to what heights as an architect Pollini would have risen, for his career was cut short a few months after the death of his master. To be exact, he was stabbed in a brawl over the daughter of a local taverner in 1581. Zilferi dal Verme, as the house is known, has one tremendously arresting feature: a winged Palladian window over the *porta grande*. Four square, deeply fluted pillars, Corinthian capped, support the arc of the central window and the "tables" or cornices of the side windows. What gives vigor and point to this fine window are the two fluidly modeled figures of demigoddesses, as large as life. Fame and Fortune. In undulating draperies, tiara and jeweled plastron modeled in high relief, these two attendants, welcome, I should think, above anyone's door, seem about to depart to a gala. The whole central part of the Palazzo has enormous style.

The Teatro Eretenio in a narrow side street behind the Palazzo Municipale has a simple but rather handsomely proportioned exterior, although it is miserably cramped and ill-lighted within. A series of nine arches of plain dressed stone have rather unusual square supports between. These are three and one-half feet thick and seven feet across the front. Each one has a square-topped door cut through to the loggia behind, which forms a corridor in front of the doors letting into the theater. These pillar-doors were, I am told, a sort of shadowed hiding place for the *polizia* who were out in full force on nights when some piece or other was being presented at the theater. Footpads and all manner of undesirable *bravi* always gathered around places of amusement during the Renaissance and in the early nineteenth century in Italy. The most memorable features, architecturally, about Teatro Eretenio are the carved marble plaques set in the plain wall of the second story between the windows, and also in the upper part of the supports between the arches of the loggia. These lower ones are round, about two feet in circumference; in each is an intaglio head, soft ivory-white against indigo. These depict Roman playwrights or actors. The panels in the upper wall are rather fantastic and very flowingly modeled. Masks of Comedy and Tragedy alternate. Each holds in his teeth a swag of silk. From this swag tumbles in fine confusion the bladder of a Commedia dell' Arte Arlecchino on its beribboned staff, the high cothurns of an antique tragic muse, and musical instruments such as Pan's pipes, flutes, and mandolins.

The Palazzo Trissino-Baston is usually credited to Scamozzi, who is known to have worked with Palladio. There are stories that he, not Pollini, was the chief apprentice in Palladio's atelier. Just why Trissino should have engaged another than his protégé Palladio to build him a townhouse seems a shade obscure. It could have been that the Baston faction—undoubtedly the wife of Trissino—controlled the purse strings at that time, and of course he or she who controls the purse strings calls the tune. The façade has no great originality or arresting style. There are nine windows across the front. The colonnade of engaged pillars of the Ionic order is rather impressive in scale. One feature remains in the mind. At each end of this colonnade, at right angles to the street, there is an arched door set into the columns. Reclining on the curved cornice of this arch are the female figures of Spring and Summer at one end, and the male figures of Autumn and hooded Winter at the other. The keystone of each arch, against which the figures lean, is the head of a Titan. The effect is sumptuous. The courtyard of this palazzo is grand in scale, for the house is three stories high. Doric columns form a colonnade around the entire courtyard, and two sharply curving staircases ascend to the *piano nobile*. A balcony with fine ironwork in spearhead and scroll design follows the line of the colonnade around the court.

The Palazzo Porto Colleoni, happily facing a small piazza thus enabling one to examine closely the detail of the keystone carvings, was actually only half finished in Palladio's time. His elevations for the proposed courtyard are entirely handsome. It is a definite loss to architecture that another architect, unknown, was allowed to meddle in a style for which he had little knowledge and no feeling.

The family of Colleoni was never a rich one. The most outstanding member was the renowned military strategist of the fourteenth century, Bartolommeo Colleoni, 1400–1475. This man who rose to the highest possible military heights came from an impoverished family stemming from the lesser nobility; his mother from the ancient Venetian family Carelli. Colleoni fought in the wars with Venice and Milan, changing sides so often he was known as *capitano variabile*. Filippo Maria Visconti, Tyrant of Milan, imprisoned Colleoni twice. Both times his own soldiers managed to effect his escape. The second time he fled to Venice where the Venetian Council of Ten had offered a large price for his head. Colleoni scotched this, however, in a burst of oratory—delivered in the teeth of a *tramontana* sweeping down from the Dolomites—of such power and patriotism that the assembled army of the Doge practically ripped their throats wide open shouting for him to become the leader of the winged lion banner of St. Mark. Promptly, the Doge rescinded his order of "assassination on sight," which had been posted against Colleoni, and begged the huge-framed warrior to accept the post of generalissimo of Venice. This he did, on condition that Venice provide his family with a fine house *in perpetuita*. Colleoni remained loyal to Venice and fought her constant battles brilliantly until he died from accumulated old wounds.

In the center of the Piazza S. S. Giovanni e Paolo, in Venice, stands the arresting and widely celebrated equestrian statue of Colleoni astride a caparisoned charger. Certainly this statue, for sheer power of dominating personality and rhythm of treatment in the swing of man and animal, is Verrocchio's best work.

One morning in February a few years ago, I was in Venice during a freak snowstorm. I rose on a brilliantly sunny morning to see all the city blanketed in six inches of snow. Venetians are profoundly distressed by the sight of snow and start calling on their patron saints to remove it *subito* once it appears. In this case the remover was the sun. I streaked out of my hotel and made for the Piazza S. S. Giovanni e Paolo. There was Colleoni and his great warhorse handsomer than I—certainly the most loyal admirer they possess—had ever seen them. The stern-visaged generalissimo of a long-gone state wore a high cap and little shoulder cape of purest ermine. His horse wore a pointed cap and a sort of bustle of snow on his rump. I saluted them and returned to my hotel before the ermine turned to runnels of water.

It was the grandson of Bartolommeo who commissioned Palladio to build him a palazzo in Vicenza. In the vaulted entrance hall of this still unfinished house, a bust of the doughty warrior, Bartolommeo, who provided a fortune for his descendants, reposes in a niche painted bright red to throw in relief the waxy marble features of *capitano variabile.*

The basilica of Vicenza has four façades, each slightly different from its fellows. In general treatment the design of continuous loggias is identical. Here Palladio uses his winged arch to achieve flow of line in the most satisfying manner. Between each arched opening, a tall Ionic column rests upon a tableted base flush with the balustrade, continuing up to support an extremely elaborate cornice. This is ornamented with masks of young Roman athletes. Many authorities feel that Palladio has never used his winged arches to such stunning effect. The spaciousness of conception throughout the entire basilica is marked. Twelve persons abreast can stroll with comfort in the upper and lower colonnades. The attic is unusual for Palladio to have designed, and if one did not know to the contrary, it would seem that a French architect had taken a later hand in its erecting. There are rather thin columns of brick. Porthole lozenges of undistinguished design serve no purpose, it would appear. Neither window nor embellishment. The basilica is only two stories in height on the side facing the Piazza dei Signori, but rises two stories and a high basement on the Piazza dell' Erbe side.

This is, to my mind, an advantage. It lends power to the whole mass. The vitality of the flowing arch motif needs this power to match its weight. Inside the basilica it is dark. Little thought or taste has been employed to enrich the walls. The ceilings were once painted, though indifferently. It is the exterior of this building with its splendid movement in stone that is truly remarkable.

The house known as Loggia del Capitano has a strange history. Palladio was asked to submit elevations to a masked client who apparently came from a far place in Italy. It is said that the client spoke with a dialect so obscure that he had difficulty in making himself understood. However, he could not be denied for he bore a ring emblazoning the arms of the Pisani. Later, when approached by Palladio, the head of the Pisani family in Venice remained aloof, discrediting the man's claim of protection under Pisani patronage. But as so often happens, gold, gold, and more gold of the realm, when emptied into Palladio's palm, cleared all barriers. Loggia del Capitano was designed and built. But it was never lived in by the masked mystery man. On the day before the doors were to be thrown open for occupancy, the owner of this vastly handsome house disappeared from the world of men. At least from the Venetia. His bills were paid. He simply left to whom it might concern a completely furnished house, very much in the grand style. And he never returned to claim the house. Some say Palladio himself lived in it for a time. It would seem entirely probable. Then one day the city of Vicenza took it over for taxes. For many years since it has housed shops and apartments.

The façade is overelaborate, and most of the stucco has fallen away, giving it the look of an entirely brick house. The Corinthian columns are extremely fine. A beautifully modeled balustrade resting on heroically scaled consoles partially hides a three-quarter-story attic. The added height gives the house character. Of all the Palladian palazzi in Vicenza, del Capitano is in shockingly bad repair.

I have saved until the last the most stately, most imperial of all the palaces designed by Andrea Palladio for the nobles of the Venetia who wished townhouses "in which to pursue their private affairs," as Palladio wrote to Trissino. This is the Palazzo Valmarana. The only drawback to its perfection is that the house is built in a cobbled street scarcely more than an alley. Just why a family magnificently endowed with land and golden ducats, as the Valmarana notoriously were, should have picked this spot to build one of the most splendid houses in Italy is hard to fathom. In the light of facts pertaining to the miserliness of the head of this house, perhaps it was because the spot chosen happened to be Valmarana land.

We first hear of endless discussions between Conte Baldasare Valmarana and Andrea Palladio over expenses involved in building a townhouse larger and finer than any in Vicenza. Because the Valmarana were the outstanding breeders of Spanish Barbs in the region and maintained a coach and eight in defiance of the Doge himself, stables were to be built at the back of the courtyard. They were to be an integral part of the architectural plan. The façade of the stables had to be as handsome as the house. After three years of pro and con (during which time Palladio made his tour of Italy, measuring Roman ruins), the Valmarana decided to give over the amount of money necessary to the proposed project. Let it be said, as Palladio wrote: "I am obliged in the extreme to my noble Conte [Valmarana] that he is pleased to let me proceed with his Palace as I wish. The building will reflect my every thought and care. Few times enough is this true." Once well away on the building of the house it must have been intensely gratifying to Palladio to watch it rise from day to day, the whole conception not deviating one jot from his elevations.

The house is different in plan from any other of Palladio's that I know of, excepting only, in modified form, the villa he built near Padova for one of the Barberini, the Villa Lanterna, which was destroyed by fire in 1886. The plan is divided into two distinct parts by a central court. Each part contains ten reception rooms; many were used as bedrooms when entertainments were not in progress. The stables, marvels of spaciousness, extend the length of the back, at the end of a long garden. As at Palazzo del Strà alla Brenta, the stable front shows much the same façade as the house itself.

The first floor apartments are all vaulted, or as Palladio wrote on the margins of his drawings, "arch'd." All are superbly painted in pure color laid in varying thickness over a gold-leaf ground. The effect is at once lovely and startling. Startling because in an age that tended toward overembellishment in painted wall spaces, this grading of pure luminous color to give added height to the coves is revolutionary, to say the least. One room is pure cardinal red over gold, another violet, still another is matrix green. One that remains my favorite is as illusive in color as the wine-dark Ionian Sea: a clear chestnut brown that has both violet and rose lights in its depths. This over-gold coloring is something out of fable.

The suites of rooms on the second floor are equal in width, height, and breadth, twenty-five feet each way. These cube rooms are one of the most outstanding features of Palladio's interior arrangements. Possibly the most renowned in the world is the "double cube" room at Wilton, Salisbury, seat of the Earls of Pembroke. The room was designed by Inigo Jones, and would have delighted the heart of Palladio. There is a "double cube" room above the huge central arch in the stable block at Valmarana. Apparently it was used by the Conte to entertain his friends when he displayed his fine horses.

The front of Palazzo Valmarana is one story higher than any of the other townhouses built in Vicenza. There are a first floor, an entresol,

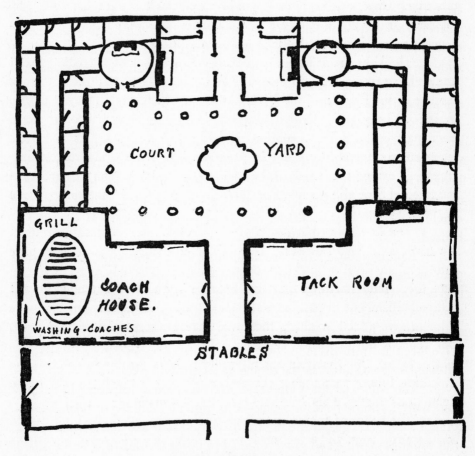

Palazzo Valmarana

a twenty-five-foot *piano nobile,* and above that a twelve-foot attic. A rustico treatment combined with dressed stone panels between forms a high barricade wall to ten feet from the pavement. This fortresslike lower story throws into interesting relief the Composito capped columns which extend from the flange of the barricade wall to the balcony of the second story. Graceful columns with flat surfaces and capitals of the Composito, or last order in Palladio's Order of Five, extend from the barricade to a line flush with the pointed pediments over the windows. The range is seven windows across. A widely projecting cornice of elaborate modeling gives a great air to the whole façade. It is said that a magnificently carved and gilded cartouche originally surmounted the attic, over the central window. At night a light—probably a horn lantern—was always placed in front of this cartouche so that passers-by or chance visitors to the palazzo would know to what family it belonged. At either side of the stable block is a sort of loggia called *loggia da vaggoni* where the painted, lumbering road coaches (the sort that so raised the ire of young Giovanni Magini) were housed.

At this point a brief description of the arrangement of the stable plan seems in order. A more felicitous atmosphere in which to house horses cannot be imagined. The one-story colonnaded frontage is high and spacious. Loose-boxes are arranged in double rows with an aisle of generous breadth between. Stallion quarters are on the right-hand side of the drive through, from street to courtyard. Quarters for brood mares line the left-hand side as shown in the sketch of the ground plan.

The colors of the Valmarana are everywhere apparent in decoration. Walls of loose-boxes are painted to resemble boldly rusticated wine-colored stone. The engaged columns of Doric order are marbleized yellow with veinings of wine and gray. *Stoia* (a pungent matting of woven rushes) is hung upon the wall to protect the horses against damp and cold. Handsome bronze staples displaying the head and shoulders of unicorns and heraldic beasts can still be seen, high up near the heavily molded cornice. These held the lengths of *stoia* in place, the like of a tapestry. A pierced bronze ribbon, in the manner of a swinging sign, hangs above each loose-box door. Such names as "Cupido," "Parnassus," "Maro," "Carissima," and "Re d'Argento" emblazon these signs.

A small circular room in the main stable block was used apparently by grooms, postilions, and pages. The tall closets for livery are still lined with purple *filoticcio*, a silk and wool material. As late as 1928 a number of rather moth-eaten liveries of the Valmarana still hung in these closets. Tailored of lemon or red-purple *stuffa*, a kind of whipcord, the jackets were intricately braided, pinked, and puffed. There is something mightily engaging, to me, about the ingenious arrogance of Renaissance or eighteenth century liveries. Brilliant contrasting colors, ebullient designs of swags, curlicues, and tassels burst into flower on the jackets of small page or gigantic major-domo. Bombastic as an Adriatic sunset, "heralds to vanity," these flunkies have been called.

It would appear that the Valmarana was the last palazzo attributed to Palladio to be erected in Vicenza. This was approximately 1555. Two years before this date he had submitted elevations to Conte Rinaldo di Branno-Antonini for a townhouse to be built in the Udine. After the usual procedure of bickering over costs, a state of affairs that seemed continually to plague Palladio, Conte Antonini decided to build a house on the very brink of a miasma-ridden marsh. Further to irk his architect he cut the size of the building in half. Nevertheless (in what frame of mind one may imagine), Palladio went to stay in the Udine until the Palazzo Mezzo, as he called it, was finished. There is an odd look about this house. Although it is situated on a small piazza, the house looks dark and brooding. Perhaps because of the eternal rains, amounting to downpour, which are familiar to this region of Italy, the eaves of the roof extend like a shed on all four sides of the house. This produces a top-heavy effect, far more like a house in Madrid or Barcelona. In short, except for a fine arrangement of two tiers of columns across the front, one would scarcely believe Palladio had had any connection with so drab a house. Even the columned entrance porch is too large, and was surely designed for the original elevation, which was twice as lofty. The *prato tristo* has been filled in and is now a rather scraggy park.

Very soon after this unfortunate interlude, Palladio was given a commission he thoroughly enjoyed. A senator from Bologna named Vaccelli conceived the rather daring idea—for those times—of building a Palazzo Tribunale in the very heart of the city, which would serve to house him and his family as well.

The palazzo is not large, but most beautifully proportioned. It is recorded that the façade was never stuccoed, for the rose-beige bricks, very narrow laid, give a most engaging sort of ripple to the walls upon which sunshine and silver moonlight play, as upon the waters of the Brenta. A center arched doorway set into an entablature of rusticated stones is flanked by four square-topped windows. A balcony extends across the house. From this balcony columns rise, single in the center, engaged (or in pairs) at the extreme ends. The Corinthian capitals have at one time been gilded. The fine pediment extends over the space of four columns and is filled in by two figures of winged angels, bearing to the city of Bologna its arms quartered with those of Senator Vaccelli. A charming touch is the pair of obelisk plinths at either end of the pediment. In Italy this touch, which denotes maritime interests, is usually seen in seaport towns.

Bologna again enters the picture at this point in an odd manner. Odd because so little is known, on any count, concerning the marriage of Palladio and a young woman from Bologna. It is said she was the daughter of a Bolognese doctor. We know only that Palladio did marry, for his son Silla was so highly regarded as an architect that, as we shall later see, the Academy of Arts appointed him to finish Teatro Olimpico after his father's death.

During Palladio's stay in Bologna, emissaries were sent from Venice laden with impressive documents heavy with crimson and gold cords, and embellished with the jeweled seal of St. Mark and the Doge. One was a commission to design a new building for the ancient convent of Carità. The other, to build on an island in the roadstead of the Grand Canal a church to glorify San Giorgio Maggiore. Palladio, accompanied by Daniel Barbero, who assisted him in building Palazzo Valmarana, and probably Bertotti, who was much in evidence during the Venetian period, set out for Venice early in the spring of 1554. Quite an entourage it was, by all accounts, as befitted *il illimitato architetto*, an appellation affectionately bestowed upon Palladio by his apprentices. These same apprentices totaled fourteen at this time. Palladio wrote Trissino from his quarters in Venice in a rage, using such words as *povero, miserabile,* and *sporcare:* "Here I am, like a beggar housed. Oh, misery and befouled air. Were it not that I have transported all my gear, along with fourteen apprentices, I should return to Vicenza within the hour."

Whatever miscarriage of hospitality had taken place through the dunderheadedness of a lackey was put right, for the next we hear from Palladio, written to the President of the Academy of Art in Vicenza (one

Filippo Danzetti), he is in high spirits. "Venice fulfills my dreams. Queen of Ocean and Madonna of the Salute. Work fires ahead. We build the Maggiore apace." The storm clouds clear. Ambition soars.

All now seems admirable to enter with Palladio his "middle period," the glorifying of Venice.

VENICE

From many reliable sources it appears that the arrival of Palladio, surrounded by an imposing retinue of clerks and satellites, in that most salubrious city called Bride of the Adriatic was marked for success from the start. True, there had been the little fracas when, on his arrival late at night, Palladio had been given "beggarly" lodgings, which he promptly wrote home to complain about. Next day all was satisfactorily arranged, for with the morning sun appeared no less a personage than Monsignore Grimani, patrician, patron of all the arts, and *persona grata* with the Doge of Venice and the Vatican. No more auspicious visitor could be imagined. Forthwith Grimani placed one of his lesser but beautifully situated palazzi at the disposal of Andrea Palladio. From that moment out, he was to enjoy the friendship and generous cooperation, in all his undertakings, of one of the most intellectually brilliant men of his day, Cardinal Giovanni Grimani.

VENICE

As Palladio and his newly discovered friend drifted down the Grand Canal in one of the magnificently carved and gilded gondolas of the Grimani (for in the fifteenth century gondolas reached a high plane of inventive decoration; not until the end of the eighteenth century was it decreed that all must be of one design, and that black), I hazard that Grimani taunted Palladio about the first time he had visited Venice and been asked by a member of the Rezzonico family to design and superintend the building of a catafalque in which to place the body of a Spanish bride of one of the younger sons. She had been Matalita Perán y Sotomáyor. Death had struck her down in childbirth. To do honor to her illustrious family in Seville, as well as the Rezzonico family, a funeral cortege of great magnificence was planned. Young and intensely eager, Andrea had set about building a catafalque to end all catafalques, it would seem. To begin with he asked for and was granted permission to build his edifice —a really splendid catafalque of the period was nothing less—in an open space on the Calle Sottoportico, behind the Palazzo Rezzonico. In this manner he would be free to soar on flights of fancy and not feel the confines of four walls. As well, it would be much simpler to move the catafalque onto the barge which would bear its weight in the procession of funeral gondolas. His imagination soared with a vengeance, no doubt of that. The day arrived for the funeral. Borne by six sturdy lackeys, the coffin was taken out of the palazzo to be slid into the chamber in the catafalque. There was no chamber. In his youthful enthusiasm to make this first commission from the illustrious Rezzonico a veritable spellbinder of design, Andrea had completely forgotten to allow for a cubicle to receive the corpse. Boys gathered on the water-steps to watch this entertainment (for the funeral of a Venetian noble family was as gala as a wedding), yelped with delight, and called out, "Imbarazzo, non corpo, non corpo!"

For a few weeks it appears that Palladio luxuriated in idleness. Physical, not mental idleness, for a brain as active as his would be constantly stimulated by all he saw in Venice and the environs, where he was taken by Grimani to visit his friends. Many of these had small, rather flimsily constructed villas built years before, along the reaches of the Brenta Canal. For over one hundred years various landlords, many of them Venetians, had tried to make this narrow waterway popular, fringed as it was for miles in those days with plane and hazel trees. But so far no success. In two years Palladio changed all that.

During his first visit to Padova he met the ebullient brothers Foscari. Nicolo and Alisio were the astonishingly handsome twin sons of old Federico Foscari, whose gaunt bent figure and beetling brows were so familiar to all who frequented the *scala grande* of the Palazzo Ducale, unofficially the greatest money exchange in Europe in Palladio's day. The Foscari had held a few acres of land along the Brenta since the year 1200, when a Foscari had acquired it from the neighboring monastery of San Illario. The engaging brothers begged Federico to settle this plot of land upon them as part of their portion. This he did. Immediately Nicolo and Alisio drew up a document. It was read and duly signed by Palladio. In his *documenti architettura*, preserved at Vicenza, one reads: "Villa Foscari [later Malcontenta], erected on the festa of Corpus Domini 1555 to the order of the two brothers Nicolo and Alisio Foscari, sons of Federico Foscari of Venice."

Thus, two dilettantes of the fashionable Venetian world fired the first gun as a salute to herald a new style in architecture: the Palladian country villa. Many more were to follow in succeeding years, along the

Catafalque for a Noble Venetian Lady, 15th Century.

Brenta and scattered over the hills and valleys of all Italy. Ireland was to know this type of house at its best. England, Scotland, the continent of Europe, and America all adapted this dignified and immensely elegant style to their needs.

For a time Palladio devoted his talents to building, in Venice, probably the most architecturally beautiful convent in the world, Della Carità of the rhythmic colonnades, and the churches erected to the greater glory of God.

Many chroniclers differ about which of his churches Palladio worked on first. It does not signify in the long run. We know that he designed the façade only of San Francesco della Vigna. The main body and sort of temporary front were built by Sansovino, who had changed his name from Jacopo Tatti out of admiration for the Florentine sculptor, Andrea Sansovino. This Palladian screen against a long rectangular building resembles the portal of Palladio's San Giorgio Maggiore, but it lacks the sweeping scale that so instantly identifies this architect, whether in church, palazzo, or villa.

It is said that when the Council of Ten demurred a space, not wishing to spend public moneys on designs from an architect who was unknown to many Venetians, Monsignore Grimani paid Palladio out of his own pocket to proceed with his idea for a new front for San Francesco della Vigna. The result apparently pleased the reluctant Council, for they immediately commissioned Palladio to design San Giorgio Maggiore, on its water-bound island.

To me it has always seemed that no buildings anywhere present so magic a picture as those grouped, easily, with no sense of crowding, on this tiny square of land, reflecting in the Grand Canal the entire length of the rose and silvery white of the Campanile San Giorgio. It is like a shaft that always beckons one's eyes to the green-gilt dome of the basilica. "Look well," it seems to say, "you will never see a lovelier sight."

Many times I have been asked by persons who have carried away from Venice treasured memories of her palaces and churches just what quality the winged portico of San Giorgio has, more than another, that causes it to remain gleaming in the mind, seeming brighter in memory than all the other buildings. I tell them to what I attribute this recollection. The intense white of the pillared façade, as it is seen from Piazza San Marco, the Guidecca, or from a gondola in the Grand Canal, is framed in bright pink brick. This is the nave of the monastery church, wherein the marble and gilt wood of the altar is housed. A miracle of placing, surely, for at all times of day, whether a brilliant Venetian *particolori* or a soft pearly mist, when all Venice assumes the quality of a dream world, this backing of rose-red brick surmounted by the gold dome throws into sharp relief one of Palladio's supreme gestures.

I have never ceased to marvel at the basalt floors in the nave of San Giorgio. So satin sleek, so deeply rich in color, the curious dark green that is like a pool in the depths of a forest or as brown as spar. Why should it not be, indeed? A million years ago this basalt was water and spar. How cunningly has the hand of Palladio's chosen artisan cut the pointed slabs of stone to resemble the floor of a forest primeval. Yes, Palladio designed this church from his heart. *Con grande.*

In Il Redentore, as Venetians call their favorite church, in San Giorgio, in San Francesco della Vigna, and in the now destroyed tomb for the Pisani family near Strà, Palladio employed the same basic design of a pillared portico flanked by wings which are half of a pediment. Being cut in half at the apex of the pediment, these are generally known as "broken pediments" or *frontone rotto,* as Palladio indicates this motif in his decorative calligraphy on the margins of his drawings. And the very mention of these handsomely executed elevations which have been pre-served in Padova, Vicenza, Venice, and Rome, bring to my mind the envy I am always prey to when I see them. Envy not only to own one, but also because the paper on which Palladio drew will never be seen again in this world. Huge sheets of rough-edged handmade paper which in the course of centuries have taken a beautiful tone of *crème brûlée.* In many cases a smaller, quarto sheet of the same heavy white paper is covered with black notes, describing in minute detail just how a given doorway, pediment, or architrave must look when finished. When I held one of these sheets of intense black script in my hand in Padova one day, I felt as if I were actually in the room with the master who had written them. I turned a little toward a door at my back, fancying I heard his step and his voice.

Just as Persian script is sheer decoration, as Chinese and Manchu writings are so flowing and interesting in design, so is the writing from the hand of Palladio an integral part of his drawings. Regard this fragment that I have attempted to reproduce to give point to my story. Black as the day he wrote it—some sort of dye must have been used instead of the

Ta VII
Spaccato della Rotonda.
Portico occidente
0 1 2 3 4 →

usual ink of the period, which more often than not turns pale brown and is sometimes scarcely legible—the script concerns the Villa Capra (Rotonda) at Vicenza: "A view of the western portico." There are four pillared pediments at this villa. The dash and spirit of his writing is as full of infectious vitality as his buildings are today. There is a lift that even those who are not completely sold on Palladio admit intrigues them. So long as art in any form "does something to you," there is a reason for its being.

The interior of San Giorgio Maggiore is lofty and in every way worthy of the splendid quality of the entrance. A long aisle with a series of five groups of engaged columns, in nests of three, leads the eye to the altar screen which is both rich and simple. Rich, because the detail is carefully considered for placing. There is no attempt to fill all available space with ornament, as in baroque churches. Simple, because the design uses only one motif: engaged columns and a winged kind of loggia behind the altar, surmounted by two marble columns capitaled in the Corinthian order. These support a pointed pediment and two angels with particularly beautiful wings poised for flight.

A tiny church in an equally tiny piazza in Venice is most charmingly called Il Zittelle, the young spinster. It is a shade baffling just why this is so, for Venetians will tell you with some spirit that the name has nothing to do with the Virgin. The tall narrow façade is a charmer, no matter what spinster was so highly regarded that Venice chose to name a church for her. Again this small edifice tends to show what a truly fine artist Palladio was, for this commission—apparently paid for by public subscription—could not have meant very much to so popular and busy an architect as he was at the time Il Zittelle was built. In 1565, Palladio employed, by his own words, thirty-eight apprentices. He wrote to Trissino, who at that time was living in the old ramshackle villa at Meledo, built by his grandfather nearly one hundred years before:

I am forced to employ more Scribes and Youths who feel the call to Architecture. For my own ease of mind these seem to be plentiful, though it is a Taxing Life. I would more lief live the Country Life of yourself, even if the roof over your head does leak in a hundred places. Soon I shall quit Venice and build you the Vitruvian Palace you want at Meledo. Though for my Own Taste a Big Farmhouse would be fitter.

When Il Zittelle was finished, it presented a gay front to the world. A dome, painted clear blue overlaid with silver leaf, supports a lantern type of belfry, octagonal in shape. This belfry displays, in miniature, flying volutes in carved wood, painted to resemble pale blue marble. Surmounting the lantern is a figure of a rather bulky young woman, holding in her left hand what from the street looks like the enormous pipe carried by a traditionally correct William Tell making his entrance down the valley. I have been inside only once and found the interior unimpressive, or, rather, greatly altered since the church was first built.

The church of Santa Lucia in Venice was built just before Palladio started on his famous Redentore. In fact, so engaged did he become that after the main shell was roofed over a number of years elapsed before Santa Lucia della Musica, as the church is called, was finished. Over the vestry door there is a carved marble plaque, which informs all who read it that Palladio died before he finished the façade. By whom the church was finished the message does not reveal. Whoever he was (perhaps the apprentice Ranolli, who finished some of Palladio's work), he must have adhered strictly to the original design, for it is pure Palladio, if I ever saw it.

One of the fine touches that grace the interior of Santa Lucia della Musica could, I am convinced, have been designed by no other hand than that of Palladio. Over the entrance door, facing the altar, is a beautifully scaled choir loft for the nuns of the near-by convent of Santa Lucia. The proscenium of this small masterpiece carries in effect the lines of an open shell; the arched top is cut into the plaster in graceful flutes. The heel of the shell is a most imaginatively carved balustrade. This becomes a sort of sublime *vitrine*. A frame for saintly music.

One day, the story is told, an extremely haughty nobleman arrived in Venice from Bologna. Pompio Cardenosso by name, Conte by title. A god from Olympus by nature. He had come, he said, to offer Andrea Palladio the greatest honor ever tendered a mortal: a commission to design a basilica to the glory of San Petronio, patron saint of Bologna. After a talk with Conte Pompio, Palladio remained unimpressed. He had heard all about this precious "basilica" in Bologna. In reality it was a ratty old pile of Gothic jiggery-pokery. For years the Bolognese had cried out against this monstrosity. Now that Vicenza and Venice were building one magnificent Palladian church after another, they could barely hold up their heads for very shame. So Pompio Cardenosso was delegated to approach Palladio in Venice with an offer to design a basilica that would be supreme in church architecture. Pompio was a bad choice for ambassador. For in a fit of pique at Palladio's seeming lack of interest, he let the cat out of the bag. He said that actually the city of Bologna was nearly bankrupt. What they wanted was a Vitruvian frontage to extend across the old Gothic pile. The interior would have to remain, for the time being, as it was. Palladio heard about the same time that any number of architects had been invited to submit designs for altering the existing church. A sort of *concours*.

Finally Palladio, after asking a prodigious fee—of which he received only the first payment, or retainer—drove to Bologna in his traveling chariot drawn by the six horses that had been given him by a Venetian contessa who admired him vastly. He was interested to find on arriving at Bologna that a kind of workshop had been fitted up in the north aisle of the drafty old church and there were on display at least forty designs by Giulio Romano (pupil of Raphael), Vignola, Sansovino, and many other lesser architects, sculptors, and painters.

At least an amazing *galleria dell' arte* had been gathered with the greatest masters of the last twenty years in full force. Palladio caused his apprentice Aprilio Contini, an expert carver in wood, to fashion a model, which may still be seen in Bologna. It is delightful in a rather fantastic manner, for the carved masks used to decorate the frieze across the pediment and the superstructure rising from it are all distorted as if in agony.

Marvelously carved, these masks for sheer variety and daring cannot be matched in any other Renaissance façade I know.

It has been said they show various expressions assumed by Palladio when he was forced to meet Pompio Cardenosso. The basilica, finally finished, is rich in appearance but seems muddled and has little dignity. At night, when a full moon shines upon the portico and the clusters of engaged obelisks on the pediment, the sharpness of *chiaroscuro* is dramatic in the manner of drawings by Palladio.

The lack of space in Venice has been, in the last century, a great detriment to civic expansion, as it was with one flange of the portico of San Francesco della Vigna. A dwelling built about the year 1800 juts so far out into the small piazza in front of the church that one can see but half the entrance. Just so, it is impossible to get any kind of effect from the delicious little Santa Maria Nuova, built first in Venice by the Porto family, later copied in Vicenza. Many people do not know that this small distinguished templelike building any longer exists. So it is better to see it in Vicenza. A high arched door is set in a niche which was once painted madonna blue, powdered with gold stars. A pointed pediment rests upon four columns, Corinthian capped. A porthole window centers the pediment. Two niches flank the entrance door. These were once painted blue and doubtless contained statues. The church is a triumph of elegant simplicity, worthy of a far more important situation. In San Lorenzo in Vicenza, Palladio designed a magnificent tomb for the same Porto family. In many ways I find it the handsomest funerary design in Italy. A portico resembling the Roman temple to Mars projects from the wall for ten feet. Three huge but graceful and powerfully modeled sarcophagi in the form of urns, the covers enriched by acanthus leaves and an artichoke finial, are arranged to build a pyramid. Remembering his first *blague* with the Rezzonico catafalque, Palladio kept this tomb simple.

For a number of years, ever since Palladio had finished the church of San Giorgio Maggiore in fact, there had been talk among the Council of Ten and others of the Venetian nobility to the effect that a church honoring San Marco, their patron saint, should be built. But where? Every available plot of ground was occupied, and there was little of that. Except in the wind-swept outer harbor or near the old rock where the Fortezza Laberinto scowled upon all passers-by, there was no place to build. Some hardy soul suggested the Guidecca. No, that was the ghetto. Too crowded.

Then in the year 1576 the plague struck Venice. It was a particularly horrible sort of Asiatic plague out of the stews of Constantinople via China. No plague before had ever been so sudden, so violent, so putrifying. It was holocaust. Palladio and as many of his apprentices as he could gather together—many died from the plague—fled overland to the Dolomites, and the high pure air of Cortina di Ampezzo. Here an odd thing happens. For the first time a mention of his wife is made in document (C. Tridenti writing in *Giornale d'Italia,* Rome, in 1925): "Angela Palladio left Vicenza at the outbreak of the plague of 1576 and proceeded to Cortina where she established residence for him." That is all, though he goes on to say that Palladio visited Rovina where he designed a Palazzo Municipale, "accompanied by his wife and children."

The enforced months away from his various projects in Venice and villas along the Brenta—he was just finishing Villa Valmarana at Lisiera as well—were not idle ones. Far from it. With the help of Antonio Pignani, his secretary for twenty years, he compiled the wonderful treatise on three of his "Five Orders of Architecture." This volume is (or was) preserved in a private collection. I often called upon its possessor when I was in Venice. Taking this perfect book, which reposed in a velvet-lined teakwood box, out into the light of day seemed drastic at first. But I was assured the book was sturdy and I had nothing to fear. Later this friend who owned the book really took my breath away one day when, as I was leaving to return to Ireland, he handed me a parcel wrapped in dark wine-red velvet, the kind of velvet with warp of gold-colored silk. In this superb wrapping was a book said to have belonged to Palladio. It came into the family of the donor soon after the death of Palladio, in 1587 to be exact. The book is an *opera lingua greca,* telling the tales of ancient Greece. Monks at the monastery of San Illario compiled it in 1521, when Palladio was three years old. It is just the kind of book he would have loved and may as well have belonged to him as any other.

In the book he wrote while sitting out the plague in Cortina, he tells in brilliant manner how the *Corintio* order came into being. Actually Palladio, left to his own devices, seemed to prefer the *Ionico* capital. However, he realized fully the magnificent fluidity of the foliated Corinthian cap. He writes:

Most ornate of the three Greek orders is the Corinthian Capital. The purely Legendary Originator of this work is agreed to have been a Metal worker,

Callamachus of Corinth by name. The Graceful foliations rising in tiers to unroll as Volutes to support the overhang, suggests the craftsmanship of a Greek Sculptor. In measuring the Temple of Vesta at Tivoli, I found this Corinthian order in Perfection. I prefer this Temple to the far more Imperial Temple to Olympian Zeus in Athens. No one can be Insensitive, however, to the Finer Position of the Latter.

Although Palladio never says that he visited Greece, either as a young boy or later, he continually mentions temples in Athens and at Delphi as if he had seen them. Surely it was no difficult feat for a healthy curious youth, such as Andrea most definitely was, to ship out of Venice on one of the hundreds of ships sailing to Constantinople and the Greek Islands all during the Renaissance. While the raging of the plague in Venice, which continued with unabated horror for over a year, decimated the city by fifteen thousand inhabitants, Palladio kept his talisman of Parian marble ever within reach. The five-inch figure of the winged Nike of Samothrace had been given to him when he was in Rome; at least it was while he was measuring Roman ruins that he was first discovered wearing it around his neck on a leather thong. He wrote to Grimani, who was in Milan during the plague: "To think that my Small Nike from the Blue Island of Paros should have such power for Good in my Life. I Caress her until she begins to lose form. To Her I owe Health, Fortune and my Winged Device."

As suddenly as it had struck, the plague spread its Hecate wings and flew away. Venice was a veritable shambles. Whole quarters near the Merceria and Sottoportico were silent of all life. The Rialto was shut and drear. Scores of the great palazzi bordering the Grand Canal were shuttered, their owners living elsewhere. Some of these families did not return to open their houses for five years. The island of Guidecca, which had been terribly crowded as are ghettos the world over, was swept clean as a wheatfield after the harvesters. The blackest harvester of all had dwelt upon the sad waters of Venice. But, as human nature has done since the primordial ooze, the city gathered its purple and sharp-pink tatters together, opened its port for shipping, and the Doge gathered what men of his Council he could find and issued an edict that a church of heroic proportions should be built on the island of Guidecca, consecrated to the Redeemer for deliverance of the city from the plague.

Andrea Palladio was invited to come out of his mountain retreat. Actually he was in Vicenza, living in the half-finished Palazzo Colleoni, which had been empty for years. At this time Palladio's son Silla was

Sobiri Palazzo, Sottoportico.

about the age Palladio had been when first he went to Rome. Eager Andrea had written to Trissino later: "Rome, my Mistress. Vitruvius, my Master. Architecture, my Life." As the swaying coach jogged along the road from Vicenza to Venice, it is probable that Palladio wondered if this tall youth at his side, whom he was taking to Venice as an apprentice, would in turn take to his heart the trinity that had made life so full, so glorious, for his father: Rome, Vitruvius, Architecture.

And now full flight ahead went plans for Il Redentore. There are hundreds of buildings along the canals of Venice equally impressive. Some far more exotic in mingled Gothic and Renaissance detail. Others simple in line, ingratiating in color, the true golden pink seeming to throb and burn in the setting sun, the color that is only found in Venice. But not one of these churches or palaces—for there is little else to be seen—arrests one's sight and holds it so spellbound as does the church of the Redeemer. Or so it has always seemed to me. So stilly the winged white portico rises from the very brink of water, as if the white columns of luminous Istrian stone have but lately marched up the flight of wide shallow steps leading to the dark chestnut wood door. With pale-hued Venice spread out on every hand, one looks again at this house built to the glory of the Redeemer. It is the most beautiful of all, in this strangely beautiful place.

Palladio wrote, after he had first looked upon the pillared entrance to the Temple of Vesta in Tivoli, of his emotion, his instant love at first sight. "Là dove io t'amai prima." I feel this way about Il Redentore. The fact that this is a church has nothing to do with my feelings. That it is a triumphant gesture in arranging shimmering Istrian stone, does. Soaring façades anywhere, reflected in water, have always excited me. I find myself wishing for a moonlight night, that I may witness the reflected beauty in reverse. Once in my life I was presented with this wish in a manner never dreamed of.

On the night of the Feast of the Redeemer, all Venice is *en gala,* as at no other time. Enormous floats are towed out into the "pool" known as Guidecca. These heavy wooden platforms are capable of carrying fifteen to twenty men who are to set off the fireworks. Huge screens of wire and piping are set up to hold the big set pieces of myriad-colored fire. Many private dinner parties are given in this manner. There may be two or three gondolas with trestle tables set in the center from which serving men will hand you food and wines; or boards covered with gay cloths are lashed to the gunwales of the gondolas. Candles, wine-coolers, both cold and hot foods, and all kinds of favors such as confetti, serpentine paper, whisks, and spangled fans for the ladies, are piled about. Comes ten o'clock, and the Venetian populace by now at fever pitch with excitement, you glide in a gondola to the dinner party where your host or hostess sits enthroned. The fireworks start to hiss and blaze. Toasts are drunk. Wandering musicians pole past, or for a fee will attach themselves to the party where you are. The spangled fans of the ladies catch and reflect the red, green, and violet flame of a bowl of "fiery flowers," which blazes forth on the wire screens. Roman candles and zizzing rockets split the heavens. Always, like an obbligato heard through the din of bursting rockets, the music plays, now soft as in the barcarole, now loud and impassioned, as in rigoletto. Never has a scene acquired so much the quality of a dream, because of the fierce light on the fronts of the buildings around the fireworks, and the gradation, until it fades entirely, of light as far off as Lacuna Morte in the shadows of the night.

Verily, I have seen Il Redentore at its best.

The building is in the form of a Latin cross. In the long arm are three chapels situated in the aisles on either side of the nave. A dome crowns the crossing, supported on the four arches defining the nave. As one enters, there is a chapel on the right and the left of the pediment; these are in the wings flanking the portico. A touch of originality occurs in the four columns of the Corinthian order in the façade. The two outer columns are square, the inner are round. Supporting the base of the half-pediment of the wings are engaged flat columns. The massive entrance door is magnificent. It was designed by Palladio to be made of slabs of chestnut from the forests of Monte Cimino near Bracciano di Lago. The twelve-inch planks—each leaf of the door is five feet wide—did not arrive in Venice until two years after his death. So like him are they in design and scale one would think he had carved them himself. They are carved only in the sense that the enormous diamond-shaped bosses are so richly modeled. The color is incredibly handsome, so dark a red-brown as to be nearly purple. Centuries of hand-polishing—that is, using olive oil on the heel of the palm and a vast amount of elbow grease—have given the doors a patina like the most exquisite lacquer.

A square plaque is let into the wing on the right of the doorway as one enters. The plaque is on a level with the stair balustrade, twelve feet

CHURCH OF THE REDEEMER IN THE GUIDECCA, VENICE.
DESIGNED BY ANDREA PALLADIO.

from the bricked landing-stage. In letters of gold over black are the words CAMPO DEL SANTISSIMO REDENTORE. Originally these letters were of finest gold leaf. They blackened over rapidly, and later the letters were just gilded cheaply. Then the black paint one sees today was decided on. From now on black is good enough. But look closely. Scratch a bit of the black paint with your fingernail. Yes, that is pure gold leaf underneath. Various persons put forth a variety of reasons for this strange occurrence. I believe the long-dead monk who was originally chosen to apply gold leaf to the deeply incised letters still tends them. If these moderns want black, let them have it. Gold leaf they were when Il Redentore was built. Gold leaf they will remain as long as the edifice stands. Black or no black.

CONVENT OF LA CARITÀ

One of the most ancient orders for nuns in existence today is the order of La Carità. Indeed, some say that old documents found in the ruins of a nunnery when it crumbled to dust in 1889 in the outskirts of Rome gave extraordinary information. The first abbess of the order was abducted by Ostian pirates who wandered the rabbit-warren streets of Vespasian's Rome seeking victims. Although nuns were always in attendance on the abbess, somehow the kidnaping was accomplished. After being held for heavy ransom against her entreaties, the abbess' reason fled; and although the ransom was paid by the distracted nuns, she died soon afterward, raving. In perpetual penance these sisters of the Carità spend the years.

Palladio designed a most dignified building to house this order, utilizing his beloved colonnades to the finest effect. The front is long and three stories in height; the first two stories are colonnaded three-quarters of the length. A two-story portico, with a flat entablature and balustrade but no pediment, occupies this end portion of the front. The grand scale of the arched windows on the second tier of colonnades is the finest Palladio ever did. Each is separated from its fellow by a three-quarter-round column of the Ionic order. On the first or street line of arched windows, which do not have the splendid fanlight of the others, the columns are Doric. A rather flat and extremely simple third story—not an attic—has square-topped windows and flat Corinthian-topped pilasters. The finishing cornice is heavily molded. One detail only enriches this austerely beautiful façade.

In the Greek manner there is a wide band, sculptured in a flowing design of bleached skulls of bulls whose horns are draped in the classic swag; in the loop of each swag is a sun motif, myriad rays lending to it the effect of a huge flower.

It is believed by many authorities that Inigo Jones used this design for Houghton Hall (dismantled in 1794), in Bedfordshire. The north front was most certainly an almost exact copy of Palladio's graceful sequence of arched windows and columns capped in the three orders, Corinthian, Doric, and Ionic. The recessed portico used at La Carità formed the principal entrance at Houghton Hall. The use of the open loggia, so much favored by Palladio for his country villas, rather startled English eyes, for the raw winds sweeping across the channel were still hard opponents to keep at bay. However, Inigo Jones used the open loggia most successfully at the Queen's House, Greenwich. What leaps to the mind as most strange and ironic is the fact that almost identical copies of La Carità in England and Ireland should meet and succumb to the vagaries of man. Houghton succumbed to pride, the urge for a "greater" dwelling. And Harro Court, built by Richard Castle in County Carlow, was put to the torch one demented night of wind and weather by prowlers during the Troubles. The contents went whirling away to the Carough Mountains, and all lay scarred, in tears.

Many persons wonder why Andrea Palladio never built a palazzo or dwelling house of any kind in Venice. If one knows the inner mind of Palladio, this is not difficult to understand. First he had had quite enough of building palaces in Vicenza, Bologna, and even Padova. He said in no uncertain terms that he never felt at ease building his sweeping porticos and winged cubes and colonnades in mean streets and *cul-de-sacs*. He loved the country and the warmth of trees and rivers to shade and reflect his houses. He once wrote his son Silla, then at school in Padova: "Weary I am of Town Men and their Warped Sensibilities. I long for the Hills around Lonedo [where he later built Villa Piovene]. When I have done with La Carità, I shall Leave Venice with a Glad Heart. If I return to her canals again it will be as a Visitor but no Architect."

Very soon after this, Palladio did finish the convent of La Carità and returned to Vicenza. After a short visit to his three farms, he started on one of the most simple and lovely of his houses, the Villa Porto at red-earthed Vancimuglia.

THE BRENTA

Waterways—a lovely word, a nostalgic word. In everyone's life waterways have played a part, for good or for ill, at one time or another. While I venture that many rivers of the world are so narrow and so lazy flowing they may easily be taken for canals, few canals are taken for rivers. The Brenta Canal, flowing in undulating curves, so nearly straight as makes no matter, through the fertile farmlands of the Venetia, is very often taken for a narrow river; as such it has frequently been described by writers. In early documents the Brenta is said to have started its career as a deep, fairly wide irrigation ditch. A farmer living near the spot where the village of Strà now stands caught his shepherd in a spot of smuggling, *delitto di contrabbando*, sending a few carefully culled ewes and lambs to Venice by small boats that were pushed along the ditch by ragged urchins running along the bank. For a few *soldi* the boys would hide the sheep by day, traveling the boats at night. After putting immediate stop to the thieving of his flocks, the farmer conceived the idea of widening the ditch in order to ship food, grain, and livestock legitimately.

Thus were born a few miles of ribbonlike water, which have for centuries reflected in their shallows houses that have become legends. Most of the houses bordering the Brenta are on one side of the canal, the left side coming away from Venice. The extravagant palace of the Pisani, Palazzo del Strà, in magnitude and impressive impact a palace, not a villa, stands alone for miles, on the right-hand bank.

Andrea Palladio did not build the Palazzo del Strà. The present house was built around a much smaller one, designed in both instances by an architect named F. M. Preti. The man was so under the influence of Palladio—almost bemused by him—that many persons, until they are enlightened, believe Palazzo del Strà to be one of Palladio's greatest gestures. The almost incredible sweep of fairly simple façade, embracing an elaborate portico displaying eight columns of the Corinthian order, was built in 1735 for one of the most cultured and vainglorious Venetians who ever lived, the Doge Pisani. Later I will describe the Palazzo del Strà more fully.

Writing about the villas built by Palladio along the reaches of the Brenta Canal, I shall not be able to give the exact dates of building. No one knows for certain just when some were built, for if elevations were kept by Palladio in his famous portfolio, with dates of construction, they are gone from this world forever, destroyed in the raging flames that consumed the house of his son Silla two years after his father's death.

A story told me in Venice by a man who would know as much as anyone alive about Palladio's life and death—because documents concerning both are precious possessions in his family—says that among the notations Palladio gave his secretary regarding the disposal of various effects was one concerning the white oxhide portfolio that contained his elevations for country villas. These were to be sent by packhorse to Aprilio Pisani who was in residence at his townhouse, Villa Pisani at Montagnana. For some unexplained reason nearly two years elapsed after Palladio's death before any activity was shown by his son to settle his father's estate. Finally matters began to move. Silla Palladio saw various boxes corded and labeled, then he left for his villa in the hills near Meledo. In some manner, either from haste or stupidity in reading the label, the saddlebag containing the white portfolio of elevations destined for the Pisani at

Montagnana was loaded onto a packhorse in the string going under guard to Silla at Meledo. Apparently the bales and boxes on arrival at Meledo were hastily thrown into some corner for unpacking at a later time. A few nights later they were unpacked with a vengeance. The Eumenides unpacked them. A demented wind had howled around the hill of Meledo all day. Suddenly a brand broke away from the parent log in the huge fireplace and slithered into the room, flames licked up the loosely woven *stoia,* a reed matting that covered the walls of the room in which the saddlebags lay. Alecto, Tisiphone, and sister Megaera screeched and danced about the floor. When the Furies burn, they burn to the foundations. Had it not been for an error in dispatching a portfolio to the wrong house, priceless drawings of Palladio's Brenta villas and some built in the environs of Montagnana and Meledo would have been preserved today. All that were entrusted to the Pisani have been carefully guarded through the centuries. Some of the houses still stand. A few do not.

I believe the best way to tell of the villas along the Brenta—either built by Palladio himself or so strongly influenced by his style that a marked family resemblance is apparent—will be to catalogue them, beginning with the most widely known of all his Brenta houses, the lonely, romantic Villa Malcontenta.

VILLA MALCONTENTA

What a lovely lingering word to say—Malcontenta. What a dreaming pile of stone and frescoed plaster to gaze upon, this house of the discontented woman; for it was she, malingering, golden-haired daughter of Federico Foscari, who gave the villa its haunting name. Among the many legends surrounding this unhappy lady of the Foscari, the tale of the fabulous collection of jewels, so mysteriously delivered to her one starlit night during her imprisonment in the tree-embowered villa, deserves retelling. She is called Magdalina by some chroniclers, by others Francesca Magdalina. It is very probable that she was known in earlier years, before her long captivity, as Francesca, because she was great-granddaughter to Doge Francesco Foscari, who had held the Venetian Republic in a vise of blazing prosperity that culminated in its sudden downfall, after he had ruled longer than any preceding Doge.

The Doge Francesco Foscari had acquired, during the long years

CROSS SECTION· VILLA FOSCARI-MALCONTENTA.
AFTER PALLADIO.-1555.

of his stewardship of the richest seaport in Christendom, a collection of jewels of incredible quality and value. Many were from Asia and the Orient. When the Doge died, a woman from Rovina, Maria Buccelli, raved and tore herself and most of the family Foscari into pieces trying to locate this horde of jewels. She contended, bolstered by a written will she waved for all to read, that they were to come to her. No jewels were found. And the Foscari, to the last ramification of that widespread family, were shaken but tireless in their efforts to find the hidden jewels. At last, frustrated at every turn, they concluded that the vast treasure had been stolen.

Then came the punishment of Francesca, decreed by her irate father because she had disgraced the family by flagrantly displaying her golden charms in Venice. She was sent to the Foscari Villa, which had been lately finished by Palladio on the banks of the Brenta. Here, under the constant care of a duenna, she was to meditate until her father saw fit to bring her back to Venice. Some say she died before this recall came. In any event it would seem she languished deep in melancholy for a time, whatever the release.

On a night of fair heavens and trillions of stars, the saddened lady walked the terrace under the wide portico. Pausing to gaze out across the canal, she noticed how bright the stars appeared, so brilliant and so many, doubling their beauty in the still water at her feet. One star seemed to move across the water toward her. Yes—it was a light, either on the prow of a small boat or in the hand of someone signaling to her from the opposite bank. She turned and sent her duenna into the house on an errand, then went to the iron bars that had been set up across the front of the portico to prevent her escape. Calling softly to the unknown bearer of the lantern, the lady Foscari watched wonderingly as a man crept out of the shadows of the plane trees. In the brilliant starshine she noticed that he was young, tall, and of a gypsy cast of feature. He smiled, pointed to a leather pouch in his left hand. With his right hand the tall man made the gestures of decking oneself with jewels, describing the placing of the stomacher, necklace, bracelets, earrings, and finally coronet, with deft movements. Then the man smiled and tossed the pouch through the bars. It landed almost at her feet. Francesca stooped and grasped the pouch. Carrying it to a small table which stood in the brilliant light of the stars, she pulled wide the thong and emptied upon the cold marble such a flood of lambent flame that she hastily drew back. There it lay, the lost treasure of the Doge of the Venetian Republic. Crimson, purple, emerald and rose-white fire, the faceted stones caught the starshine. Trembling with incredulous excitement, the lady turned to where the man had waited. He was gone. Only shadows and patches of starlight where he had stood.

Quickly Francesca separated the jewels. Dark sea-green emeralds she hung about her neck. Bracelets of smoldering pigeon-blood rubies encircled her wrists. Long ropes of Bahreinian pearls she slung in festoons about her throat and bosom. The pale colored fire of diamonds swung from her ears, and last of all a high tiara, intricate and tall as the miter of a Byzantine bishop, rose in icy splendor from her brow. Standing in the full light of the midnight stars, she searched the far bank of the canal where the moving light had first caught her attention. She felt the gypsy might still be watching, waiting for one look at the jewels he had returned to her, worn now as he had motioned. Beauty, jewels, and the starry night to give them luster. A bird called in the thicket. A dog barked in a distant farmyard. There was the soft *lap-lap* of water against the reeds. The enfolding night and the jeweled woman in the portico. Silence.

When word was carried posthaste to Venice and the assembled Foscari that the recalcitrant Francesca walked the iron-barred portico blazing with jewels, from the gods alone knew where, the reaction of her father and brothers was formidable. Where and when had she got them? No answer. Where had she hidden them, since not a sparkle could be found? Only a pout in answer. Desperate means are said to have been employed to make Francesca tell the story of the night of stars. Only the duenna, who was on the side of her charge, under duress related a few of the facts. The gypsy, whom she had seen from an upper window, and the fact that not a word had been spoken between her lady and him. To no avail did father and brothers threaten. At times, it is said, Francesca would deck herself in jewels wondrous to behold. When bargemen poled their laden barges past the portico of the Villa Foscari on the evenings when the lady chose to walk in splendor, they marveled, and called out one to the other, "Aspetto, La Malcontenta, amicizia sta sera." When she wore her jewels, she was prepared to be friendly, as the bargee said. At other times she screeched maledictions at them. They bit the end of their thumbs, and spat into the canal, in the classic manner against the evil eye. Only after her death, it is told, did the hiding place of her mysteriously returned jewels come to be known to the distraught Foscari, along with a statement telling a few of the recorded facts.

The canal path from Fusina in the direction of Malcontenta is a pleasant tree-bordered stretch to walk along on a spring morning when the world about is drenched with sun. As I approached the belt of tall trees that screen the house from this side, I realized that something was very different from the usual Italian landscape scene. A tall chimney. A very handsome chimney, rather like a domed minaret on some Tunisian sky line, but very rarely seen in Italy. One of the questions asked most often by persons looking over my portfolios and scrapbooks devoted to reproductions of elevations by Palladio is: "Did he never design chimneys on his houses? What becomes of the smoke from all those fireplaces?" It is true. In none of his elevations does a sign of chimney or any outlet for smoke appear. I expect he did not wish to interrupt the flow of line of his roofs, for they are always cleanly limned and carefully shaded. Chimneys were added later. I have a drawing of the Villa Manin at Polesine. In this ink and wash rendering of a singularly well-proportioned portico, he draws his chimneys—a decidedly decorative feature of the finished house—in a line, like a frieze across the top of the drawing.

Only one chimney of four original ones remains on Malcontenta, or did when I last saw it. The owner, Mr. A. C. Landsberg, is still at work on the house, slowly, but with immense sympathy restoring it to Palladio's original splendor. This tall lighthouse of a chimney is lovely in color. Pale fawn-rose terra cotta is used to fashion it and is again used in the Ionic capitals of the portico, the architraves around the superb entrance door, and for the main cornice.

The four-square block of the house forms a cube, from one wall of which projects a templesque Ionic loggia, grave and calmly beautiful,

Original Terra-Cotta Chimney,
Villa Malcontenta.

like some Attic goddess standing hesitant for a moment, reflected in the mists of time. Reflections in clear water or the miragelike play of silvery mist are very much a part of Malcontenta. For the house stands almost on the threshold of change from Venetia to where the vast plain of Lombardy merges into the Adriatic. Indeed, so near the sea is this house that when sudden storms break, the lashing rain from off the Adriatic is fused with salt spray, and flocks of drenched gulls shelter momentarily under its soaring portico.

Wind and rain, hot summer suns and hostile invaders (Austrian troops quartered here in 1848 during the blockading of Venice) have draggled this wondrous house, but harmed it little. The essentials that make Malcontenta one of the most memorable houses on earth are unscathed. The balustrades that once followed the L-shaped curve of the magnificent flights of steps rising fifteen feet on either side of the portico are gone, I hope never to be replaced, for the majestic rise and turn of these broad steps is not matched in sweep, anywhere. No iron grille or marble balusters should break the line.

Brick is used to build the cube, which is cut in half horizontally. The two sections rest on a base half as high as the whole house. The large entrance hall running through the center of the building rises two stories between these separated cubes. On the bricks is a mixture, one that seems to appear only in Palladio's country villas, called *marmorino*. Compounded from powdered sea shell and whitest marble, the whole was mixed with travertine lime before it was applied over the bricks. A flat iron spadelike implement on a long handle was then heated, and the hot spade-end was rubbed in circular motion over the *marmorino*. This method, which is still used, imparts an oyster-white semigloss to the surface. The fifteen-foot first floor is of *pietra d'Istria*, white as alabaster. Above the main pediment rises a sort of superstructure composed of a row of three square-topped windows of generous proportions. Four flat pilasters with plain band capitals support a small pediment. This whole arrangement is rather like a penthouse or large dormer.

In Scamozzi's edition of *Andrea Palladio*, he gives the main floor plan and a section, as if cut straight through the center of the house. The Villa Foscari was built as a *mietitura padiglione* to be visited for the enjoyment of the pleasures of the harvest. Its greatest charm is the elegant simplicity of the house, both inside and out. Rooms large and airy, windows arranged to catch every latent breeze blowing across the plains from Lombardy or the Adriatic. The letters written by Lady Mary Wortley Montagu during a visit to Venice (1739) to a friend in England, often mention Malcontenta. In her wittiest manner—and none surpassed Lady Mary in that attribute—she says:

> Gaiety abounds. We are moved hither and yon over Waterways, each Lovelier than the last. Fusina, adorable spot, where I bought a White Jennet for Arlie [her niece] made me eager to visit that Old Pleasure House of the "furious" lady, whom I Refuse to believe was as discontented as we would be assured. Even two hundred years ago the Villa must have been a Dream. And all those Jewels. Do you suppose she never saw her Benefactor again? I vow she did.

Lady Mary calls the Malcontenta "an old pleasure house"; surely it was built for such a purpose, and I for one do not believe that Francesca Magdalina spent any appreciable time in duress. It would have inconvenienced the family Foscari no end to have had her moping about their pleasure house, at harvest time.

At Bergamo in the Accademia Carrara there hangs an entrancing painting. The name it bears is *Giardino di una Villa Valeta*, and it was painted by a pupil of Veronese, one Benedetto Caliari. I would sell my eternal prospects to own this picture. What is more, I've just the place to hang it. Never has the indolent country life of the Renaissance in Italy been so rapturously pictured. In the foreground flows the Brenta. One is in it, so to speak. Water-steps lead up to an arched loggia-pavilion with entrances four ways. Smiling and amazingly chic caryatids uphold a canopy of thickly growing grapevines, the green fruit glowing like clustered emeralds. In the background is a sort of *tempio d'amore* with two shadowy figures in embrace. In the middle distance, set in flowery borders, is a large pool encircled by standard rose trees. Under the deep shade of the loggia a servant in violet and pink livery lays a table with silver plates of food. While waiting for lunch to be served, two ladies decide to fish— not seriously by the flimsy look of the tackle, just to pass the time. A gallant in ruff and slashed claret doublet arrives on the scene, scaring the fish. One lady is amused, one piqued. Never have I seen the very fabric of a lazy, perfect summer day so well suggested.

Apparently all these Brenta villas had water-gardens. One still exists in a much depleted state, at Villa Barbariga, more often referred to in Fusina and Strà, the two largest villages on the Brenta, as Villa Lunga

Type of Large House Often Seen in Italian Cities.
Four Cubes or Two Oblongs and Two Cubes.

Plan of Italian Townhouse. Built around Courtyard in the Middle of Which
Is a Fountain. Two Tall Arched Doorways Afford Entrance from Two
Streets. Palladio Used This Style of House in Vicenza.

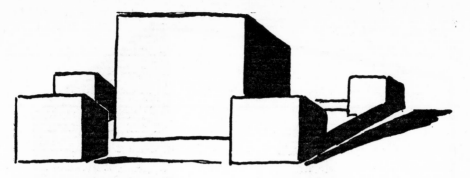

Using Five Cubes and Three Balustrades. Style of Grouping Outbuildings.

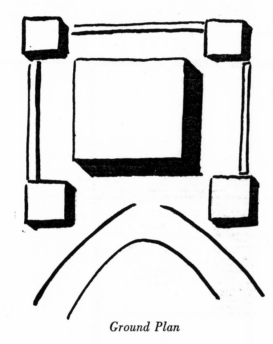

Ground Plan

*One Cube, Two Flexible Oblongs, and Two Oblongs Up-Ended. A Formation
Much Used in England.*

Verde. Probably for the wide strip of bright green lawn flung out in front of its extraordinarily long façade. No record is left of a water-garden at Malcontenta. Undoubtedly there was one, for elaborately constructed water-steps still glow dimly under the water.

The interior of Malcontenta is renowned. For many years architects from all over the world have come, as on a kind of pilgrimage, to study the grand scale and wonderful simplicity of construction. From time to time more frescos have been discovered under layers of whitewash and colored distemper. The now famous fresco of La Malcontenta was discovered in the *sala,* the most spacious room in the villa. It appears that the late Queen Mother Margherita of Italy was visiting the villa one day. She saw what appeared to be the fingers of a hand under some gesso peeling from the wall panel opposite the entrance door. With her fingernail and later a cloth dipped in water she removed the gesso from a porion of the figure of a woman. Dressed in a richly heavy costume of the period of 1560 is a full-fleshed patrician lady with a most forbidding expression on her face. She is painted in a clear yellow gown with an elaborately jeweled girdle. A pomander swinging from one hand, she stands level with the person in the room, and a dark curtain is draped behind her. A painted border like a door frame encloses the figure. La Malcontenta seems amazingly tall, until one sees that she is elevated on extremely high pattens that are nearly hidden under her long skirt. When one enters this great hall, the sense of lift and perfection of scale is extraordinary, so striking that it caused Lord Byron to write: "Its proportions are an architectural paean."

Malcontenta was built to be reached by water. One of the most vibrant memories of a happening in my life is the night I engaged a barge at Fusina. A night when all the gods on Olympus were hung with stars. As we drifted around the slight bend in the canal nearing Malcontenta, I saw it looming, pale gray jade among the shadows of black and white trees. Timeless beauty lay all about me. This was the way Palladio had dreamed the villa would be approached. A light breeze rippled the stark reflection of portico in water. As the barge slid under the trees that border the canal, I heard a tapping, faint but still distinct. Was it the high, gilded pattens of La Malcontenta hurrying across the polished *pavimento rosso* of the great hall?

VILLA MALCONTENTA ALLA BRENTA.

VILLA VALMARANA–*Lisiera*

A long, two-story farmhouse faces one across water. Only the central block was designed by Palladio. It is a house to be proud of, for an illusive quality of brightness, of pleasant days spent within its walls pervades the place. Some houses instantly spell danger, a repellent quality strikes out at the beholder. The sooner he leaves it far behind, the better. Not so is the look of this house. A more generally engaging portico I have never seen. When Palladio writes in a letter to Grimani in Venice about his elevations for this house, he shows his enthusiasm for the project. "If it were a House for Myself in which to end my days I could not proceed with greater Joy. I leave the old [a hundred years only] wings. An ancient, rickety Castellated affair has done duty so far to House and Protect, but Drafty and Ruinous. I propose a lightly set portico with a large Loggia cut into the lower face of the Front."

All this he carried out, but before he had started on the wings, Palladio died. The house and a great deal of the interior was finished by Scamozzi. It is much deeper than most of the houses designed by Palladio: ten windows deep and ten across the front, all in one block. The reason for this was to allow for a generous *cortile* where sweet lemon trees from Sorrento were set in summer. The first glass houses ever seen in Italy were built by the owner in 1889 to stand in the big grass court behind the house and protect his lemon trees in winter. The first floor of Villa Valmarana is three-quarters as high as the whole building. Six columns of the Ionic order form a cut-under room, as we call them in Ireland, or loggia, in the center of the house. The loggia has five windows across the front, each protected by a balustrade. The pediment is extremely attractive, for it displays richly imaginative plasterwork combining fruits of the earth with the elements: clouds, lightning, winds, both friendly and adverse; rain, hail, and fog. Five figures of bucolic demigods laughingly stand guard on the pediment and corners of the roof. An engaging deity, a young Father Time I should judge, raises one hand in eternal salute as you walk up the path from the canal.

VILLA BISSARI–*Relorgole*

Set amid silvery green lime trees, undulating wheatfields, and orchards of delicious quinces, this villa, now a farmhouse, is most pleasing. Palladio nicknamed it Villa Cotogno; to this day the peasants thereabouts will direct you to the House of the Quinces. One of the many joys to be encountered here, as I have good cause to remember, is the superb quince marmalade, which has been made here from the same recipe for three hundred years. Some people fill their cellars with wine. At Villa Cotogno the cellar is filled with stone crocks of jellies, jams, and marmalade from the huge golden quinces that resemble the apples of the Hesperides, and exude a fragrance as subtle as the flavor. Ginger and a dash of cognac go into this ancient recipe, and a twist of sweet lemon-rind.

I have eaten great slabs of fresh bread with "lashin's" of quince marmalade in the arcaded kitchen of this house, on a cold wet day after I had ridden miles in a teeming downpour astride a horse that should have gone for glue, long, long ago. This house has so much to offer. Companionship, *cucina grande*, within walls that are an architectural gem.

The house is three stories. Farm and stables form an L at either side of the entrances. The ends contain dovecotes, and two walls branch forward to pilasters on which swing a wide entrance gate. The large front court is gracious, completely a farmyard. Geese waddle across one's path in the classic manner. Cows look you straight in the eye and will not give an inch. A shaggy Piedmontese shepherd dog greets you and invites you to enter the portico.

This is supported by six square pillars of the Ionic order. Over its entablature is an attic of windows crowned with a shallow pediment. This is an unusual treatment. The color of Villa Bissari-Cotogno, to do the house full honor, is delightful. The walls are washed a luminous wheat color with dove-gray and white trim. From far off one sees this whole farm with its outspread buildings lying in a gentle hollow, backed by gentle hills. The whole effect is that of an early Italian painting of a Venetian farmstead.

At one time great state was kept at Villa Bissari. When Palladio built it for the Conte Bissari about 1570, the hunting preserves of Venetian nobles who maintained villas along the Brenta were the scenes of gay parties. The hunters would repair to whatever villa happened to be nearest the end of the chase. For memorable hospitality no one shone more brightly than the Bissari. In the sala, as one enters the house, there may still be seen a huge fresco of a staghunt that took place in this valley, immortalized in paint by an artist of the period named Donato Diziani, whose grandson Antonio Diziani had a vogue in Venice in the eighteenth century. The color of this spirited painting is fresh and vibrant as if it had been painted recently. The stag is in the front of the composition. The strength of his last efforts to gore the hounds is magnificently painted.

VILLA PISANI—*Montagnana*

The house Palladio built for Francesco Pisani at Montagnana is so close to the Brenta that it may well be included in this chapter. When the first elevations were drawn, the house was much larger, in many ways grander, than it turned out to be in the long run. For many reasons I like the villa better the way it now stands, although Palladio felt great grief when he was forced to cut down the scope of the frontage, the two wings and squared towers that flanked the original conceptions of the villa. There are plenty of houses with that general plan that were carried to completion by Palladio. We know what he could do, and superbly. What signifies is the fact that by the very simplicity of design and integrity of building, in scale and proportion, a most harmonious house has been achieved; one that, as I have already said, has influenced architects down the years more than any other building designed by him.

The plan is a rectangular block of Istrian stone, three stories in height. But the stories are higher than a good many of his country houses of the pavilion type. The dignity of the *frontone del Vittoria* facing a small piazza is largely due to the placing of the windows. Never have I seen windows that are simply tall or medium rectangles with small oblong ones under the cornice add to the design of a façade so effectively. At the height of the first floor a wide kind of stringpiece follows completely around the building. This has a massive richness which, with the exception of the sculptured pediment, is the only embellishment used to relieve the plainness. The entrance porch is arranged flat against the stonework. Four three-quarter columns of Ionic order are widely spaced, with a square-corniced door and two windows supporting arched lunettes on either side between the columns. The pediment is unusual; only one other time have I seen Palladio use the motif of a beautifully incised entablature proclaiming the name of the owner. Here it announces to the world at large: FRANCISCUS PISANUS JO. FF. The Roman letters are massive and amazingly decorative. In the wedge of the pediment two reclining handmaidens,

75

straight from Olympus, steady at a rather perilous angle a scrolled cartouche, emblazoning the Pisani lion rampant, and tree.

The garden side of the house is a gem of manipulation in stone, for which Palladio was famous. Never has he achieved the degree of lightness of "airy pavilions" as in this instance. There is always the chance that I might be prejudiced because of my overweening admiration for this house. But I have heard many architects and laymen of great taste say the same.

In all but this cut-under loggia the façade is the same as the front. This alcove is stunning in proportion, at least fifteen feet deep and twenty feet across. It becomes a room of many uses. At Shirley, in Charles City County, Virginia, this upper and lower pillared loggia is used with outstanding success. The rooms are not entirely cut under as at Villa Pisani, but they answer much the same purpose since they are spacious and open to the play of breezes.

The interior of Villa Pisani is of an elegance and breadth seldom achieved in a house not overlarge, and full of rooms. The *atrio*, which is splendidly proportioned, is shaped like a T, extending straight through the house from front to back, where it branches to form the crossbar of the T. Two staircases wind to the floor above, one on either side of the house.

Tall columns with Doric capitals support gracefully arched vaultings in the entrance hall, the *atrio*. Four niches indent the corners under the columns. In these stand the famous terra-cotta figures of the four seasons, which have been so much photographed. They were sculptured by Alessandro Vittorio, who modeled the female figures in the pediment. Pale beige terra cotta in color, the figures have a warm patina so subtle in finish that the fluidly molded drapery of La Primavera and L'Estate seem luminous, as with hidden light, against the pale almond green and dove gray of the walls. L'Autunno is a nude youth crowned with grapes and vine, while L'Inverno is a heroically muscled Titan, a furred skin thrown around his loins. The grandly modeled head is bearded and crowned with wreathed locks blowing in a sharp north wind.

Concerning the other houses along the Brenta, only two are attributed to Palladio. These were both built after his death. One house, Villa Contarini d'Este, was his suggestion. A preliminary sketch was sent to Il Consiglo Contarini, but nothing ever came of it. Years later, roughly

1682, an architect named Coronelli was commissioned by a member of the d'Este family to build them a villa. It is immediately apparent, when one sees this beautifully mellow old house, that if Palladio did not design it, then his ideas were tapped to a fare-ye-well.

The house is inventive in design, very much like some of the last country houses Palladio worked on in the Udine. It is in the pavilion style, a style very close to his heart, as we know. The principal front has majestic sweep, the "imperial plan" of Vitruvius, which Palladio speaks of so often in his book on architecture. One passage bears this out: "Magnificence of mass and line may assure an Architect that he has found the Lodestone for composing houses of interest to all men." In other words, "grandly simple" or "simply grand," take your choice.

Set upon a high basement of rustico stone, water-pitted in effect, is one long, rather high story, seven windows across. The entrance door has been made to look like another window. The windows are supported upon richly modeled consoles. Each window has a square lunette and a pitted keystone above. A pediment over the three center windows is heavily trimmed in overhanging moldings and the center pierced by a porthole window. A flight of ten broad steps without a balustrade wends upward to the entrance. The long, high *sala di ballo* is one of the most sensationally beautiful rooms, ballroom or any other, I have ever seen. Of spectacular proportions, every inch of wall space is painted. I have always loved great painted rooms in the Italian *bravura* style, and have managed to have one in some form in every house where I have lived, even if I had to paint it myself, which has often been so. In the *sala di ballo* at Villa Contarini the painted room reaches the very height of romantic beauty.

The illusion, first beheld, is of all shades of geranium red, gray, dark green, and white. Once the first astonishment has subsided, other colors float into the picture. One realizes there are all variations of the colors first seen and many more. The effect on the senses, when one is dancing in this room with only the light of the moon and a few candles, is magical. Greek myths in marble-framed panels make up the subject of the mural. I counted fifteen kinds and colors of marble painted in various arched perspectives in this room. The dove-gray marble veined in black and white is always nearest to the eye. Oddly, the painter of these panels is unknown, at least much in doubt. Some say Dario Voratori. Whoever did them, the room is a *tour de force*.

Winged Portico at Villa Giovanelli.

Four Cubes and Four Flexible Oblongs.

Ranfurly, County Tipperary, Ireland.
Four Shaded Porticos, Open and Spacious, to Catch the Latent Breezes.
The Brenta Type of Country Villa.

One other villa on the Brenta recalls Andrea Palladio in his earlier style of a four-square block, with an entrance in each side. The Villa Giovanelli is a sort of hybrid in architecture. Yet undoubtedly there is the grand air coupled with a sense of spacious comfort that distinguishes these Brenta villas. Ideally placed on the very brink of the canal outside of Fusina, nearer to Padova, the house was originally built for a Hungarian, Count Giovanelli, baron of the Holy Roman Empire. The older and larger villa most probably bore more resemblance to Palladio's designs, if indeed they were used at all. In the museum at Vicenza there is a sketch by Palladio, dated 1567. Written across the right-hand corner of the paper is: *Giovanelli, Conti di Morengo, Baroni del Sacro Romano Imperio.* At least Palladio was interested.

It is the interior of Villa Giovanelli that is of greatest interest today. The scale of the *salone del primo piano* is staggering. Sweeping forty feet, from violet and black *terrazza* with insets of white marble stars, the walls curve to an enriched cornice surrounding a domed "lantern." The room is full of crystals, and the enormous painted panels depict in rich color scenes from the dramatic history of Hungary alternating with equally vital moments in Greek mythology. The play of light and shade in this room is very like the water pictures on the ceilings of houses in Venice. When a house stands so close to water, the sunlight plays charming tricks with reflections. No other house in Italy has so fine a collection of the gay, curving painted furniture of *sette-cento* Venice as Giovanelli today, for one is scarcely able to move in the crowded rooms, huge as they are. Each article of furniture is a museum piece, but it is downright impossible to enjoy all its fine points in the *mêlée* of curves.

So many houses along the Brenta Canal, or in the lovely countryside lying on either bank from Venice to Padova, are purported to have been designed by Andrea Palladio. It just isn't so. Many of the seventeenth century villas, for example Palazzo del Strà, Villa Giustinian, and the Villa Venier, are directly influenced by Palladio. But so were many houses built in the eighteenth century in Ireland, England, and America. Some Brenta villas are huge and arrogant. Others are set in sweeping gardens. One or two have world famous frescos, of unimaginable beauty. But to my mind, Palladio evoked the Golden Age of Greece and the glory that was Rome when he built Villa Malcontenta.

HOUSES IN THE HILLS

Hills fascinated Palladio. "Look to the hills" might easily have been a motto for him. Some of the finest houses he ever designed lie quietly along the crest of a hill. The Brenta flows for a while, after leaving Venice, through flat country. On either hand fields of grain wave away to the horizon. Small holdings comprising a two-room house, a cow-byre, low sheds for fowls, and a small circular roundabout for grinding millet (a staple of this region) huddle together, backs crouched against the

Adriatic wind. The general scheme is much the same today as it was in the years when Andrea Palladio left the Venetian scene—whenever he could tear himself away from building churches—and sought the relaxation of the hills.

Soon after one leaves Strà, the Brenta forks; one branch flows to Padova, the other through the hills of Bagnoli and Perarolo. In dense groves of lime, plane, and hazel trees one may still see hunting-lodges or a dignified farmhouse, even a half-ruined villa in the grand style with a long, two-story loggia. Remote, mislaid, houses drowsing away the centuries. A score of these half-hidden houses were designed either wholly or partially by Palladio. Many owe their existence to the fact that they were the *barchessa* (stables, kennels, winehouses, and the like), that were turned into living quarters when the big villas were destroyed by fire or neglect. Whenever Palladio conceived a plan, a layout, or a *dominio campagna* or *ritirata*, far from the maddening crowd of cities, he always made any building on the place, be its function ever so humble, as attractive as the house. These buildings presented themselves fully equipped to house whoever wished to remain on the land.

VILLA ZENO—*Casalto*

The peach-colored village of Casalto lies on a gentle rise of land three miles inland from the Brenta. Padova may be seen through a gap in the rolling hills. It might be a thousand leagues away, for Casalto retains a classic simplicity. So little does the life of Padova interest the Casaltese that an old shepherd, whom I chanced to meet one day ambling along a cart track near the village, seemed affronted when I asked him how far it was by the highroad to Padova.

"How should I know, forestiero? I have never been to Padova."

If he was affronted, I was bewildered, for once I took another look at my map, which was faded and much travel worn, I realized the distance could not be more than fifteen kilometers, about twelve miles, down a gradual slope for half the distance.

"No," he told me, after I inquired just why he had never felt the urge to visit this big historic town, "I was born here in the hills. I have tended my sheep for sixty years, and watched the sun rise and the moon fade at morning. Whatever men do in big towns does not interest me. I do not like what comes out of them."

Standing in the shaded path, gnarled brown hand clasping his tawny homespun cloak across his chest, the man was like the wanderers one sees on the plains of Thrace. He looked intently at me, we both smiled and murmured "Andare pace." I realized I had been so fascinated by this relic of antiquity, I had forgotten to ask him the way to Conte Zeno's hunting-lodge.

Later in the day I found the house, closed now but not actually deserted, for a caretaker told me that members of the family who lived in Genoa came there for autumn shooting. The snipe, the juicy quail, and hare were plentiful in October and November. A dreamy house it is, redolent of good sport. One senses the famed hospitality for which this hunting-lodge is known the length of the valley.

Palladio built this lodge-villa-farmhouse (it is truly all three at once) for his great friend, Nobile Marco Zeno. Wide and spreading, the house has a graceful pillared porch set twenty-five feet from the paved entrance court. This allows for a delightful series of arched doors that lead to a stone-paved banqueting hall on the ground floor. The main block of the house is three stories high with a central dormer embracing three pedimented windows. The two wings, which contain stables, granaries, orangeries, and farm offices, are returned L's. The focal point of the whole grouping is, however, the rusticated gateposts surmounted by two magnificent stags in mortal combat. These battling monarchs of the forest are really in earnest. Antlers locked, front hoofs pawing the air, the stags form an arch over the entrance gate, through which has passed many a tired but happy returning huntsman.

The tiles of Villa Zeno-Casalto are interesting in color: a dark hunter's green, tinged with rusty mold. The house is washed a pale lemon, the windows and doors outlined in the dark green of the tiles. Style oozes from every pore of this Palladian salute to the hills.

VILLA BASTARDO—*Casalto*

Not far from agreeable Villa Zeno-Casalto, just over the shoulder of the hill towards Strà, glowers a most forbidding house. Palladio is said to have designed the main block only. His elevation was a simple long frontage, two stories high. The first floor was a continuous arcade, nine arches with brick pilasters eight feet wide between. Porthole windows of generous proportions let in the light and air to the second story, which is not very high. More of an attic. In many respects this house resembles the stunning guesthouse at Villa Foscarini alla Brenta. What ever possessed a later member of the Bridalo family (1772) to add the badly proportioned, heavy portico, which now seems to huddle against the long Palladian façade, eludes me. Italians have an uncanny way, amounting to positive genius, for finding the chink in the armor of a person or house to give it a nickname. Why, I wonder, did the peasants roundabout not call this house (after the depressing portico was added) Villa Pupilla, for the one huge circular window set with convex glass that bulges from the pediment resembles nothing so much as a jaundiced eyeball. However, the name borne by the old monstrosity is as venerable as the main house built in 1578 by Palladio. Villa Bastardo. Thereby hangs a tale.

It appears that Casimiro Bridalo, the builder of this hunting-lodge, held the open championship as stallion of the countryside. No woman whom he cast his lecherous eye upon ever evaded his embraces for long. The upshot of all this dalliance in glades and haymows was that the countryside for miles around was awash with his bastards. No one minded, for the fifteenth century regarded a man poorly if he was not lusty. Finally, as the various boys and girls fathered by the noble Conte ran wild in the valley, Casimiro decided to herd them all together in his hunting-lodge and look over the lot of them. Those with any pretensions to beauty, wit, or breeding he would take into his household, those who did not measure up to his standards would be sent to work in his silk mills at Pavia. The day of choosing came. Casimiro was awakened early by such a din of voices and scuffing feet that he leaped from his bed and peered out of the window into the front court. What he beheld nearly gave him apoplexy. Literally hundreds of youths and maidens, ranging in age from fourteen to twenty, milled about the courtyard, even spilling over into the gardens and hillside. Suddenly the stallion of Villa Bridalo was worsted. His twenty to thirty, at most, bastards of the surrounding countryside had, like the Hydra, put forth ten and twenty heads for every one lopped off. Every woman who had a child, whether she had ever seen the Conte or not, was taking advantage of his offer to recognize his offspring in princely fashion or at the very least to set them up in a profitable calling. The tale goes on to tell that he was first enraged, then amused. Choosing six boys and six girls, one for every month in the year, the Conte engaged tutors for them, and in time these twelve youths and maidens of disputed birth became a credit to all concerned. It is quite natural, considering everything, that the crumbling, dark blue villa on its wooded hill be called Monte Bastardo.

VILLA BAGNOLO–*Lonego*

Palladio was never happier in mind, nor were his remarkable talents more happily displayed than when he was designing country houses or town palazzi for members of the family Pisani. To begin with, Pisani seem to have had then, as now, great taste, that most illusive quality in human sensibilities. Where does the desert divide the sown? Why is it, I often wonder, that one rarely meets a person who, in conversation, in choosing wearing apparel or furniture for his house, effortlessly displays great taste, while others just have no taste at all.

No one has, of course, ever been able successfully to define taste. So often I hear the phrase, "Oh, well, that's not *my* taste." For a given object to be in good taste, it must "hit you where you live." In the case of Andrea Palladio, the kind of taste displayed by the various Pisani had just that effect on him. In the case of the writer, Palladio never fails to hit him a wallop right where he lives.

Palladio wrote to Trissino about the time the Conte went to live in an old ramshackle barracks of a castle at Trevisi alle Rovo: "What Cheer the Gods send Me. I am about to begin erecting a Great House for Conte Rinaldo Pisani. I have profited by my Mistake in the Stairs at Villa Emo. Henceforth I Strive to make all staircases Lightsome and in Convenient Places."

This is a one-story (and attics) house in the pavilion style. A handsomely conceived portico of Doric order invites one to enter this pleasant prospect by a magnificent sweep of steps, twenty feet wide at the base, tapering to ten feet as the curve in three raised terraces ascends. The steps are sixteen feet in height. It can truly be said of this house that a *scala grande* is the architectural motif which makes the façade singularly memorable. For it is just that. To a friend visiting Ireland I was showing Russborough, the finest of all Palladian houses built by Richard Castle in the Irish counties. Of a sudden my friend said, "What wonderful stone steps. Such sweep. They remind me of those at Villa Bagnolo at Lonego." And well they might. For Russborough is very like, in many ways. Both houses, once seen, are never forgotten.

The vaulted rooms at Bagnolo are full of light and summer breezes. Primarily a summer house, the Conte and his family and guests came here only to escape the hot months of midsummer. Palladio had built, fifteen years earlier, a big rambling villa for Rinaldo Pisani at Strà. Not the now famous villa of the Doge Pisani, which was built later. The one I refer to was three miles nearer Brentella. It was destroyed by fire in 1696. Stone and rubble from the ruins were carted away whenever a wall or byre needed mending. Now only grass-grown mounds proclaim the spot of one of Palladio's most ambitious villas. Oddly enough, the houses built either entirely or partially by Andrea Palladio have been treated gently by the Fates. A few are ruinous. A very few suffered oblivion due to fire. The house of his son Silla, near Meledo, where so much of Palladio's data was burned, was not designed by him. It was a rented house.

One room at Villa Bagnolo deserves special mention. At the end of a long gallery—actually a fifty-foot room in one of the wings—there is a feature I can never remember seeing anywhere else: a raised pool with a latticed cover, which was spread with trays of fruit during the summer days. A great curling conch shell is set into the arms of a sculptured naiad, and from this shell cool water from a mountain spring flows over the fruit. A wide cornice or lip of white marble, veined in violet and black, surrounds this pool. One can easily evoke the picture of a hot summer afternoon, the family Pisani, their guests, and chance callers sitting around this pool, partaking of the fresh fruit cooled by spring water. A languishing air would prevail. The ladies of the household, as well as callers, would be dressed in the sheer tissues from Constantinople, vividly striped and shot with gilt and silver.

VILLA LA FRITA—*River Adige*

For the Nobile Francesco Badoero, a house was designed by Palladio. It took ten years to build because the Furies pursued everyone who had anything to do with the undertaking. First the Nobile himself was horribly gored by a young bull that broke out of his pen when Badoero was inspecting his livestock. The huge dairy farms along the hurrying River Adige have been famous since the tenth century for the excellence of cheeses made from the rich cream given by herds grazing on its banks. Another product from the Adige country is her stalwart, handsome sons. Tall and magnificently made, these youths were much in demand as models for sculptors and painters during the Renaissance. Michelangelo is said always to have specified when engaging a male model that he must hail from the *campagna Adige.*

Badoero survived, but was an invalid for the remainder of his life. The second misfortune to strike during the building of the villa was the dread disease that seemed to attack so many young women in the Middle Ages: *ammalata amore.* Victorians called the condition "a decline." In highly emotional Latin races this "love sickness" is often accompanied by extreme mental disorder. Not far from the villa, closed away behind a screen of alders, there stands a small two-room building, so charmingly constructed one thinks at first glance it is a *tempio d'amore,* seen so often in the grounds of Renaissance villas in Italy. In effect it is just that: a temple to thwarted love, where Badoero's daughter was guarded. The unhappy girl is said to haunt the garden on summer evenings, wringing her hands and moaning piteously.

Again, after construction had been halted on the villa for three years, Badoero decided to proceed. An elaborate scaffolding had been erected for Vittorio (who modeled all the figures at Meledo and Villa Pisani at Montagnana) to work upon his famous grotesques in the pediment. A few days before the villa was to be pronounced finished, Palladio and Vittorio walked out upon the narrow boards of the scaffolding to inspect the finished work at close range. Suddenly there was a sound of rending wood, and one end of the platform broke away from its moorings and hung dangling in space forty feet from the ground. Both Palladio and Vittorio were thrown against the wall of the house, where they clung to ropes until they were rescued by workmen. Vittorio seems not to have suffered more than bruises. Palladio tore ligaments in his thigh which caused him much pain for years. After this fall all his journeys were made in a litter borne by two horses, or by barge.

Once Villa la Frita was finished, one hears of no more catastrophes. However long it took to build, the house is worth it. The main block is a generously proportioned rectangle, with a high portico. A pediment rests on Ionic columns, six in number. Two demilunes spread out from the center block like welcoming arms. Nearest the house three arches pierce the demilunes. Three tall arched windows complete the crescent. Half-mythological figures in the pediment are strange and certainly unique. Italians call such figures *mostro fantastico*. Satyrlike, these figures caper about, holding in front of their faces masks that mimic the fox, the snake, the lion, and the ass.

VILLA ARCUGNANO—*Environs of Vicenza*

This extremely reticent almost prim house is one of the many pointed out to visitors in Vicenza as having been built by Palladio for himself. I for one do not believe he did for the simple reason that the man who built Villa Capra (Rotonda) according to his own wishes would never have built so ordinary a house as this to live in. The one reason for its existence is the beautiful articulation of the whole. Like a creamy intaglio, the house is too perfect in detail. Yet it bears the unmistakable thumbprint of Palladio's master hand. The roof is shaped in a low peak which reaches its apex at the exact spot and height as that of the pediment. Six columns with Ionic caps rise for two stories from the first floor, which is reached by a graduated flight of stone steps. A two-story cut-under room has a closed balustrade across the front. The color is delightful: pale aquamarine-blue wash, with pale mauve in the lunettes over the first floor windows, and covering the three walls of the cut-under room.

VILLA TORNIERI—*Environs of Vicenza*

Villa Tornieri, almost across the highway from Villa Arcugnano, has terrific style. If I were asked what this house has that its *vis-à-vis* has not, I should say, "Style." It is built in the form of a long, widely spaced E, with the back of the letter facing the garden and the ends of the three prongs toward the roadway. The central portion is high and rather narrow. There are four Corinthian order columns across the portico. The extreme height of the first story, which is laid off in long, narrow bricklike stones, gives an immense reach to the unusual arrangement of the steps. Twelve steps rise in the middle of the portico, branching off on both sides to a landing, where they double back to rise again in the middle to the center of a two-story loggia. Figures of three exceedingly plump nymphs rise from the pediment, while two curious fauns crane their necks from the center of the pediment, missing not one voluptuous curve so frankly displayed above.

Two garden loggias, a story and a half, with three tall keystoned arches across the front, complete the façade. The house is washed with pale yellow and the interior of the loggias is cerulean blue, painted with drifting white clouds. Primarily a pleasure house, the mood is gaiety personified.

VILLA ERO-QUERINI—*Environs of Vicenza*

Alas, the big Vitruvian villa designed by Palladio for the immensely rich and fashionable *famiglia Querini* of Venice—originally from Rovina—no longer exists. Left to decay in the arms of wind and weather, the house fell to ruin and was carted away for building material during the early nineteenth century. The magnificent gardens remain, and the lyrical *casa madre*, or dower house as it would be called in England. This is a six-room house of gleaming white Istrian stone. All the rooms are on one floor, each one in line with, and opening into and out of, the other. They are actually a long corridor of cube rooms. Each is twenty-five by twenty-five by twenty-five feet. A long line of six steps continues along the façade, and a gracefully arched door leads from each room down the steps to the loggia. This repetition of architectural features, each one perfection in scale and detail, gives the lyrical quality of a Scarlatti *bandero* to the building. A broad avenue of cypress, tall and exclamatory, leads away to a syringa bower, skirting the River Trella. Placed half embowered in ilex trees that line the broad walk to the river are rustico pedestals. On these stand the gods of Olympus. I counted twenty. Eros, from whom the villa takes its name, occupies the place of honor. Inside the pavilion a romantic atmosphere prevails. On a bright day, such as the one in early autumn when I wandered unhindered through the garland of high cube rooms, a limpid light fluttered across the painted ceilings as doors were opened. No furniture remained in the house, all having been divided among members of the family. Some rooms had built-in cupboards with carved and painted doors. One room, which I suspect had been a *sala colazione* originally, for it is at the end of the line of rooms, faces the rose garden. This room is pale primrose yellow, and valances of chestnut brown and pink taffeta, old and frayed but of miraculous quality, still outline the tops of three windows. Along the wall, above where a mirror must have hung, is painted a procession of dwarfs, each dressed in fantastic livery, green, violet, pink, with traces of silver sashes. Beturbaned and beplumed, all bear trays on which are painted chocolate pots wreathed in steam. Jars of *marmellata*, high-piled tiny loaves of bread, plates of butter, and a Capo di Monte bowl of crisp green cress—all the ingredients for a country breakfast. Christina of Sweden found harbor and a brief happiness in this gay house when she first came to Italy. From this vantage point she ranged the provinces until she found a villa to her liking near Anzio.

VILLA LUNA MOROCCO—*Treviga*

For Leonardo Mocenigo, certainly one of the wildest eccentrics of any age, Palladio built a villa, which, when completed, was immediately torn to pieces stone by stone by its owner because he was jealous of a far grander one built by Palladio for his rival, Conte Giorgio Cornado. It is told that in the dead of night Mocenigo would ride over to the barred gates of Villa Piombino, shake his fist, and call down obscene curses on the grandiose Cornado house. Finally, by selling his wife's jewels and precious altar gear—sacrilege in itself, and a distinctly bad omen—he was able to reconstruct his shattered house even larger than Palladio's Piombino.

As soon as the second, larger house was finished, Conte Mocenigo again summoned Palladio to witness how much cleverer he was, having built a house twice as large as the first out of the same material without so much as a basketful of new stones or mortar. Naturally this did not impress the man who had spent years of his life solving every problem of building. Upon entering the front door of this huge square house he found it to be a hollow shell, indeed only a series of empty rooms built around a courtyard. He prevailed upon Mocenigo to allow him to proceed with the house so that a completely finished building might be a credit to them both. As mild as milk, suddenly, the noble eccentric gave orders to proceed. Palladio then designed what was to be his finest pillared hall, copied many years later, almost to the last vein of pink marble, by William Kent for the world renowned entrance of Holkham Hall on the north coast of Norfolk.

This great atrio, as Palladio called it, is a vast cube, seventy feet each way. Thirty soaring columns of the Ionic order spring from a sort of terrace, raised twelve feet from the floor. The once gilded capitals support a magnificently sculptured dome of coffered alabaster. The design of the cornice is dancing *amorini* bearing an endless swag of ribbon-bound fruit upon their shoulders. The Villa Luna Morocco hall was fashioned from six kinds of marble: two gray, two yellow, and two pink. Where old Conte Mocenigo, notoriously impoverished—periodically, at least—came by the immense amount of money for all this grandeur, is not told. One hopes Palladio was paid in full. It is just as likely that he was not.

The series of rooms opening off this astounding Vitruvian dream of pomp and glory are not at all noteworthy. In fact one feels the money actually did fine down to a trickle by the time the atrio was completed, for little architectural detail is found in them. The façade has a portico of six Corinthian-capped columns, and a superstructure containing a fine winged window, poised as if for flight, directly over the pediment. When I last saw Villa Luna Morocco in the summer of 1946, the main house was partly ruinous, although the roof remained intact.

A farmer who raises the huge razor-backed hogs, for which the locality is famous, showed me about. One curious sort of pen looked like the private bullrings one sees around Arles in the Camargue de Rhône. The farmer grinned, shook his head, and said, "A good thing this baiting-pen is not used now for the purpose of the old days." When questioned further, he told me the crazed barbarian of a Conte during some of his more erratic spells would emulate the holidays of Roman emperors. Traveling nomads, mountebanks, itinerant musicians, *et al.*, were gathered into a camp near the enclosure. Then the Conte and his guests would assemble on the bleachers arranged in tiers. If the session took place after dark, giant flambeaux were carried around by linkboys. Then the orgy commenced. Masks depicting wild animals and monsters of every lewd description were handed round to audience and performers alike. A trumpet blared. Bands of wine-maddened ragamuffins and strollers dashed into the ring. Except for the masks, men and women were naked to the

buff. Often the guests became so intrigued they too joined this bacchanal.
Grand romps at one of Palladio's greatest houses.

LARGE HOUSE AT QUINTO

This rather haunting title is all that one finds labeling what is
undoubtedly one of the most flamboyant conceptions of Palladio. Only
on paper, alas. We see, in a set of six completely spellbinding drawings
preserved in the Museo Municipale at Vicenza, his dream of what the
"large house at Quinto" was to have been. Some say the reason the dream
never materialized but had to be built on a much reduced scale was the
age-old one of financial reverses which strikes all and sundry in any era.

The wind-wracked, rain-blotched old house, crouching on its
rocky ridge today, has a strange, compelling majesty of its own. "I'm not
finished yet, *per Bacco*," the old hulk growls, shrugging its rafters. "I was
built like a fortress. When I see fit, I'll crash down to dust; not before.
Go away."

The long crescent-shaped frontage of this house without a name is
in the true style of Vitruvius as interpreted by Andrea Palladio. Two long
wings, with attendant gate pavilions, were to have carried the line even
farther. Guesthouses, *due foresteria*, as the original plan calls them, were
abandoned along with the elaborate detached portico which resembles
the triumphal arch of some long-dead Caesar. In his book *I Quattro Libri
dell' Architettura*, Palladio quotes Vitruvius, Book VI, Chapter X: "In
well considered Country Houses, especially those remote from Towns or
Cities, guests stopping for any length of time should live apart from their
Host. Complete liberty being afforded them during their Sojourn."

I heartily agree to this, and always have. To me one of the most
disconcerting things in life is "visiting round." Particularly in small
houses with large families. After a few days—in most cases a few hours—
the urge to run away, if only for a few minutes, sweeps over me. I may
suddenly want to write, to paint. Guest rooms apart are the answer. I
can hear my readers murmuring at this place, "He must be a lethal
guest." How right they are.

The Spaniards, a morose race at best, have a saying, probably
from the Moors: "Crowded caves lead to murder. Solitude to madness."

A happy medium is to be desired. Apparently this house at Quinto was designed with just that thought in mind.

Big as the house is, there are no attics and no hall, as such. The absence of stairs of any kind leads one to suspect that the servants who slept in remote parts of the second story used ladders which were pulled up after them. This was in fact a custom in many Renaissance country houses. Annotations on the original sketch for the second-story floor plan point out stores, granaries, wardrobes, servants' rooms.

The whole conception of this house, even half derelict as it is today, is of the most profound interest to architects, in fact anyone at all interested in integrity of design. The sweeping colonnades at either side of the hexastyle entrance and the interior court were to be used as entrances to the house as a sort of reception foyer for visitors. This idea stems from the Greek custom of "court for audience," which was often the most beautifully decorated room in the house. Stabling for horses, kennels for hounds, and an outdoor bathhouse—all pretty run down now—attest to the real splendor, intelligent splendor, which characterized this country domain in its heyday. Far more pleasantly planned than many a royal domain I have seen.

One day fairly soon, I expect to walk up the long weed-tousled avenue leading to "the large house at Quinto," hoping the old barracks will still growl at me, "So—you back again? Not much change in me. My roof's sagging. Getting old." I shall reply, "Yes, but still grand. I have a present for you. A name. No one has ever called you by anything but the large house at Quinto. I noticed, last time I was here, a pair of gray owls who-o-o-o-ing in the plane tree by your gate. I shall call you Villa Gufoni."

VILLA TOMISERI—*Campagna Lodino*

On the dusty white road to Verona stands, far back among the canebrake, the deserted villa whose dignity and powerful proportions weather the centuries unimpaired. So much character has this pile of carefully cut stone and stucco that it has become a place of pilgrimage for artists, architects, and many writers as well. To describe this house is an exciting challenge, a gage thrown in one's path.

The façade is long and infinitely graceful, supporting a double colonnade of Ionic order. The whole structure is not unlike some of the great Creole plantations along the bayous of Louisiana. Demilunes flank the main block of this engaging house, adding to the lightness which is carried over into the immense scroll-like foliations that ornament the wide cornice under the roof and between the upper and lower colonnades.

At the extreme end of each demilune a long building of one and a half stories, colonnaded, was used for stables, coach houses, and offices. In one of these extremely pleasant pavilions lived a daughter of the family who owned the domain, at the time I made drawings of the house. She was intensely interested in what I was doing and insisted on taking me through the big villa standing empty and rather forlorn in its arid fields.

The painted *salone grande* is lovely in sweep and color. For eighty feet the walls on two sides of the room carry the design of gods, goddesses, nymphs, satyrs, fauns, all the hierarchy of Olympus in a revel amid sylvan scenes. How often one sees this subject in paint! The Renaissance in Italy, France, and England fostered the infinite variety of moods pertaining to this theme. Some are atrocious, some utterly delightful, some show great draftsmanship. In this rather dim room—for all its size there are not sufficient windows—the eternal subject of everyone in the Olympian throng hugely enjoying himself or herself, except Aphrodite, is engagingly painted. Aphrodite and her pique seems to top the composition. The floors of yellow marble from the quarries near Verona are ingeniously patterned in high-lighted and shadowed cubes of moss-green quartz. There is a *grotto marina*, dripping with dank, shuddering shadows. Shells of all kinds are stuck in every conceivable wall space and over the coved ceiling. Two huge allegorical figures, twin river sources I expect they represent, pour water (not running at this time, like all the once elaborate mechanism for water effects) from weed-encrusted jars into an elliptical pool. A soft pink and violet blur hovers in the air. Once, I was told, the room had been painted pink and purple.

VILLA CLOTILDA—*Verona*

A bijou, if ever I saw one. Palladio is said to have designed and built this house for a charming widow for whom he formed an attachment while building the Villa Tomiseri. There are four rooms only. And quite enough, so handsomely are they proportioned. A square house. A very miniature Villa Pisani at Montagnana. Instead of the conventional doorway, a fine winged window allows entrance to the hall connecting the four rooms. In the garden at the back are a small cookhouse and a graceful *tempio d'amore*, where a slightly infatuated architect sought dalliance, I presume. The cavernous and mightily smoked fireplace attest to huge dinners being cooked to satisfy Palladio, who is said to have taken enormous interest in food after his accident on the crumpling scaffold.

VILLA TRISSINO—*Meledo*

During the devastating plague in Venice, a miserly old fellow named Corcacceli Vido, a Levantine Jew, died, as did thousands of others. His body was put into a sack and burned on the pyres erected for the purpose on the wastelands near Mestre. After some sort of life was restored to Venice with the ebbing of the plague, a strange document came to light that completely changed the fortunes of two brothers from Vicenza. They were Francesco and Ludovico Trissino, cousins to Giorgio Trissino, whom we already know as the patron of young Palladio as well as his lifelong friend.

It appears that the old usurer Vido had held a bill of sale against a shipment of colored quartz to be shipped in blocks from the Dolomites to the House of Fugger in Vienna. Vido had advanced a third of the money, the remainder was advanced by the brothers Trissino. With the horrors of the plague foremost in the minds of men, this transaction had been forgotten. Suddenly the brothers Trissino, through the unearthing of the document, found that the quartz had been duly shipped to the Fugger warehouses at Daltbrück (which occupied ten acres of land for the enormous Fugger enterprise), and a huge sum of money awaited. The Trissinos had only to call for its transfer. This manna from heaven was received with untold joy by many people concerned in the building of the great Vitruvian country house, started ten years before. Palladio had lavished every facet of his talent upon this villa, which, because of its lofty contours and wide-spreading frontage, has always been called by peasants and townfolk alike, Palazzo Meledo.

Rising in four distinct levels, the house crowns a hill, giving to the whole plan a quality of lift, lyrical in the extreme. The conception, carried to completion without a change of any kind once the edifice got going under the impetus of added money, is ambitious and unusual and bears no resemblance to any of Palladio's country house designs. This is due largely to the rising terraces that cause the bulk and rotunda to silhouette against the sky.

Seen from the foot of the hill, especially on a misty day or by moonlight, the house seems a retreat for Fata Morgana, floating in space.

If any similar building can be found, it is the Villa Rotonda, built by Palladio for his own use, near Vicenza. At Meledo quadrant wings support the block and add the necessary weight to the structure. The frontage is one hundred and eighty feet, the depth ninety feet. A circular entrance hall is fifty feet in diameter, surrounded by various rooms and four staircases. A colonnaded portico of Corinthian order draws admiring attention to each face of this building. It was placed thus, says Palladio, "so that Every Front shall have a Fine, Far Prospect." He continues, "I find, on inspection, the situation of Meledo Supremely Satisfying. Set like an Attic Temple on a little hill, the lower terrace is Washed by a little River in the midst of a Spacious Plain, relieved here and there by a glossy Forest through which winds a Frequented Road."

The rotunda crowning the mass was intended to be made of sheet copper, but was later gilded and spatter-dashed with vermilion and silver. Wind and weather have mellowed this metal to a most lovely quality of muted color, neither gold nor silver, but some of both with hints of red. The immense quadrangle forecourt, which was finished in 1579, has disappeared. Now field flowers and scattered swaths of wheat and barley blow in the warm wind. Bees hover over the barley, black energetic honeybees, causing havoc amid swarms of aimless yellow and mauve butterflies. Acres of cobbles, once sending out sparks from the hoofs of Barbs, hump under a rime of lichen and gray moss. Palazzo Meledo, inspiration for half the great houses in the world, lies leanly on its hill, silent and withdrawn.

VILLA REPETA—*Campiglia di Monte Berico*

Just over the hill from Villa Piovene, yet hidden from view from the terrace of this commanding house by a mound overgrown with hazel trees, drowses one of the most architecturally attractive of Palladio's country "farm-villas," as this form of house is called to differentiate from the palazzo type, such as Villa Emo.

This house was built for a Venetian doge, Mario Repeta, soon

VILLA ROTONDA, VICENZA.

after Villa Piovene was finished. Though it is not nearly so gracious and spreading in plan as Villa Piovene, there are a number of features which remind one of that house. The portico is rather higher and set upon a first story of rustico stones, vast in scale and deeply indented to form stalactites. Oval windows, set the long way, pierce the first story at intervals. The hand-wrought iron gratings of these ovals is extremely original, an interlaced vine design with thorns and leaves. Between the *piano nobile* and third floor, a double set of narrow slit windows form a decoration where the usual stringpiece would be, and are the means of admitting light and air to a series of tiny boxlike rooms, a sort of cramped entresol, given to the unfortunate servants of this period of the Italian Renaissance. The cut-under room at the back of the house, overlooking the garden, is enriched by deeply incised shells forming a canopy over the two doors and three tall windows that let into the rooms opening off the porch.

Now rather faded, but still discernible in design, are the frescos which enrich every room in the house. Haunting in color and subject, these painted rooms, by the imaginative painter Maganza, depict every form of the many kinds of entertainment to be found in the chase.

In the *salone grande* at the back of the house the ceiling is oval and extremely beautiful in design; cloud forms in raised stucco are tinted pale mauve, rose, heliotrope, and primrose. "The Awakening of Aurora," painted in sweeping style, forms the fresco subject. Villa Repeta sleeps fitfully these days, sometimes visited by its owners, more often left to doze through the changing seasons, but, like so many of these half-forgotten Palladian houses, it is ever ready to waken, rub its eyes, and entertain in its glowing, slightly disheveled rooms.

VILLA PIOVENE.

DEMETER'S HOUSE

In the year 1540 Girolamo di Godi sought Palladio at his retreat at Rovina. He burst in upon the sleeping architect, it is said, to acquaint him with the happy news that his marriage to the most beautiful and accomplished woman in the Udine, heiress to vast wealth and land holdings, would take place. Adrienna Copadisto had at last surrendered to his pleading. One year from that very day they would be wed. Palladio must, of course, build him a villa fit to house in state so formidable a bride as the sparkling Adrienna. Poets had sung her praises. Painters had limned her suavely sculptured features. Vittorio, the leading sculptor of the day, had imprisoned her loveliness, the long fluid lines of her tall body, in Parian marble. Her voice, when she was singing madrigals and *romanzas,* in the pale, rain-washed evenings, shamed the nightingale. Her suitors had numbered three score and ten, Adrienna wore a necklace of seventy pearls to prove it, one pearl added on the *congé* of each cavalier. Girolamo had secured *la bella assoluta* to share his life.

There was one condition to which Palladio must adhere. Work could start immediately on the villa but *must* be finished in time for Girolamo to bring his bride to her new house on their wedding day. That gave Palladio one year to build the kind of house that in the ordinary way took two to three years to build, even if the Fates laid a stone or two in friendliness along the way. Much wine was drunk to bind the bargain, and work is said to have begun with the digging of wine vaults on the following day.

So kind were the Fates that one month before the flamboyant nuptials of dark-visaged Girolamo—so saturnine he was called Il Malinconico —and richly golden Adrienna, the long, grandly proportioned Villa Godi-Porto was finished. Lighted with flambeaux and candles from stem to stern (it was often called *barca grande* because of its resemblance to a huge galley), all was ready to christen the finished house.

Girolamo and Adrienna arrived in a blazing hot sun; a series of heat-blanketed days had enfolded the region of Lonedo, causing the two rivers that flowed through the valley to sink to a rill. Everyone except the new mistress of Villa Godi-Porto drooped to the point of collapse in the shriveling heat. Not she, however, for always the pale, slim Adrienna from the Udine had been cold and remote, like the summer moon. "The warmer the night, the cooler the moon," say the Arabs, and in very truth this lady resembled a crescent moon, sharply lithe, pale, and far-drifting. Madonna della Luna.

The great villa on its ridge overlooking one of the most fertile stretches of farmland valley in all Italy caught the fancy of everyone who heard of it. French cavaliers, returning from the signing of some maritime treaty or other in Venice, would halt, reining in their caparisoned horses in awe when they sighted this veritable palace on its red-brown terraces. Prelates, cardinals journeying to Rome in scarlet splendor, as well as simple lay-brothers of the church, turned in at the plinthlike gateposts for refreshment and shaded rest. Not the religious occupations of Madonna Adrienna but her interest in herbs and simples caused a guarded curiosity in the minds of all who saw her. It was rumored she was a sorceress. A few years passed. No children were heard shouting through the vaulted corridors of Villa Godi-Porto. The *padrone* was much away, hunting, sailing in the Adriatic, or traveling in foreign parts. No entertaining livened the huge painted rooms wherein Madonna Adrienna wandered. She hated the house. "I stifle in houses," she said, "walls crush my heart." And so through the days, the lost lady ranged the fields gathering flowers and herbs. From the flowers she wove garlands to deck balustrade and portico. From the branched leaves of dark green or dusty silver plants, *basilico, camomilla, timo,* and *salvia,* she brewed medicines that she stored in amber flasks. Farther and farther afield ranged Adrienna. Shepherds saw her skirting the woods near Fanzolo, many miles to the west of Lonedo. Days, nights, time made no difference to La Luna. Then one evening she disappeared utterly. A farmer standing on an upland near Caldogno told a strange story a few days later when a party of men-at-arms from the garrison at Godi-Porto came searching the countryside.

The farmer had been looking for a stray lamb. As he breasted a rise of ground overlooking a sweep of meadows, he was startled by singing, a strange song rising and falling in the cadences of a chant. Something like the Greek chorus in the theater at Padova. Out of the light ground-mist that rises at evening in these parts had come a tall young woman in draperies the color of the wild hyacinths she stooped to gather. A large bunch of mixed flowers and leaves overflowed her arms. Always she seemed to see a fairer flower farther away, out of reach. When she came to it, on she went to another clump. As the man watched, wondering, a dark shape like a great stalking man in armor, a wreath of red flowers in his hand, emerged from the mist and approached the palely fair woman. That was all. The mist, rising in swaths from the grasses, had struck the pair invisible.

Not far from the half-plundered hulk of once majestic Villa Godi-Porto, lies, lovely and serene, what is to my mind, as I have said elsewhere, the last word in farmsteads. The word farmstead seems to fit this house. After all, the ancient *luogo stemma*, to place the beginning of a family, is a heart-warming way to designate a farm. And I learned, during the weeks, even months as I remember, when I stayed at Villa Piovene, that a "stead" or "place," wherefrom to farm the rich surrounding land, has endured in this spot for many centuries.

As a dwelling, it is a house in the great tradition. For it has three important qualities: spaciousness, architectural integrity, and warm personal character. Springing from the good earth, the house seems one with fertility. Fruits of the earth garland the place. Plowed fields, sowing, growing, and harvesting follow one another in sweet succession. Suns rise and set. Moons wax and wane. Trees and meadow burst into leaf and flower, then the winds of winter sweep the ground clear until another year. What is more contenting than to watch the seasons change, fusing mood, color, and light. I saw them change in power and glory from the spreading portico at Piovene. After I had spent a few weeks in this farmstead, I called it Demeter's House.

There are two reasons for the name. One is a legend told me on the Island of Crete, when I was making drawings—reconstructing treasure, such as gold headdresses, armor, battle gear, and ceremonial trappings— for Sir Arthur Evans who was excavating the subterranean palace of Minos at Knossos. The story had to do with Demeter as she appeared at the Festival of Fecundity, held at Eleusis each spring in the temple built by Triptolemus (whom Demeter had rewarded by crowning with the diadem of Agriculture). This ceremony, under the name of the Eleusinian Mysteries, surpassed in solemnity and splendor all other religious celebrations among the Greeks. I made a large black and brown crayon drawing of the Earth Mother in her tiaralike headdress of bronze, wreathed in corn and chained by the heads of yearling bulls; symbol of fertility. When Demeter had searched from one end of the earth to the other to find her lost Persephone, to no avail, she strode to her dragon-drawn chariot and rose to Olympus, where she beseeched Zeus to restore her daughter to her side. He feigned helplessness, saying that because Persephone had eaten of the pulp of the pomegranate in Pluto's realm, all he could do was to bid the King of the Dead to let Persephone return to earth for six months of the year. Enraged at this craven evading, for Demeter accused Zeus of cowardice, she vowed to return to her realm of Earth and dwell among courageous mortals, keeping her daughter by her side in a flowery landscape during her half-year restoration. When Persephone returned to her dark world, Demeter would shrivel the leaf and lay bare the fields. But not entirely did she mourn, for she taught men to husband their harvest and preserve fruits, vegetables, and meats, to last them in abundance through the long cold months. It is told that Demeter found a spot in a fertile land that is now Italy. There she dwells amid beauty and plenty. I know where she lives. For I have seen her. Stately, the embodiment of grace, Demeter moves at night among the furrows. Bronze and wine-dark purple are her robes; they trail the earth, become one with its fragrance. Her draperies wind the trees and start the sap flowing. Sometimes I have seen her a deeper golden figure, heroic among the golden corn.

The other reason for naming the farmstead Demeter's House is the legend that persists in the neighborhood of the Villa Piovene. Down the years, by word of mouth—the route by which our most richly embellished folklore descends—the country people in this locality sing at harvest festivals an ancient song of the abduction of Persephone. From miles away, the song goes, she came in misty draperies, gathering flowers in their valley, disappearing later into the mist from whence she was snatched down to the underworld. Any black animal in the region, I found, was called Pluto. Bulls, stallions, watchdogs, tomcats, pet ravens, black roosters, all. Huge black ravens perch upon the cornices of lonely Villa Godi-Porto. One early winter evening I remember, I had walked all afternoon in a circle winding up behind the outbuildings, which, though they are rapidly crumbling to pink dust, are still inhabited by caretakers for the Godi-Porto. A deafening *caw-caw-caw-caw* of hundreds of ravens fighting for a roosting place among the cornices of the pediment greeted me as I crossed the terrace on my way down the valley to Piovene. One old reprobate leveled me with a beady eye. Instantly to my mind leaped the legend of Demeter and Persephone, evoked by this messenger of Poe's from "the dark Plutonian shore."

At the foot of the mountains rising sharply behind Piovene straggles the small village of Lugo. The streets, little more than alleys, are built in broad, shallow steps. The inhabitants have the carriage of antique statues, for the constant carrying of baskets and trays of fruit upon the head fosters a straight back and a firm muscular neck. The life of the village

DEMETER AS THE GODDESS OF FECUNDITY. DRAWING IN BROWN AND
BLACK CHALK BY THE AUTHOR.

appears to center around that at the villa. A warm friendliness exists between villager and *padrone*.

The outstanding feature of this perfectly conceived plan is the harmonious manner in which the broad steps of the principal street of Lugo flow effortlessly into the *scala grande* that ascends to the portico of Villa Piovene. These broad, shallow steps wend upward in nine terraces, intersected at each rise by a roadway.

One's first impression of the house is spaciousness. The ultimate of a country retreat. Six tall Ionic columns, generously spaced, lend an air of peace and plenty to the front, even before one knows that the two words, peace and plenty, are the very definition of this farmstead. The main house is a long, beautifully proportioned building, with the portico, placed midway in its length, jutting so far out from the wall (which is cut under to the depth of twelve feet, forming a room) that a coach and four can drive comfortably along the paved terrace under the pediment. Five large windows pierce the walls in this cut-under loggia, on both the first and second floors. The wings are four windows across, allowing two big rooms side by side in each wing. This feature is unusual in Palladian villas.

Almost without exception, his big square houses have only one room flanking the entrance hall. The wide hall at Piovene measures forty feet across. Vaulted and painted in tempera panels of the four seasons with a delightful bucolic touch to them, this splendid room is much used by the family, for there is always a cool breeze to be found here on the hottest summer day. In winter the great painted room in the long loggia wing to the left of the main block is the most comfortable. Two gigantic fireplaces in which ten-foot logs are burned give out more heat than anyone can stand. The vistas of ancient Venice, in triumphal pageantry during the stirring days of the Republic, give this room color and drama. To me it is one of the five great rooms in the world. On a dreary night of lashing wind and teeming rain, we often sat around the fire in this room. Firelight emphasized the singing crimson of the heavy damask curtains, light and shadow flickered over the yellow and rusty bronze of the Venetian palaces and gilded gondolas in the panels. We discussed the painter of this miraculous world shimmering all about us: Battista del Moro Veronese, who ate so much of the roast ox during his stay that he vowed he would never use red in his pictures again. It reminded him too strongly of the blood from the underdone (the way he liked his beef) steaks, which he ate until he could scarcely leave the table.

Another room in this hospitable house for which I have a tremendous fondness is the *sala di mappa mondo,* a big comfortable room at the back of the dining room on the right of the entrance hall. Four windows, two on the side and two in the back wall, give plenty of cross light. This is necessary, for in this room one looks and looks again. Big maps of the world from 1300, when they resemble a geometric design for wallpaper, down to modern ordnance maps. The collection is rare and unique. Tables as large as those used for billiards stand round the room. They must always stay cleared when not in use displaying maps. One takes the map desired out of its rack—all are stretched on heavy linen—and spreads it out or hangs it on a wall. A grand way to study them. There are racks of engravings, water colors and pencil drawings as well. The owner of this house has very catholic tastes, so the range of drawings is from Gustave Doré through Holbein, Boldini, Constantine Guys, Sargent, Augustus John, Picasso. I found some of my own drawings of thoroughbred race horses included in this varied show. The floor is strewn with the skins of animals shot in the mountains, behind the house, and in Sicily. The yellow dining room is oval, and has ten kinds of marbleizing in receding arches of gray and pale violet-beige. The vistas of mossy rocks and the foam-crested sea, painted in brilliant sunlight and glimpsed through the shadowy painted arches, is magnificent.

To either side of the main house stretch the unique loggias I have spoken of. Loggias, yes, but far different, more exhilarating, than any I have ever seen elsewhere. Two stories these loggias rise, with a half-story attic above the cornice which is supported by six Doric columns. The wall of the wing is set back twelve feet, giving a wide, long room protected from the elements. The entablature which answers for a cornice is eight feet wide and pierced by oval porthole windows, allowing light to the second-story rooms under the loggias. The raking roof line of these wings is lovely, gently sloping and formed of old green-gold tiles. In the entire façade Palladio has been more successful in bringing unyielding stone and stucco to life, in causing dry bricks and mortar to pulse with a luminous quality of movement, than in any other building he ever designed. Erecting Villa Piovene was a labor of the heart, one can see that in every tile.

104

The *scala grande* is equaled in impact and drama only by the orangery steps at Versailles, or perhaps the breath-taking flight of sea-front steps leading to the high town at Odessa. The steps are twenty feet across, the rise is shallow. Balustrades, closed, mimicking deeply pitted stone, follow the rise. At intervals are open gateways, flanked by statues of woodland dryads, fauns, and centaurs. Two lanes, arteries for the busy farm life that constantly flows hither and away, all about one, cross the steps at terraces intersecting the rise of steps. A marvelous sight it is to stand on the steps just below the first lane early in the morning and witness the coming to life of the *popolo del masseria*. Shepherds pass, boys of seven or eight years as well as bearded men, weather-beaten to the tinge of old leather. Dairymaids chatter, stool in hand, heads tied in yellow and scarlet handkerchiefs. Harvesters pull their broad-brimmed hats low to shade their eyes from a sun already brilliant in the flat, hot sky. Teamsmen walk beside their big-muscled horses, on the way to plow and harrow. Dogs bark, greetings are called to one another, a deep-toned bell calls laggards to the morning meal in the shady loggia. Villa Piovene with spirit faces another day.

However beautiful the painted rooms may be, grouped with gleaming *cassoni*, bright-woven stuffs, and crystal chandeliers, it is the kitchen in this house where the heart beats, where the pulse throbs. If ever there was *cucina grande*, it is here in this high vaulted room presided over by a high priestess of cookery.

Conte Alessandro Piovene, for whom the house was built, was a man of mighty stature, a consumer of formidable quantities of wine, and an epicure in the great tradition. It is said that from morning until late at night his table was never empty of food or of guests to partake of the smoking platters as they were borne from the kitchen and soon emptied. The aura of wide hospitality, which arches like a rainbow across the acres of this farm, is still accepted by all in the countryside. No one, beggar or prince, has ever been sent empty away from Piovene. By this same token the farm has always prospered. Droughts have seared the valley, torrential rains at the wrong time have laid standing crops low. Two rivers, swollen by mountain snows, have flooded surrounding fields. But this is Demeter's House; she watches over its destiny. Its granaries, storehouses, and cellars must be so well stocked that the bounties of the earth may stand as a back-log to help those in distress from the elements. From her vantage point, enthroned upon a massive cart drawn by white oxen, Demeter surveys the hurrying women in the great kitchen, for she is painted in an arched lunette over the double doors in the end of the loggia wing, a room entirely dedicated to preparing food. I know she is there because I painted her. The hand-woven canvas on which the mural is painted has a rough texture, very like the gesso-washed walls. Enthroned in the center of the panel, full panoplied as Goddess of Fertility, Demeter is surrounded by harvesters who gather great sheaves of corn, baskets of the topaz grapes of the region, and the pungent quince. Behind her spreads the valley, steeped in golden haze. Like the Val d'Oro in Umbria, a sheen of luminous gold seems to pervade the reaches of the rivers Adige and Bacciglione straight away to Padova. To watch long lines of carts piled high with fruits leave the *masseria* on the way to Padovan markets is a grand sight. Gold, gold, and more gold seems to shimmer. Melons, grapes, plums, nectarines, quince, and peaches, a range of yellow gold with now and again a hint of pink. The markets of Padova are justly renowned for delicious fruits.

What is that I smell? It is unmistakable. Newly baked bread. One more turn through the kitchen then, before we leave Piovene. Lucilla, who tends the huge ovens, is stacking freshly baked loaves, big and round as a Parmesan cheese, on red-painted shelves hung on the wall by ropes. Let us take one, break off a crust dusted with almond flour. No butter is needed. This is BREAD.

SCATTERED PORTICOS

I n a letter written to Monsignore Daniel Barbaro, Palladio says:

I leave for Asolo surrounded by a Retinue worthy of Yourself. My New Liveries have arrived, such Display will entrance all, along My Route. Rotonda has been a Hive of Activity for Weeks. My Roster of Apprentices is Formidable. We carry in a specially constructed litter, the Model of your House. Maser in Miniature. I throw off all thoughts of Pain from my torn thigh, in Expectation of the delights of building both Church and Villa for Your Excellence.

Andreas Palladius

This Latin signature was often used by Palladio after his election to the Academy of Arts in Vicenza. At this time he took for his livery the colors yellow and black in wide stripes. For his secretaries there was a touch of silver. Silver cords held back the curtains of his traveling litter, his seldom-used coach, and the awnings of his magnificent barge. Always

107

by his master's side these days, we find Palladio's favorite pupil, Giambattista Aleotti. It was he who fashioned the exquisitely intricate models of houses designed by his friend and teacher. Some were only projects, never completed. A few of these Palladio-Aleotti models are still in private collections and museums. One is a walnut and lemonwood model of the defunct Academy at Bassano, Italy. The model measures three feet by three feet ten inches, and still shows traces of original gilt and carved moldings. This model was a gift to the Library of the Boston Athenaeum, presented by James Amory Sullivan.

The site chosen by Barbaro was a mound, probably artificial, within the immense boundaries of land once owned by one of the rarest creatures to flame in the skies of the Italian Renaissance, Caterina Cornaro. For flame she did! She blazed a trail of luxury and intrigue, filling a roster with the names of her conquests. Her happy hunting ground was Venice and later Cyprus. Lady Mary Wortley Montagu wrote of her daring: "Caterina Cornaro, Queen of Cyprus, while sitting in her Curtained Litter at the Lists, was so Prodigal with Scarves, Ribbons and embroidered Knots, thrown to her Importunate Swains, that she Must Draw the Curtains lest she expose her unbound Charms."

In 1472 Caterina was married at the age of eighteen to James of Cyprus. The new Queen ordered a palace built on the island under her direction. The palace, never totally finished, was to display twelve towers, to celebrate the months of the Zodiac. It was one of the wonders of the age. A story is here related to give an instance of Caterina's terrific penchant for the grand entrance. After half of the palace of Cyprus was finished, the Queen gave a ball, a sort of pageant, to welcome a whole procession of ambassadors. When the entire list of guests was assembled at the foot of a tremendous staircase (kept in darkness and awaiting a given signal), a fanfare of trumpets caused scented torches to burst into flame. Down the staircase, moving slowly, came Caterina Cornaro, Queen of Cyprus, Jerusalem, and Armenia. Standing well up on the stairs, she paused. Some of the men, gazing at her, wondered: Was Caterina fat? Impossible, yet her fabulous robe of Tyrian purple embroidered in rubies and pearls seemed to look bunchy on her figure. Then she raised her arms. With emblazoned fingers Caterina unloosed a clasp. Down fell the purple robe, to reveal another of emerald damask encrusted with diamonds. And so the robes fell from her shoulders. As the Queen of Cyprus walked unhurried down the stairs, she would pause every few steps, unclasp a jewel-encrusted mantle, let it lie in a pool of faceted color where it fell, and move on toward her enraptured guests. Only when she reached the last step, slim and smiling in a gown of silver, heraldically simple, did the bewildered ambassadors realize how wrong they had been.

Titian, in his portrait of Caterina, catches a look of divine arrogance in her green-gray eyes. She carries her head regally. Her mouth is beautifully, voluptuously carved, but uncompromising. This picture now hangs in the Uffizi Gallery in Florence. It dominates the room.

After a series of treacherous intrigues, Venice annexed Cyprus, and Caterina returned to live for the rest of her life on the vast Cornaro estates at Asolo. Here, surrounded by a brilliant court of painters, musicians, and men of letters, Caterina Cornaro died, still handsome it is said, at the age of fifty-six. Just eight years before Andrea Palladio was born.

Villa Maser is delightfully placed in undulating grounds parallel to the Castelfranco-Montebelluna highroad. When one motors from Cortina di Ampezzo to Venice, this is the first big house one sees, then the Campanile of Venice thrusts upward from the horizon.

Every detail in and about this villa is engaging. The entrance gates, before which stands a fountain with mermaids spouting jets of water from upthrust nipples, are of shells and dolphins. This fountain always seems to be a magnet for the eyes of small boys. I have encountered many. One day when I was making a water-color sketch of the fountain, I had constant company. Boys from Asolo and Castelfranco swarmed around me. But only for a minute. Soon I was catalogued and disposed of. Although each boy had seen this fountain every day of his life, I don't doubt, there was something about it ever new. Like Cleopatra's "infinite variety."

A long, low building, the villa gives a deceptive effect of prodigious length. This is largely due to the rhythmic flow of continuous line from one end of the façade to the other. Sixteen tall arches, with only a break for the pillared portico embracing three windows in the center. When Maser was first built, the entire frontage was rustico stone. This was 1568. In 1799 the entire façade was stuccoed and washed with pearl, almost a pinkish white. Although this treatment does not in any way alter the lovely flowing lines of the villa, I would rather see the cross-hatching of light and shade which rustico stone attracts. So many unusual features spring to the eye everywhere one looks, there is a feeling that perhaps

Palladio knew this to be the last country house he would ever build, so he was prodigal with his ideas.

One feature, which is said to have completely fascinated Thomas Jefferson by its ingenuity when a model was shown to him in Paris, is the fountain in the back courtyard of Villa Maser. Standing in the center of a hexagonal space, the basin of the fountain drips a transparent sheet of water into a small lake surrounding it. From this lake tile pipes lead the water to all parts of the house. The plan of the hall is cruciform. Two staircases are hidden in the arcades. Palladio was fortunate to have not only so grand an opportunity to will posterity an absolutely perfect example of pavilion architecture as he visualized this style of country house, but also the sympathetic aid of many of the foremost artists of the day. Vittorio did the figures of athletes in the niches between the arches along the front of the villa, as well as the superb masks that form keystones for the arches. There are sixteen of these, giants or sea-gods, each expressing a different emotion. And Veronese caught in paint and illusion exactly the scale and lift conceived by Palladio in vaulted walls, arches, and the richness of molding. No more splendid heritage could possibly be left to succeeding generations than a country house embodying the talents of Palladio, Vittorio, and Veronese.

The frescos at Maser have been photographed and detailed in writing more often than any others in existence, I wager, except perhaps Michelangelo's monumental Sistine Chapel. Probably because the Maser panels are so spirited, so engagingly informal. No one could ever feel lonely, no matter how solitary the life led there. In place of closed doorways, or plain dark wall spaces, one has charmingly poised pages hesitating in doorways, waiting only the word to bring in a flask of cordial, a vase of roses, or a carnival mask. Elaborately costumed women, flirting, in full war paint, as only Veronese could do it, walk along painted balconies. In the room where the page halts in the door, the dado panels are great favorites of mine. The chair-rail space is divided off into oval lozenges, painted in *chiaroscuro* like white marble. Against a background of dark larch-green within the ovals are white horses with youths astride, each balancing a silver javelin. No two are alike, and the arrangement of horse and rider in the panels is ingenious.

Across the highway from the entrance to Villa Maser, Palladio built a small church. Never was a temple of worship, pagan or Christian, so enchanting. A dazzling white portico with a highly ornamented pediment is isolated at the end of a tree-fringed path. The building is circular, about forty feet in diameter. The portico, jutting out from the main block, resembles the Pantheon in Rome. Garlands of white marble flowers seem to swing eternally between the Corinthian caps of the columns. Rising in volutes and scrolls, the dome is singularly light and airy. Sunlight filtered in, the day I was there, through a high lantern crowning the dome. Whatever the day, bright or overcast, the gleaming façade of Capella della Villa Maser, sometimes called Tempietto della Barbaro, seems always dressed for a holiday.

Just before Palladio started building Villa Rotonda, "as a retreat for my retirement," he fulfilled a promise to an old friend. When a young man, he had met in Vicenza a remarkable character, Conte Tornieri-Schio. A famous horseman, the Conte was always on the lookout to show his horsemanship to advantage, that it might in some way induce a few gold pieces into his pocket. For he was blessed with a handsome person, an ancient name, but not a *soldo*. One day he watched Palladio, who was sitting at a table arranging cubes and oblongs of white wood to form houses. This was a game he seemed always intent upon. A cube here. That was the center block. Two oblongs flanking it. The wings. And so on it went. All his life this was to be his way of setting the plan of a building in his mind before he drew the elevations. Tornieri-Schio was amused; more than a little interested.

"One day, when I find a rich wife, will you build a house for me?" he asked.

Palladio replied that he would, with alacrity, *when* that day came. They both laughed and left it at that. But the handsome Conte was cagey. He lived well; he loved even better. Women adored him, but none roped him. Finally years after the episode of the white building-blocks, a greatly aged Conte Tornieri-Schio visited Palladio.

"Now!" said he. "You may make good your promise. I want you to build me a country house. I have married a widow from Padova, who owns an ancient property at Monteccio. Will you restore it for me? But do not change it too much."

The house is of a type one would scarcely credit to Palladio, though it has great charm, the charm of grandeur in miniature. While not exactly

Garden Side of Powerscourt, County Wicklow.
Three Oblongs and Two Demilunes to Each Corner of Central Block.

Entrance Façade of Powerscourt.
Five Oblongs Resulting in Extremely Long Frontage.

Three Demilunes and Two Flexible Oblongs.
An Unusual Pavilion Style of House in Ireland.
Dartry Court.

Balrennet
Four Cubes and Four Flexible Oblongs.

An Extremely Elegant House Is Balrennet.
The Unique Floor Plan of This Medium-Size Country House
Gives It Great Distinction.

a small house, it has none of the sweep of conception, the soar of portico, usually associated with this architect. It appears that a much more ancient house of the long, low fortified type occupied the site. When Conte Schio sought a new house, he stipulated, "Preserve the old house." Palladio, having great respect for the magnificent structure of massive walls and groined arches, left them intact, adding a pure Palladian screen along one wall. The other he simply left as it was, adding only windows and an entrance door. The multicolored patina of succeeding washes of color and frescos vibrates like burnished metal in the changing light. In sunlight the house is red, copper, and rose. In moonlight it is silver, green, and dark wine. No portico surmounts the majestic proportions of the entrance door, but a tall winged window does. Broad semicircular steps lead to the door. The house has a distinct air of pageantry, the blast of fanfare seems to hover about the painted rooms. The names of the twelve months are sculptured over the windows, *Aprile, Maggio, Giugno,* and so on. The whisper of silk and velvet drifts along the corridors. Color and nostalgia frost the house.

VILLA ROTONDA—*Vicenza*

In 1552 Andrea Palladio built a huge house for Signore Paolo Amerigo, Referendary to Popes Pius IV and V. He is said to have been an incredibly tall man, who was forced to stoop almost double to pass through an ordinary doorway, and had to have a specially made bed carried everywhere he went. He picked the right man, certainly, to build him a house in his immense scale. He wrote Palladio to finish his villa before he returned from Spain. In one letter he wrote:

> After having traveled for Many Years in Remote Parts as well as Highly Civilized, I tire of Improvement and Culture. Now Middle Life approaches and my days at the Vatican are Over, I shall return to Vicenza to Meditate and administer my Roses, until Death Snatches me away.

A few miles outside Vicenza occurs a sharp rise of ground. A sort of footstool to Monte Berico. Here, dominating the landscape for miles, stands Villa Rotonda. Palladio says, "We chose a situation of Dominance. As advantageous to erecting a country house as could be found. At the foot of the Terrace flows the Bacciglioni, a sweet, navigable River."

The house is immense, without being in any sense ponderous. Bulking against the sky, it seems one with the crag on which it stands. It is undoubtedly one of the best-known works of Palladio, due largely, I believe, to its singularly happy position in the landscape. Instantly one comes within a few kilometers of Vicenza from any direction, Villa Rotonda arrests the eye. Many of Palladio's finest houses are so far back in the hills or on bad, even almost impassable, roads that visitors will not take the trouble to look for them. Hence they are unknown, forgotten. But not Rotonda. So big in scale, so simple in detail is this house, that one look seems to bring all into focus, from afar off. The four Ionic colonnades projecting from each face of the square main building are comparable only to the single portico at Villa Malcontenta, Palladio's masterpiece. The porticos project fourteen feet, having a width of forty feet. A grandly sweeping flight of steps gives access to each. Kitchen, servants' quarters, and stores are in the basement. The circular entrance is one of the most impressive rooms in the world, not only because of its sublime scale, but also because of the painted decorations by Battista Venitiano that fill the eye. The Olympian crowd are portrayed in the grand, full-blooded style of Tiepolo. Four enclosed staircases wind up from the alcoves cut from the corners of the hall to make a full circle. So there is nothing to deflect the eye from the vaulted hall. At each corner of the central block is a big room, twenty by thirty feet. Two smaller rooms flank the halls leading to the north and south porticos. There are eight reception rooms on the first floor. On the second floor, one-third as high, are six rooms. Stone screens, with a high arched opening in the center, fill the space between pillar and wall in the return of all four pediments. Lorenzo Rubini modeled the many sculptured figures that crown the four pediments and flank the four flights of steps. The rotunda, which rises almost to the clouds it seems, is pierced at its base by eight round windows that light the great hall. The tiles covering the entire roof of house and rotunda are noteworthy, for the color was obtained originally by soaking them in the residue from wine vats. This method, still used today in the Touraine in France, produced a dark purplish red color, turning to liquid bronze in the fierce rays of a setting sun.

TEATRO OLIMPICO—*Vicenza*

And now we approach, down a wide shaded street, the *chef-d'oeuvre* of Palladio in Vicenza: Teatro Olimpico. It has been said that this building, both inside and out, is a very dream of *chiaroscuro*. The arrangement of engaged columns, arches, wide cornices, statues placed in diminuendo to give a sense of perspective, the rise of semicircle above semicircle, all contribute to a sense of unreality. The like was never experienced in architecture before Andrea Palladio presented it to the world. When one realizes that the Olimpico as Palladio planned it was the first theater to be built as such in the Renaissance, and has been used as a model, if not wholly, with variations, ever since, it becomes a veritable landmark in architecture.

I do not agree with some that Olimpico is cold and soulless. That it is simply a staggeringly beautiful mathematical problem in stone. In this edifice there is to me a loftiness of imagination that Palladio so often missed imprisoning in stone and marble by only a hairbreadth. In the circular auditorium the sweep of tier upon tier of seats has a sense of a magnificent flight of steps rising to the colonnaded gallery, where pillars of Corinthian order support a balustrade. Just to wander into the auditorium of Olimpico at any time of the day, quite alone, is a challenge to the imagination. There is no curtain to separate or blot out the entrancing vistas of silvery gray and fawn-brown streets in some Vitruvian city we never knew. Pale ivory or delicately pearl statues of classic grace abound: goddesses, vestals, emperors, Pretorian guards, fauns, and dryads. Some are overtall, some are shortened to force the perspective in the three vistas, which are arranged like the three prongs of a trident. Light comes from we know not where. A hush prevails. The hush of centuries, for in this temple to the Muses "Time bides, bides Time," as John Dryden said when he fell into temporary disgrace; like Dryden, Olimpico needs only an imagination worthy of its quality to restore its great days. Drama, Tragedy, Comedy, all the facets of Commedia dell' Arte seem to garland the stage. In this building "admirer takes admired by the hand." I know of no other building that breathes the classic spirit of Vitruvius as does Olimpico. For so profound adherence to coldest classicism, this theater is surprisingly alive and peopled. It was not until after Palladio at his own expense had excavated the Teatro Berga at Vicenza, an ancient relic to paganism, that he designed, *con grande*, what to his mind was a fitting temple to the Muses Melpomene and Thalia.

Five years before the Olimpico was built, Palladio had caused an alabaster model, one inch to a foot scale, to be made by one Carlo Bor-

PALAZZO CHIERICATI, VICENZA.

PROSCENIUM SEEN THROUGH SCREEN OF COLUMNS,
TEATRO OLIMPICO, VICENZA.

chetti, an itinerant sculptor from the Dolomites, glorifying his idea for a permanent theater in Vicenza. While the model caused admiration on all sides, there was no apparent enthusiasm from the council to provide the considerable sum of money necessary to carry out so grandiose a scheme. Well, "Time bides, bides Time."

In 1560 an Academy of Arts was formed in Vicenza. Of ten men chosen for the governing body, Palladio was one. Immediately he put into motion the wheels of his greatest desire, to build the Teatro Olimpico. Nowhere in Italy outside Rome was there a fitting auditorium in which to enact the resounding plays of classic authors, which were in the days of the Renaissance presented very much in the grand manner, no matter how simple the theme. Palladio considered the task of building this edifice so "Herculean," to quote him, that he called in a consultant named Daniel Barbero, whose name we often find in Palladio's notes. But what with one thing and another, important commissions in Venice, Padova, Bologna, and building country villas, it was a score of years at least before ground was broken and the Teatro Olimpico started to rise. Even then, there were months when no work proceeded. The constant delays are said to have undermined Palladio's health, and in August of 1580 he died, destined never to see the fulfillment of his greatest dream. In gratitude for his work and untiring services to the Academy of Arts, which had made him president two years before, the committee unanimously elected Palladio's son Silla to carry on the work started so gloriously by his father.

It was 1584, the celebration of the Feast of the Redeemer, when the theater was finished. The Academy christened it with the name Olimpico, which had been Palladio's original idea but had not been considered as fitting at the time by the committee.

No building I recall contains so many features that leap to the eye as does this masterly conception for a temple to the arts. For that is what it is. Music has been found a delight when concerts are given here. The *pulpitum* of classic drama, a raised platform which is flexible, can be moved to the front of the stage or far back at will. This has become universally used in theaters all over the world. At either side of the stage, in effect the wings of a proscenium, is a screen of stone. This is monumental, yet lyrical in design. Niches above and below a middle cornice contain statues, life size, in richly sculptured Roman dress. Possibly the finest sculptured panels ever used by Palladio are the large oblong ones set into the attic that extends across the back of the stage. The subject depicts the labors of Hercules, executed by well-known Venetian sculptors.

Three vistas of painted screens showing piazzas, fountains, colonnades, and buildings in perspective were designed by Scamozzi. He painted many such decorations to be used by Palladio and other Renaissance architects in frescos and arras, and as borders around doors and windows. The amazing ingenuity and variety of mood displayed by Scamozzi and his apprentices was greatly appreciated by his clients. They vied with one another to have his most fantastic work on the walls of their houses. Particularly in his screens for the theater was his color extraordinary. He would suggest the essence of a given scene with golden yellow for late afternoon; sunset, orange red; evening, violet; night, indigo; winter, silver and gray; spring, limpid green and pale lemon. An opulent palace room, by gold upon crimson or purple. Poverty, by indefinite grays and sepias in waving lines, as opposed to his usual precise, lineal mood. Hot desert scenes were gained by placing lamps behind red and orange silk scarves. While Scamozzi's effects were myriad, he never deviated from the classic scene.

The height of the proscenium from stage to cornice is forty feet. There are no flies as in theaters today, and no curtain was used.

On a late autumn afternoon, when Teatro Olimpico was three-quarters finished, Andrea Palladio collapsed in the pit as he was directing the placing of some plasterwork. Hastily his son Silla had his father carried to his litter and borne to the Villa Rotonda, where, he had said, "I shall retire to end my days." For the last three years he had lived there. As the dying architect was carried up the magnificent stairs of stone, I am sure the four winds of heaven clashed. Thunderheads piled darkly one upon another, and forked lightning darted earthward. The gods of Olympus would have marked with sound and fury the shuffling off of his mortal coil.

The funeral of Andrea Palladio was marked with sonorous magnificence, according to the chronicles of Donna Ivieratea Monti, which she wrote in 1582. The black and silver catafalque, draped with a yellow velvet pall fringed in black, was drawn through the streets of Vicenza by the young apprentices in the atelier of Palladio. Clothed in liveries of black and silver, they wore arm sashes of yellow. Four of these apprentices carried an alabaster model of the Teatro Olimpico. Andrea Palladio was buried first in the church of San Corona. Later his son Silla removed the body to a vault in the monastery of the Dominicans. In 1845 the coffin of Andrea Palladio was again moved, at the request of the people of Vicenza, to the cemetery basilica, where a monument was erected over his grave, a plain marble shaft obtained by public subscription. The only embellishment is a length of molding of Carrara marble, probably from the first burial place, the church of San Corona. Deeply incised Roman letters read ANDREAS PALLADIUS. What makes this length of carved marble particularly interesting is the line carved in infinitesimal letters *Marc-Antonio P. scultore*. Silla and Marc-Antonio, the eldest and the next to the youngest of the four sons of Palladio, are the only ones who gained any kind of prominence. Silla, architect, and Marc-Antonio, sculptor, appear now and again, fleetingly, in document in the museo in Vicenza. Of Grazio, Leonido, and the daughter Zenobia, one learns nothing except the fact that they existed, in nearly as shadowy a world as his wife Angela. It appears that Palladio had few possessions other than his white leather portfolios of sketches and elevations. For years a nobly constructed barge, with a painted and gilded deck and accommodations in the hull for eating and sleeping, was tied to a wharf at Fusina alla Brenta. No one claimed the rotting hulk, and it was finally broken up and sold for the gilded carvings. It is recorded that at a sale in Padova in 1590 "ten bales of rich silk of Orient and China, in party with some hundred lengths of pile velvet from Spain and Genoa from the collection of the deceased Andrea Palladio, will be sold." Veronese wrote to Alessandro Barbaro, after he had painted the portrait of Palladio, reproduced in this book as the frontispiece:

Andrea Palladio's portrait is finished. The fire in the man's eyes I have caught, I believe. His high forehead he insisted covering with the fashionable turban. His arrival was that of an emperor, attended by his apprentices and sons. His dress of magnificent velvets and gold galloon, was quickly doffed for a more *dégagé* suit of satin, in which he works.

119

BOOK II

IRELAND

PALLADIO'S
SPIRIT IN IRELAND

The sweeping gesture with which Palladian architecture rode into all Ireland during the eighteenth century was not merely an esthetic event; it was a social and to a great extent economic one as well. The previous century had been marked by almost continuous riots and bloodshed, bringing utter havoc to the lean resources of the country. A dark cloud of poverty and exhaustion hung over Ireland. The gentry lived in half-derelict castles of feudal grimness. It was in the cards that the beauty-loving Irish nature would demand elegance and sweep in decoration once the pendulum of fate swung back again. This came with the Battle of the Boyne Water in 1690.

Thereafter there reigned over Ireland a ninety-year period of deep tranquillity. With peace came prosperity, at least to the landowners. Each tried to outdo his neighbor in lavish sums spent on country houses and decoration. At the first hint of loosened purse strings the young aristocrats embarked on the Grand Tour through central Europe, considered so necessary in those days to broaden and give polish to a young man of position. Those with imagination and taste were mightily impressed with the classic purity, the elegance, and breadth of proportion expressed by Andrea Palladio in the villas he built for the rich Venetians along the quiet, tree-shaded Brenta Canal, only a day's coach journey from the fashionable and cosmopolitan glitter of Venice.

I venture to say that the first rocket fired in what was to prove an epic translation of architecture from Latin into Gaelic sprang from the quick brain of young Robert Fitzgerald, Marquess of Kildare, soon to be second Duke of Leinster. In his mind's eye he saw as in a vision his broad lands in County Kildare; the rich dark green of Irish yew to replace the jet of Italian cypresses so arrestingly used to point up white marble columns and pediments; Connemara stone, gleaming white in the sunlight, gray-violet in the shadows, in place of Italian Carrara. Instead of reflecting in the Brenta Canal, these soaring façades would mirror in the hundreds of streams flowing across the Irish countryside.

The vision was realized. I learn from data found in the National Library in Dublin the fact that Leinster brought back to Ireland seventy-five Italian artisans, workers in stucco (including the famed brothers Francini and Aurelio Callari, whose work is to be seen on walls and ceilings of most of the great Palladian houses in Italy, Ireland, and England), cabinet-makers, upholsterers, embroiderers, workers in gold leaf and gesso, as well as a number of architects all under the influence of Palladio. Among these was a young man from the duchy of Saxony, named Richard Castle, who had received his training in Vicenza, the birthplace of Andrea Palladio, where many of Palladio's finest buildings and houses are found. The Duke commissioned Castle to build Leinster House in Dublin, and Carton at Maynooth, in the County of Kildare. With the completion of these houses, Palladian character became the rage. It swept from the fastnesses of the bleak glens of Antrim, to the gaunt dramatic Sligo, along the towering promontories of Connaught to County Limerick, into tree-shaded Waterford, Wicklow, and the plains of Meath and Tyrone. It ran like wildfire, it put quicksilver into Irish blood.

Curiously enough, it ran to extremes in the South of Ireland, reaching vast proportions in such great gestures as Russborough, Carton, Rathgannonstown, Caledon, Castletown, Kilra House and Inishvara, again turning to perfection in miniature, Kilshandon, Arrow Hill, and Templeshallard.

Palladio is known to have said frequently that his great love was to design the country house. It was surely his province, in it he was superlative. He had tremendous sympathy and feeling for the country, often making use of simple country forms for enrichment, as in the wide band in quarter relief of fruits, corn and melons and grapes, just under the cornice supporting the closed balustrade at Ballysaggart House, in County Wicklow. Travelers returning from Ireland, having motored through the counties, wax lyrical describing the placing of the generously proportioned classic houses in relation to the countryside.

Scarcely a site was chosen to build these houses but that had water of some sort to reflect the breathless lift of white column and portico; a lough winding in from the sea, or one of the countless rivers that form a pattern of silver lace over the richly turfed meadows of the greater part of the island. If no water was at hand, there might be a false lagoon, either guarded in architectural formality by a balustrade or planted with trees along its edge to give the natural look, as at Russborough near the village of Blessington, in County Wicklow.

The grandly conceived, many-windowed façade of Castletown rises above the spreading fields of County Kildare. In late summer stooks of golden wheat are casually piled in front. As one walks toward the house backed by towering yew and wine-dark beech, there is a sense of festival about; one expects to encounter Demeter among the corn.

There seems to be an aura of pleasure hovering continuously around these Palladian country houses, past pleasures and pleasures to come.

A friend, whom I had given a list of some of the houses along the magic reaches of the Blackwater in County Waterford, wrote me as she was ending her visit to Ireland that she had gone late one afternoon to Cappoquin, a lovely riverside village, and on to old Ballynatry dreaming away the years among the most magnificent lichened oaks to be encountered along the richly wooded Blackwater. The letter reads:

We pulled up at the gates of Ballynatry in a hired pony trap. As there was no one about to answer our shouting, we tied the pony and walked up to the house. The oaks are, of course, indescribable. Our pull at the bell handle was answered by an amazingly tall, cadaverous butler, who, turning to a wide stairway, said, "Here is the Captain now." Riding-crop in hand, Captain Holroyd-Smythe welcomed us into the most unspoiled and romantic house I have ever seen.

The length and breadth of Ireland yields many romantic houses, but to my mind none compares, for sheer unbridled excitement and swank, with the assembling and dismantling of Ballyscullion. Seemingly it existed for a few dramatic years, aloof, a frozen classic dream, dedicated by its builder to a curious purpose, at once a dwelling house and a temple to the arts.

BALLYSCULLION—*1778*

No house of folly ever built has a more daring history or a more startling fate than the great classic pile Ballyscullion, built by the Earl–Bishop, Frederick Hervey, Earl of Bristol, Bishop of Cloyne and Derry. Ballyscullion rose upon a rocky promontory on the shores of Lough Beg, in the County Antrim, circa 1778. The huge house formed a sweeping crescent, or more rightly a sharp steel scythe, which promptly swung and cut through its own foundations, reducing them to dust. It commands a superbly beautiful sight, the sparkling reaches of the Lough Beg, with the added prospect of the intensely green Mountains of Mourn that come down to the sea. From all accounts Ballyscullion was on every point arresting.

In 1777, that remarkable eccentric, Bishop of Derry, returned to Ireland from five years in Italy, France, and Spain. It was his intention to build a country house that would be a museum to house the art treasures he had gathered during the five years he wandered back and forth across central Europe, possessed by an acquisitive instinct second to none on record, and accompanied, happily, by an open, apparently bottomless, purse.

The two great wings of Ballyscullion spread like those of an eagle, unfolding from the main bulk, an enormous circular rotunda that contained the living rooms and offices of the household; corridors and galler-

PALLADIO'S BROKEN PEDIMENT AND ATTICS USED SUCCESSFULLY IN
IRELAND BY RICHARD CASTLE.

BALLYSCULLION IN COUNTY ANTRIM, IRELAND.

ies in the wings held his priceless loot. Writing to his daughter Lady Erne in Paris, March 8, 1779, the Bishop describes Ballyscullion:

> The house itself is perfectly circular, the Drawing Room 84 feet x 74 . . . the Dining Room and Library 48 feet x 36 feet; total length of whole, including Corridors and Wings, 360 feet. I think too small. Were I to build it again I would double all footage, at the very least.

Surprisingly, he kept his word.

In 1797 the Bishop left Ireland and Ballyscullion in anger. Returning to his estates in Suffolk, he built the gigantic Ickworth. As it stands today, Ickworth is beautifully lived in and tended by the fourth Marquess of Bristol. Its frontage is 680 feet, nearly double that of Ballyscullion, ruined and wind-wracked on its Irish lough.

Architecturally, Ickworth is an exact replica of Ballyscullion. Although the gardens are splendid, wooded and strewn with flowers, the house loses in drama, since it stands in a flat landscape with no Lough Beg to reflect the luminous sweep of pillar and portico. Accompanying the Bishop of Derry to the Continent on his first Grand Tour in 1765 was a brilliant young Irishman, John Shanahan, officially tutor to Augustus Hervey, the Bishop's son.

Shanahan was intensely interested in Palladian architecture. A scholar of distinction, he had assisted the architect Richard Castle during the building of Leinster House in Dublin, Carton at Maynooth in County Kildare, and the great Shanganagh Castle in County Wicklow.

Oddly enough, while compiling drawings from Palladian houses in Italy, to be used later when actual work on elevations for Ballyscullion started, the unpredictable Bishop bade Shanahan acquire from the profligate Duca di San Valedo of Vicenza Palladian elevations that the Duca had intended using to build a villa for himself at Brenta. Drowning as he was in a sea of gambling debts, the Duca offered these family heirlooms to the highest bidder. The rolled and sealed elevations under his arm, the Bishop returned with Shanahan to Ireland immediately.

In the spring of 1767 the Bishop started building a house in the County Down, employing the elevations Palladio had designed for the San Valedo. These designs reached the very pinnacle of classicism. Downhill, as the house was called, rose rather bleakly on a bare rock facing the sea. From under the portico one looked out and away across the gray Irish water.

127

The Bishop wrote Lady Erne: "The shell of my new house, Downhill, stands facing the sea. It will be a large and convenient edifice when finished. It stands on a bold shore where a tree is a rarity."

Downhill was started as a fairly small house, small, that is, for the Earl–Bishop, whose soaring ideas plunged him wildly forward, regardless. As the years went by, large additions were made. With the suddenness so characteristic of the Bishop, he tired of the house, and with John Shanahan he again started out for Italy, fully agreed to gather fresh ideas for his new and grander house on the Lough Beg.

From Rome he wrote the Duchess of Devonshire: "I have combed Italy, purchasing treasures: paintings, sculpture, brocades, crystals, miniatures, and intaglios for Ballyscullion that is to be, which, I flatter myself, will be another Tusculanium."

In the great days of the Earl–Bishop's tenure, life blazed brilliantly at Ballyscullion. In many ways it probably did rival Tusculanium. Travelers sailing up the lough by boat were surely rewarded when they sighted the great range of Palladian façade flung out against the drifting Irish sky on the rocky eminence. The Bishop never approached the house by land. A fleet of sailing boats and twelve oared barges were always kept in readiness at Portglanone, at the head of the lough. Today one sees traces of an elaborate landing stage. Little remains save stained and broken marble water-stairs, and graceful Italian urns toppled into the clear water.

After the angry Bishop took himself and his treasures out of Ireland forever, Ballyscullion stood lone, crumbling in neglect for years. In 1802 the house was stripped from cellar to roof; the superb mantelpieces of alabaster and rare Italian marbles carved by the greatest artists of the day—even the bronze, silver, and painted porcelain hardware—were removed to Ickworth.

In chronicles and memoirs of the period, the witty, well-informed Mrs. Delany and the sporting buck Lord Mountgarret tell of high doings at Ballyscullion. For five years the Bishop of Cloyne and Derry lived in princely style, suiting his manner of living to the grandeur of his great house. Entertainments were prodigious. Mrs. Delany writes to Mrs. Middleton in London:

Hardly a fine day passes without coaches and carryalls rushing to and fro on the roads from Antrim, Portadown, and Moneymore bound for my Lord Bristol's vast demesne of Ballyscullion. He keeps great state at all times. Surely a King could do no more.

I am told over three thousand wax tapers burn to their sockets each night, and I believe it, for at a rout last week the odor of burning French wax was overpowering. The extravagance beheld on all sides renders one speechless; at table and buffet, every delicacy out of season.

Lord Mountgarret wrote his son, who was in Italy enjoying the Grand Tour:

That Prince of Elegance and Prodigality, Bristol, entertains continuously at Ballyscullion. He seems never to tire, though some of us do, mightily.

For all his lavish casting about of money, he does nothing to improve the vile Irish roads. Overturned and bogged coaches litter the ditches nightly. However these remote counties now enjoy gaiety extreme, I doubt it lasts long, for as you know we say of Bristol "Everything by starts, and nothing long."

Ballyscullion was built of pearly white Connemara stone. The texture seemed not to please the Bishop, and he wrote his son Frederick from Italy during his third journey to the Continent:

I am decided on covering Ballyscullion with a wash of ivory stucco. I shall follow, as always, dear Impeccable Palladio's rule, and as no building should be without a crust or covering in our raw damp climate, I shall cover house, pillars, portico, all, with Palladio's stucco, which has lasted on the Villa Vennaro in the misty, wild Abruzzi for two hundred and eighty years.

It has succeeded perfectly well at Downhill, that Temple of the Winds, and on my Casino at Derry, it resists the frosts and winds of Vicenza and Ireland alike, *c'est tout dire,* and deceives the most acute eye till within a foot.

At this time the Bishop sent to Ireland the Venetian brothers Carabelli, masterly workers in stucco. Many of the richly fluid ceiling designs seen today in Irish Palladian houses were done by these brothers who spent twelve years in Ireland.

Lady Templemore of Castle Clon writes in her Journal, which is preserved and included among data on "The Wide Streets Commission" (drawn up by the Duke of Leinster, and Lords Charlemont, Caledon, and Belmore in 1741, the object being to "Rebuild, Improve and Widen the Streets, Squares and Parks, of the City of Dublin-on-the-Liffey"):

As one walks from room to room at Ballyscullion, the freshness of color, the grace of ornament continually fills the eye, the yellow of primroses, the pink of hawthorn, touches of gilt and black marble, create a scene too lovely to describe in mere words. A brush and the color spectrum are needed.

In 1830, Lady Templemore, then an old lady, writes further: "Sad to relate, Ballyscullion is abandoned utterly, by that wicked abominable fellow Lord Bristol."

A last gesture before his truculent departure from the Irish scene was made by the Bishop. At the ceremony of the convening of the Dublin Parliament in 1791, Ireland was reveling in and vastly enjoying one of her periods of wishing to be a nation, succeeding for a time in freeing the Dublin Parliament from the domination of Westminster. Lord Charlemont, a moderator, was holding the reins lightly, but suddenly the apple cart was kicked over with a resounding crash when in stepped the arrogant Earl–Bishop of Cloyne and Derry thrusting for dramatic effect.

The picture we are given by a contemporary is typical. Astride a curvetting black stallion, the Bishop headed a considerable retinue. His costume, half military, half ecclesiastical, was flamboyant and pure fancy dress. Along the road from Ballyscullion to Dublin he had ridden a veritable Triumphal Progress; fanfares and loud blasts on brass trumpets had frightened pigs, geese, horses, and country people alike. Later his entrance into the courtyard of Dublin Castle to attend the Viceregal Ball was wildly theatrical, causing a near riot. The Earl–Bishop sat as enthroned, in a yellow lacquer landau made by Cesarini of Mantua, the equipage drawn by six gorgeously ribboned black horses. The Bishop wore a flowing robe of Vatican purple, with gloves fringed in gold, a golden cap upon his powdered hair.

It was at this ball that the Bishop created a situation that made his relations with Dublin Parliament impossible to continue, and his further residence in Ireland intolerable. Within six weeks the fantastic Earl of Bristol had assembled a fleet of forty cargo ships at Kilkeel on the Irish Sea, to transport his fabulous collection of art to England.

On moonlight nights the waves that lap the ruined water-stairs at Ballyscullion tell the same tale so many shattered houses whisper: "We were built by the grandiose dreams of men, we die a little each day, but some part of us, some fragment, will always remain, for we are the stuff dreams are made of."

RICHARD CASTLE, DISCIPLE OF PALLADIO

In a tall, rather narrow house in Venice, a young man was angrily cording a big oxhide traveling box. Other boxes of various sizes lay bound and labeled for the long journey by coach across Italy, hot and miserably dusty at this time of year, into the cool forests of Thuringia. The rather florid, blue-eyed young man was Richard Castle from Saxony, and he emphatically did not wish to leave Venice. But he had no choice. His father's last letter had had a ring of finality about it. "Come home, Richard. I can send you no more money. Times are bad. My business does not prosper, for the Court is still in mourning for the Elector. Come home, I bid you, and build your houses in Dresden." Not an angry letter, to be sure, mused Richard, but further pleading would be useless.

The late summer day was fading, and all his candles had long since been burned to the last spatter of wax. One more glance around the bare room with its slit Gothic window looking out onto the teeming Rialto Bridge. Tonight he would row to Mestre in a market boat. Tomorrow start the long overland journey home.

As the creaking old coach, seeming about to split at every seam, lurched down a mountain pass into the plain of Roibas, Richard Castle woke with a start. Shrugging his cloak higher about his shoulders, he peered out of the rain-grimed window at the gray landscape. France. France, which he, the Italianate Richard, had never cared to see; he wanted only to be allowed to live in Venice or Vicenza. To live from day to day, a little bread, a little wine, endless sheets of white paper and sticks of black *carbone*. That was all he had wanted. Sometime, of course, he would like to build a house. A huge Vitruvian pile, like Villa Rotonda or Palazzo Thiene. Just so long as he might live and work in the atmosphere that breathed Palladio. To Richard it seemed very little to ask. Apparently it was not so simple as he thought. The month was now October. He had been nearly three months on the way. At times, like the days spent in Turin, he had enjoyed himself. There he had drawn sharply contrasting sketches of Palladian houses, churches, and a big decoration in attempted *chiaroscuro*, showing the three aisles of diminishing perspective on the stage of Teatro Olimpico. That drawing had aroused great interest at the palazzo of the Duca di Tenio. A few gold pieces had chinked in his money pouch when he sold the drawing to the Duchessa. After that he had been taken to see the wonderful *scuderia* where the famous racing stallions were bred. One day he would build stables as well as houses. Palladio had loved horses. Why, he had even made a huge mathematical chart of one, a towering stallion, jet black with strange markings of eight-pointed stars on either rump. This was one of Richard's favorite drawings among the Palladiana in the Museo Municipale at Vicenza.

A few weeks later, through clear blue and russet autumn weather, Richard arrived at Dresden. In a month or so he had settled more or less contentedly into his father's porcelain atelier. Here the delicate designs of trailing vines, berries, rosebuds, and pastoral scenes, so desired by the Electoral court, were painted on fragile cup, platter, and chocolatepot.

Two years went by. Richard designed a small hunting-lodge near Plütten in Thuringia for one of the cadets of the Wettin family. This is, by the way, one of the most perfect Palladian pavilions in existence. It follows the long line of frontage (very like the *foresteria* at Villa Foscarini della Brenta) with a continuous line of eight arched windows, which, when open, form a loggia for use as a room in fine weather. Each rusticated arch is topped by a keystone carved in the image of some animal sought in the chase. Inside this comfortable retreat the rooms are all fitted in red or green leather and the walls and woodwork, white gesso. This extremely sophisticated forest house, simply bristling with style, was built when Richard Castle was only twenty-three years old.

Here and now I wish to make clear the way I shall spell the name of this rising young architect, henceforth. One finds it written Cassels and Casels as well as Castle. I find the form most frequently used is Castle. That is how, for the sake of clarity, I shall refer to the builder of Leinster House in Dublin—his first Irish commission—and many other Irish houses.

When Richard Castle was twenty-six years old, a legacy flowed into his pockets, unexpectedly, and none too soon. For he had been getting restless; he and his world were not in tune. The aunt who died and left him not only a small property in the bustling market town of Leipzig but also coin of the realm in fair quantity was his father's sister, always known as an admirer if not a patron of the arts. Indeed, for all her money she did not possess one article at her death that interested her heir Richard. He wrote his sister Betta from Leipzig: "Aunt Gundorpt left a house full of lumber. Not one article would I take for my own, save a long-handled copper warming pan." As a collector, Aunt Gundorpt's taste seems to have been in her mouth.

As one might easily guess, the first move made by the now exultant Richard was to procure coach space to return to Italy and his beloved

Vicenza. It is a grand thing, I have always believed, to have so strong a desire in life that it must not be gainsaid. Sometimes people fight against this consuming urge in their life, and usually to their eternal undoing. For this tall, broad-shouldered, fair-haired visionary from the baroque splendors of Dresden, one thing and one only meant a life worth living, according to his lights. This was to keep alive, to perpetuate, the Palladian spirit in architecture.

It is in Venice we again encounter Richard. Not in the tall mean house beside the Rialto Bridge. This time he is well housed in a Renaissance palazzo on the Grand Canal, the house of Monsignore Rinaldo Pisani. While in Vicenza, Richard had met this man, who, following in the footsteps of his ancestors, had made a kind of career of art. A patron of the arts, par excellence.

In the pale carnelian palazzo of the Pisani, hospitality was a fetish. All visiting foreigners of rank were invited to dine and view the extensive collection of paintings and rare sculpture from Greece and the Florentine marbles but lately become the fashion. It is reasonable to suppose that Richard Castle met these leisurely traveling foreigners and found they had much in common when discussing pictures, architecture, music, and the comedy and drama of the nightly carnivals Venice was addicted to.

From 1715 to 1740 the gambling and banquets indulged in by the pleasure-loving Venetians became a scandal in Europe. Fortunes and inheritances were lost nightly across the filigreed tops of card tables. A cast of dice determined whether a young man would return that night to a house still his, or be allowed only to gather his clothes before the winner took possession. The entrancing pictures painted at this time by witty Pietro Longhi show all the twists and turns of this scintillating life to perfection. His collection of cartoons for a mural decoration—never executed—called *Carnevale in Maschera* has a vitality of line coupled with wit and color that he never equaled again, even in his superb staircase fresco at Palazzo Grassi-Stucky. This immense decoration is absolutely living. All sorts of persons are depicted. Cardinals, advocates, courtesans, masked ladies, and cloaked gallants. Turbaned blackamoors hand round cakes and cups of chocolate. All the rank and fashion of the brilliant city of tall palaces and deep, dark waterways seems to walk abroad. Standing beside a black-masked lady in cherry and white panniers is a red-cheeked young man in dark green satin; he is "wearing his own hair," clubbed and tied with a white ribbon. On his shoulder sits a tiny monkey, to which he feeds a cherry. On the broad cuff of the green coat the initials R.C. are painted. Riccardo Castello, as the architect from Saxony was called in Italy.

For three years Richard lived in Venice and Vicenza. At times he traveled to Rome, to Florence, and even to Sicily. Always he made measurements of buildings that attracted his eye. In Rome it was the Vitruvian ideal that entranced him most, just as it had Palladio.

One day there came to Palazzo Labia, where Richard Castle was engaged in restoring the arches of a loggia, an Irish milord of splendid address and, as Richard had great cause to know later, unparalleled vision and enthusiasm for Palladian architecture. The Pisani suggested to Richard that he escort Lord Robert Fitzgerald—within a few weeks to become nineteenth Earl of Kildare—to the Pisani palace at Strà. From there they could make daily visits by barge along the shaded Brenta Canal to such Palladian villas as Malcontenta and Valmarana at Lisiera.

For two months Lord Robert and Richard Castle resided at Strà, making frequent trips into the hills around Padova and Meledo. When Lord Robert was suddenly called back to Ireland by the death of his elder brother, which occurrence placed him in direct succession to the dukedom, he extracted a promise from Richard that he would arrive in Ireland within the year to begin building a house in Dublin for Kildare.

Perhaps one reason for Kildare's enormous admiration, his *simpatica,* for Italians and all things Italian was the fact that his own family, the FitzGeralds, were originally Geraldines, descended from the Gherardini of Florence. Later the Barons Fitz-Gerald (1350) became great princes, ruling over the broad and grassy meadows of Kildare. Of all this tribe Geraldine, the greatest by far was Gerald the Grand Earl and Danger Man of Maynooth Castle. The townhouse of the arrogant FitzGeralds was in a dark side street in Dublin, almost an alley. It was built of timber, as was then the custom. But the new Earl of Kildare would change all that. He would import an architect imbued with the Vitruvian style of building, the sweeping lift of pillar and arched window, pediments against the sky and long corridors with niches for statuary, copies of the priceless Greek and Roman sculpture used so freely in Italy to enliven and enrich the vista both indoors and out. The Geraldines had ever been arbiters; now

Dublin, all Ireland, would be treated to elegance and power in architecture such as the country had never seen.

So, on a spring day there stepped off a French packet berthed at Dundalk, a tall, portly young man wearing a greatcoat of rather absurd cut. Warm though the April day was, the coat was almost an ulster, more fitting for wild, demented weather. The pockets bulged with what looked like a huge assortment of building blocks painted white. Why should they not? That is what they were. Ever since the day in Vicenza when Richard Castle had been told of the manner in which Andrea Palladio had juggled his cubes, oblongs, and demilunes, placing and replacing them one against the other to get the desired plan of a house, he had done the same.

As Richard drove through the fertile Irish countryside, he was intensely interested in the crowns of trees, richly foliaged oaks, shimmering beeches both green and copper, ash and chestnut, plane trees and bog-myrtle; all seemed to him to weave and cluster into the lovely semblance of the forest of Arcadia. Everywhere was water to reflect the trees, the sky, and whatever castle or mill or farmhouse stood on lough or river. Rivers, rivers, rivers, some as narrow and shallow as a brook, others rather like the Brenta Canal, many much wider. What a delicate tracery of silver web these waterways wove upon the land. By the time Richard had reached Dublin he had planned many country houses and knew just where he wished them to be placed. In the following years, more than one of these dreams came true.

Arrived in Dublin, Richard was taken to Lord Kildare's house, which privately he thought shocking-mean and dismal for anyone to live in, appalling for the residence of so great a nobleman. The next day Lord Kildare drove Richard around the city. A few new houses were springing up here and there, mostly hugging the quarter near the Liffey River which bisected the town. After a turn or two through fashionable Capel Street and Abbey Place, the coach turned and drove along what looked like an unfrequented road. Finally, skirting Dawson Street, very new and paint conscious, the coach groaned to a halt in what was surely a suburb. The end of Molesworth Street, called Molesworth Fields. A friend who had accompanied Lord Kildare and Richard exclaimed in amazement at the idea of stopping in so vulgar a spot. He nearly had apoplexy when informed by Lord Kildare that this was the location of his new townhouse, to be built by Richard Castle.

"But you cannot live here," expostulated the man. "What will Dublin say?"

"They will follow me wherever I go," haughtily the Earl answered. How right he was we now see.

TOWNHOUSES:
DUBLIN CHIMNEY POTS

Crossing from New York to Cobh one winter, I met a Canadian architect on board the steamer. He was extremely interested in hearing all I could tell him about Dublin, where he planned to spend a few weeks later in the spring. One of his remarks, pertaining to information he had already received about the Georgian city on the Liffey, amused me. For in a way it was so right. "I hear," said he, "Dublin is called the city of chimney pots and areaways."

Between the areaways and chimneys there are of course houses, rising from the former and supporting the latter. But I must confess that the deep wide areaway, large of window and flagged with stone, is much in evidence, and the thousands upon thousands of chimney pots, row upon row, dominate the sky-line wherever the eye roams in Dublin.

Almost without exception, the red brick Georgian houses are five stories high. That is, a deep areaway, which is the first story (basement), then there are four stories above the sidewalk level. Palladian houses, as for example Powerscourt House in William Street, Aldbrough House in Portland Row, Clanwilliam House in St. Stephen's Green, and Charlemont House in Palace Row (now Rutland Square, Upper), are three stories above the sidewalk level. A deep basement contains kitchen, servants' rooms, stores, and wine rooms. Sometimes, as in Powerscourt House (not to be confused with Powerscourt in County Wicklow, the country house of Viscount Powerscourt), a high superstructure across the front of the pediment allows for an attic of such height as to be termed a story. In all other Dublin houses in the Palladian style the attics are low, generally hidden by open or closed balustrades.

Regarding chimney pots, I consider them essential in finishing off the top of a house with any pretense to proportion and balance. As soon let a well-groomed woman appear appropriately turned out for some occasion without any eyebrows above her eyelids. Other than for the very practical outlet for smoke, one can gain a pleasant bit of color by using either terra cotta or tawny yellow chimney pots on a gray or white house.

One singularly smart house I know of in the large town called Waterford Old Port in County Waterford (well known for its handsome Georgian and Regency houses), is built of stone, whitewashed. A four-story and basement house, it is five windows wide. In the center front there is a pedimented doorway of extreme grace, above that a winged Palladian window. The height of the stringpiece, dividing first from second floors, is painted jet black with white trim. From there up, the walls are white with black trim, the roof is painted a soft rust pink, and the chimney pots are black. When this house is seen in spring or summer the window boxes are always planted with yellow daffodils or primroses, or perhaps wallflowers. In winter, stunted holly bushes fill the boxes. All weather, the black chimney pots, marching against a turquoise or cloud-harried sky, arrest the eye and cause a nod of the head in approval.

139

When Richard Castle was well away on his first important building job in Ireland, Molesworth Fields became suddenly as fashionable as it had heretofore been shunned as the "wrong side of the tracks." Various builders, always on the lookout for the whims of the fashionable world, waited just long enough to be assured that this curiosity was not a nine-day wonder. When interest in building a house near Kildare's new "palace" (even when it was later named, with much ceremony, Leinster House, Dubliners still called it Kildare's Palace-in-the-Fields) became really potent, ground was broken for streets running in all directions away, to what is now Fitzwilliam Square, and in the direction of the Liffey River. Coote Street and an alley were thrown into a *cul-de-sac*, St. Patrick's Well Lane. The name given the wide and fashionable thoroughfare was Kildare Street.

Leinster House took nearly three years to build, and Lady Kildare waxed "monstrous impatient to be settled in her Grand, Great House in those Bare Fields," according to Mrs. Delany. And if the indefatigable Mrs. Delany, Chronicler Extraordinary in matters concerning the world of fashion in Dublin—all Ireland as a matter of fact—says so, we may believe it. Married to a brilliant and immensely handsome doctor, Mrs. Delany led a sort of charmed existence. Her life seems to have been spent in constant activity, visiting in succession friends situated in the four extremities of Ireland. One wonders how she managed it, considering the perils and discomfort of coach travel in the mid-seventeen-hundreds, made hideous by the appalling state of Irish roads. Nothing daunted, Mrs. Delany wrote reams of letters to friends, and in her *Chronicles*. Her husband maintained houses in Dublin and at Delville and Mount Panther. She "drove today through Good and Safe roads in Hospitable Country, where Stately Houses abound." She went as well, "by coach to Dangan, my Lord Mornington's fine house in County Meath, which I find flat but Verdant. Castle, the German Architect, so costly to Employ, accompanied me back to Dublin. He is heavy, and his speech guttural; however he is the fashion at the Moment."

Although Leinster House—the erstwhile Kildare House—is generally conceded to be the first house built in Ireland by Richard Castle, this is, to be exact, not true. But the tremendous importance and scope of the house, with its pure Palladian façade and magnificently proportioned rooms, puts completely in the shade a much smaller house built by Castle for Sir Marcus Beresford (later Earl of Tyrone), two years earlier, immediately on his arrival in Dublin. It appears that one of the many Irish gentlemen making the Grand Tour in Europe was Sir Gustavus Hume, a close friend of Sir Marcus. It was Sir Gustavus who asked Richard Castle to accompany him on the packet from Dieppe to Dundalk. And it is said that on the tedious journey from France to Ireland, Castle drew the elevation for Tyrone House. Not particularly distinguished, of stone and purported to be the first stone house built in Dublin, the house is oblong, three stories and basement. A winged doorway supports a pediment, above which is a Venetian window—the name given a Palladian winged window by Georgian architects—and above that a porthole niche containing a Roman bust. Inside, the house is said by Tyrone himself, writing to his brother in France, to be "dark and ill planned, the stairs at an unholy pitch."

Far and away the most interesting feature of Tyrone House is the fascinating ghost story told of Lady Catherine Power, Countess of Tyrone. It is said that she had an altercation with a member of her family, one John Power, both being ardent devotees of deism. The first one to die vowed to return and explain the world beyond the grave to the survivor. In 1693 John Power, who had succeeded to the earldom of Tyrone, appeared to Lady Catherine in her boudoir saying he had died the previous Thursday at six o'clock. He went on to relate in a sepulchral voice all the events in store for her. A son would be born; her husband die; a second, unhappy marriage, and the birth of four more children. She would, soon after the last child's birth, die at the age of forty-seven. Refusing to believe that he was a shade (she had not been told of his death), she scoffed at him. He, in turn, to prove his story, touched her wrist and it shrank; the sinews withered before Lady Catherine's horrified eyes. All during her life, from that moment out, she wore a wide black ribbon to conceal her deformed wrist.

All happened exactly as Tyrone had predicted. After her fourth child was born, Lady Catherine thought perhaps she had outwitted the curse, for she flourished, even to bearing a fifth child. Then arrived what she fancied was her forty-eighth birthday. At chocolate that evening, a doctor who had attended her birth was present. A glass of wine was pressed upon him by Lady Catherine, for, as she said, "This is my forty-eighth birthday." "Oh no, my dear lady," he replied, "you are forty-

seven years old this day." Lady Catherine blanched. "My God!" she exclaimed, "you have signed my death warrant." Within the hour she was
dead. To this day in the house, which is now a National Education Building, a beautiful, delicate lady dressed in a costume of the period of Queen
Anne walks aimlessly through the rooms and passages of Tyrone House.
Looking closely, one sees a wide black silk ribbon encircling her left wrist.

The work on Leinster House proceeded rapidly, largely due to a
veritable army of workmen bribed away from other builders by the arrogant Kildare, who desired his house to be finished as quickly as possible,
so that he might put Castle to work building a country house for him at
Maynooth, in County Kildare.

When the time approached to decorate the interior of Leinster
House, Castle prevailed upon Lord Kildare to allow him to send to Italy
for workmen in stucco and carvers in wood, as well as men skilled in the
art of gilding and painting arabesques and romantic scenes upon walls
and ceilings.

The upshot of this move, readily agreed to by Kildare, was the
fortunate arrival of two brothers, Paolo and Filippo Francini. With them
came approximately three score artisans of various talents. The complete
success of this bold venture to import foreign workmen was assured from
the start. The sureness and virility of line, the sweep of design manifest
in their work, captured the imagination of the Irish mind. All ranks of
men applauded the Italian artists. Clients fell one over the other to obtain
their services. Irish women fell violently in love with the handsome young
Italians. Many an alliance was formed, both via the altar, and by skirting
it a mile. One sees today descendants of these Italo-Irish matings in names
displayed on signs over the doors of cabinet shops or frame-gilders—
Randolfo Murphy, or perhaps one reading Patrick Buccerelli.

For a while the Italians were dazzled by so much adulation and
demand for their services. Then, not being congenitally energetic, *dolce
far niente* set in, and a good long rest was indicated. To keep bread and
wine in the larder, the Francinis opened a school in Dublin to teach the
Irishmen employed as assistants the Italian method of *brio-brioso*, as they
laughingly called their dashing, elegant style. Songs were sung in the
streets *con brio-brioso*, even behavior took a turn *con brio*; a period of
lighthearted gaiety took Dublin by storm. On the crest of this wave the
Lottery was born. For twenty years this baiting of Fortuna was added to

the chancy Irish manner of making a living. The Lottery both supported and destroyed half of Dublin.

Aside from the ills caused by the Lottery, the benefits gained by architecture were astounding. Using the huge sums of money won by chance, many builders started to cut wide streets through what amounted almost to the city dumps. Certainly some of the regions that bloomed as fashionable sites within a year's time had recently been a wilderness. For example, the ground that the houses of Henrietta Street stand upon was originally a portion of the property of the Cistercian Abbey of St. Mary-in-the-Meadow. Great George Street was a reclaimed stew, where bawdy houses flourished and murders occurred daily.

When Leinster House was finally finished, the sweeping view from the front windows on the first floor—*piano nobile* in Italian houses—was magnificent. Merrion Square was not built at this time, nor were any houses near it. An unobstructed view could be had of Dublin Bay. The plan of the house was Palladio's best. A long façade of eleven windows. Four three-quarter columns of the Corinthian order support a pediment in the center of the oblong main block. The tall windows on the second floor alternate pediments, segmental and pointed. For the width of the portico the first story is rusticated. Two one-story wings, colonnaded, flank the oblong block, and a rusticated stone wall enriched by arched niches, which at one time contained statues of deities depicting the twelve months of the year, extends at right angles, forming a courtyard. An elaborate triumphal arch answered as porter's lodge. Gateposts in the center of the stone wall ran parallel to the street. This is now superseded by an iron fence. The garden side of Leinster House facing Merrion Square is the same as the Kildare Street side, save that there is no portico. A double flight of balustraded stone steps lead down from the center window on the first floor, which is ten feet higher on the garden than on the street side. The stone used is Ardbraccan, quarried in County Meath. The urns, plinths on the gatehouse, and statues are Portland.

The interior of the house has a suite of superbly proportioned rooms. The hall is lofty and serene, rising two stories; a rich molding answers as a cornice, supported by engaged columns of the Doric order. The plasterwork by the Francini brothers is bold and graceful. Foliations and sea shells predominate.

At either end of the oblong are rooms extending the depth of the house. One was called the supper room, the other the dining parlor. In both of these rooms, forty feet by twenty feet, sixteen fluted columns of Ionic order support a beautifully carved entablature and ceiling, arched and painted in the *Triumph of Amphitrite* by James Wyatt.

Several apartments on this floor are noteworthy because of the richly ornamented ceilings, the plasterwork being extremely brilliant in conception and execution. The Francini *brio* was never more in evidence. Lunettes and over-mantel paintings in the great drawing room are dark glowing fragments of the chase, by Luca Giordano. White and ecclesiastical-scarlet damask was used throughout these rooms, with touches of gilt and crystal. The supper room was in bronze velvet and pink damask. Curtains of the original materials remain on view.

At the time Leinster House was built, a gazebo was erected on the roof, a sort of *plaisance* for Lady Kildare. Mrs. Delany writes: "So pretty a View may be seen from Atop Kildare's house. The Hills of Dalkey, Killiny, Clontarf, the Seat of Black Rock, and on a clear day, a British Frigate."

In the eighteenth century Ireland took so sudden a turn for the better in the matter of individual taste that one wonders why so much inherent knowledge of line, color, and proportion in building and furnishing houses had lain so long dormant. With great wealth and education, we find the gentry making the Grand Tour of Europe, studying various branches of art in a dilettante way. Many fine examples of sculpture, paintings, and carved alabaster and colored marble mantelpieces were brought back by these travelers to place in their Irish houses. Mrs. Delany speaks with disgust of two huge group pictures in Castle Oliver, County Limerick: "Saw I ever such hideousness. Hercules and Samson, both dark and horrid."

The next houses built by Richard Castle were a pair, almost identical, at 15 and 16 Sackville Street. Castle built these houses for Robert Handcock, Esquire, of Watertown, County Westmeath. He died in 1759 and his widow, a staggeringly handsome and eccentric woman, married a man much younger than herself, Edward Pery, of whom she was insanely jealous. Speaker of the Irish House for three successive parliaments, he was elevated to the peerage as Viscount Pery. Life with his new Viscountess became, after a few tempestuous years, unbearable. Pery moved into the corner house, which had a frontage of sixty feet, abutting on Findletter's Lane. High jealousy-wracked stories are told of Lady Pery, who lived in a continuous state of "raw anger, 'till she looked red and mottled," as her daughter Diana Knox said. Part of the time she lived in the house next door, which was particularly noteworthy for its fine curving staircase. Whenever she saw a woman, be she duchess or washer-woman, hovering anywhere near the house of her husband, she would rush to the window, throw it wide, and hurl such a flood of invective at the woman (probably innocent), that the unfortunate fled as though scalded by more than words.

Lady Pery lived to be ninety years of age, outliving her husband by a score. Until her last days she would rise with the lark, plaster her face with paint and powder, adorn her person in bright yellow satin and laces, arrange an enormous plumed headdress on her high wig, and take her accustomed place in the window over the pillared porch. No one pass-ing in Sackville Street below was safe from her scathing tongue. Part of the time she played off key on a French harmonica. Paneling in chestnut wood, lightly touched with gilt, is a feature of this house at 16 Sackville Street, as well as doors of Domingo mahogany in the first-floor reception rooms.

Castle built a handsome house in this same street for Lord Netter-ville, who married Sally Burton of County Carlow, one of the touted beauties of the day. Mrs. Delany says of Lady Netterville on her marriage, "The bride is credited with £9000 for her portion, and a pretty person, much in vogue." Of the young bridegroom she is not so charitable, saying, "A fool and a fop, but a lord with tolerable estates." The plasterwork on the ceilings of Netterville House are richly imaginative, probably done by pupils of the brothers Francini. The rooms, *en suite*, are in Castle's best manner.

There can be few houses in any city on earth that have survived time's vicissitudes and emerged in so perfect a state of preservation as the large house built for Provost Andrews of Trinity College after his appointment in 1758. The architect of this singularly imposing house was a pupil of Richard Castle, John Smith, who, after the death of Castle, became Ireland's leading architect.

No other house outside Italy seems to bear so unquestionably the stamp of Vitruvius as this mansion, a lyrical arrangement in spaces, of rusticated and dressed stone. By far the finest room in the house is the saloon, occupying the entire front of the house on the second floor. The gracefully coved ceiling is beautifully carved and gilded. At either end of the room, a screen consisting of two fluted columns of the Corinthian order upholds a cornice, wide and sweepingly designed. The motif is chestnut leaves and ribbons. The carved pine mantel, displaying caryatids in full court dress, is handsome. Five tall windows across the front, the center one being of Venetian or Palladian style, make the room immensely light and pleasant.

Twin Houses for the Perys.

A gem of architectural distinction is the small house, number 9, at the corner of Sackville Street and Elephant Lane. It was sold by Richard Dawson to Charles, sixth Earl of Drogheda. Charles, a tall, thin, extremely handsome and winning man, was a great beau and had in his youth been one of the wildest bucks of the Hell Fire Club. Of impeccable social position, his marriage to Lady Ann Seymour quieted him down considerably. As life progressed, he devoted himself more and more to collecting rare silver while at his townhouse, and breeding thoroughbred horses at his countryseat, Moore Abbey.

The elaborate plaster ceilings are rococo (1777) with a spirited design of a phoenix in the center. Vast dinners were served at this house, for Lord Drogheda delighted in providing so many tempting dishes that his guests could hardly leave the table, so replete were they after sampling the viands prepared by his chef. A simple repast, a sort of snack to entertain a visiting Viennese nobleman arriving off the Dundalk packet late at night, consisted of:

First Course	Second Course
Fish, Creamed	Turkey Pout, Oysters
Rabbits and Onions	Terrene Peas, Terrene Mushrooms
Fillet of Veal, Pork, Fried Apples	Quail, Claret Sauce
	Apple Pye and Cream
	Cheeseballs
	Ginger Foam

Clanwilliam House in St. Stephen's Green (number 85) is that rare specimen in architecture, a perfectly planned and proportioned medium-sized townhouse. Grandiose, sweeping buildings to house great collections of art treasures dominate the fashionable quarters of every city of note the world over. Every now and again we find exquisite small dwellings such as Montbijou in Potsdam, La Peri in the old town of Buda (Buda-Pest), Crewe House in Curzon Street, London, and the ravishing Petite Aiguille with its conelike staircase tower, for Marion Delorme, the mistress of huge Cinq Mars. This fantasy in stone, close to the Place des Vosges in Paris, was, under the Fronde, a meeting place for the enemies of Mazarin. All these and more are perfection in miniature, evoking the period in which they were built. It is the medium-sized house, whether for town or country habitation, that is the hard one to design.

In Clanwilliam House the challenge has been met with signal

success by Richard Castle. The façade is unique among Dublin houses. Only two stories, and they immensely high, are faced with Wicklow granite of a pleasantly silvery tone. The first, or street floor, is heavily rusticated. Above a richly molded stringpiece the large blocks are so smoothly dressed as almost to shine. An arched doorway is flanked by two tall square-topped windows with superb iron grilles in the manner of Italian townhouses. The second story is tremendously effective, due to the placing of the Palladian winged window in the center, flanked by wide single windows crowned by segmental pediments. A fine cornice supporting a white marble balustrade completes the picture. A small boudoir on the first floor has enchanting panels entirely covering the walls, which are pale smoky green, the subject being the nine Muses. Draped swags floating from the cornice are truly Francini, in lightness and feeling of movement. The Francini brothers modeled the extraordinarily powerful ceiling in the saloon of this house as well. A wide-coved border shows Greek harvesters lunching, drowsing, working, or disporting themselves in tree-shaded pools, the scenes and figures confined within appliqués in the manner of *toile de Jouy*.

Number 86 St. Stephen's Green, is a very large, rather gloomy house, designed by Robert West for Richard Chapel Whaley, whose famous profligate son, "Buck" Whaley, lived here; his father died before the house was completed. West was under the influence of Castle to a marked degree, but his sense of line and lightness was never in the Vitruvian tradition, nor had it the Palladian elegance of detail that so instantly characterizes the work of Richard Castle. West leaned more toward the rococo, and it is in the interiors where he shines. His own house, erected on a hundred-foot frontage in Dominick Street, is unimpressive outside, but within the rooms are spacious, and as a *stuccodore* he seems to have shone second only to Francini. He designed a number of houses on the west side of St. Stephen's Green, which was known as French Walk, for here lived a number of emigré Huguenot families such as the Rouville, de la Chélle, Le Fanus, Berangers, Le Forét-Bique, and Vicomtesse de Casalto de Loches, half Portuguese, half Breton. The Vicomtesse, when receiving visitors, wielded a painted gauze fullface mask of a delicious young woman's face in front of her own, until she died by choking on a Damson plum at the age of eighty-eight years.

When St. Stephen's Green was laid out, the year was, roughly,

1711. The Green probably still retains its original title of being the largest square in Europe. Soon afterward, other squares were laid out with gardens, lakes, and temples, each plot surrounded by red brick Georgian houses, all more or less uniform in design and bristling with chimney pots. Merrion Square, Rutland Square, Mountjoy Square, and the last to be planned and still my favorite, Fitzwilliam Square. Five enormous gardens, for in effect that is what they still are, made Dublin one of the most flower-strewn and tree-shaded cities on earth.

In 1757 the Irish Parliament set up the Wide Streets Commissioners, a body of men whose names shone brilliantly in Parliament and Society. In those days Society meant wealth, culture, elegance, and appreciation of the advantages to be enjoyed by living in a spacious and dignified city. Dublin fairly bristled with iron palings around parks and gardens. Serene red and pink houses showed beautifully designed doorways, the one spot of variation in the uniformity of façade. Pale violet-blue turf smoke or wreathed gray smoke from applewood logs drifted off and away over the Dublin Mountains, from tens of thousands of chimney pots. Sedan chairs gleamed in lacquer and enamel. Coaches ground hub against hub in the narrow alleys of old bystreets only to swing to broad cobbled thoroughfares where my Lord Bishop of Cloyne and Derry drove five horses abreast with no fear of hub scraping.

Severity in line and proportion in architecture has always appealed to me. In fact, when I am left to my own devices, houses—both outside and in—designed by me are said by many persons to be "gaunt and haughty." That statement may very easily be true. I like elegance of line, fine free spaces with shadows of trees, or say, the shadows of magnolia leaves cast on the walls of a room to give strong but subtle pattern. For the very perfection of severity in line and proportion, one will go far before he finds the equal in distinction of the large brick house bearing the address number 53 St. Stephen's Green. Four stories rise above an areaway. The windows graduate in height but not width as they elevate. There are eight windows across. This is the style of house built by rent companies. For example, the books of Messrs. Gatty and Perk show that the most affluent and aristocratic Dubliners rented the big Georgian houses by the year. These people were the kind of floating population that follows courts.

Timothy Turner, Iron Monger—so read his shop sign—who died in Dublin in 1765, was one of the richest men in Ireland. His wealth was acquired by designing (with the help of his two nephews), forging, and casting most of the fine ironwork and indoor hardware used in hundreds of the houses in Dublin. The name Timothy Turner appears constantly in the order books of Trinity College. He supplied all the enormous amount of iron palings, hardware, and grilles required in the assembling of thirty college buildings. Timothy married for his second wife a "black-headed shrew" with high social ambitions. At her insistence he tried to install her in Baggottrath Castle in County Dublin. Failing to acquire this house, she set her heart on regal Bective, in County Meath. Rebuffed, she tried to get Richard Castle to design for her a great house at Blessington, but he was too occupied with building Carton, Russborough, and Finn-riggin Court in County Fermanagh. In rage, thwarted ambition, and just generally boiling in her own bile, Mrs. Turner ran off one dark night with a young man apprenticed to her husband. It is said the two joined a traveling circus in France.

POWERSCOURT HOUSE—*William Street, Dublin*

Just what the reason was for imperial-minded Richard Wingfield, on his succession to his brother's title of Viscount Powerscourt, to build one of the most architecturally satisfying townhouses in existence in a narrow, unfashionable, rather puny street in Dublin, eludes one. Whatever the neighborhood was in 1759, it is now given over to rooming houses, which are small and, as they antedate the great house looming beside them, could never have displayed any particular tone in the days of Viceregal Dublin.

As one turns into William Street from Dame Street, the grandeur of Powerscourt House leaps immediately to the eye. I once questioned two old loiterers in William Street to find out what their reactions were to so flaunting a pile in these days of bogus enlightenment. One old fellow twisted his cobeen pipe, spit across the street, and replied, "That auld hulk. What good is it, surely. A haunt fer rats and others. Better made a chinhouse." Chinhouse is flophouse, in the vernacular. A block farther on I questioned the other man, a cut above the last. He smiled, wagged his head, and said, "Oh, gorgeous, gorgeous, the like ave it they'll not build agin." That, I reflected, might be said of Dublin entire.

The house was compiled from many Palladian elevations supplied

POWERSCOURT HOUSE, WILLIAM STREET, DUBLIN. FROM A
CONTEMPORARY PRINT.

to Robert Mack, a little-known Dublin architect, who, before he received this princely commission from Viscount Powerscourt, had built only in the country: Farhill in County Carlow (burned in 1892), and ill-designed Jessytown House in County Wicklow. Old documents say Lord Cloncurry had sent Mack to Italy to collect all the elevations he could lay hand on pertaining to Palladian villas. For Cloncurry intended to follow the Duke of Leinster to Molesworth Fields. The Cloncurry house never materialized, however. What happened to the Palladian elevations no one knows. A contractor's building book among Mack's papers is preserved.

On 6th and 7th April 1771, Lord P. approved elevations for his house, drawn by Robert Mack. Agreed to pay said Robert Mack at rate of 5 per cent for constructing same. Mack will hereby instruct all workmen, stonecutters, diggers and plasterers to live in tents, all found.

Signed, J. Doyle.

On another page: "Intense damp and rain. Workmen miserable, for tents leak, food moulds, and DRUNKENNESS prevails."

For a while all seems well, then October 10, 1772: "All work held up to find where money for plaster has been mislaid. Thievery suspected." Again, December, the same year: "Most workmen paid and departed. Hardware allotted throughout house. Lord Powerscourt inspected today. Showed great pleasure."

Built of granite from Powerscourt demesne in County Wicklow, the arched gateway to the right of the entrance led to the stables surrounding three sides of a courtyard. The arch to the left led to kitchens, offices, and servants' quarters.

Some idea of the magnitude of this immense townhouse can be gained when one glances through house account books kept by the steward.

October 9th, 1772
Thomas Marley, Steward
Today all house servants answered roll call.
22 men. 4 lads. 6 footmen. 2 linkboys.
2 pages to answer out and indoor calls.

The entrance has a lofty columned room, oblong and as nobly planned as any I have ever seen. The stairway of carved mahogany, from the inventive hand of Ignatius McDonagh, is probably much handsomer today than when Powerscourt entertained in the house, for the patina of

151

time has given the richly carved spandrels and tread consoles the look of
Phoenician bronze. To my mind the sweep of vibrant plaster scrolls and
trefoils which seem fairly to leap up the stairs ahead of one, cannot be
bettered anywhere.

Some persons feel that the large dining room is the finest room in
the house. This is on the first floor and measures thirty-six by twenty-four
feet. Again the panels seem alive. Greek youths run in a rocky landscape.
A border of oak leaves and startled birds are as deftly modeled in high
relief as Grinling Gibbons would have done.

The exterior is extremely pleasing. At night, in starshine or in
the slant of a riding moon, it is dramatic, no end. The stunning height of
the building is augmented by a four-pillared superstructure rising directly
above the pediment. This is the Palladian touch we see at Villa Malcontenta and at Villa Maser at Asolo. The reason, aside from decoration, was
to hide the attics. Over the entrance door is a magnificently articulated
Palladian window of immense scale. Probably the most noteworthy feature of this house is the tremendous style and lift of the wide flight of
stone steps leading from the sidewalk to the front door. The movement of
balustrade as it curves back from the foot of the steps to meet the pilasters of the entrance gates is terrific.

At number 80 St. Stephen's Green, south, rose the most imposing
of all the houses in the "new" part of Dublin, as all south of Merrion Square
was called in 1730. At the time Richard Castle built it for the erudite Dr.
Clayton, Bishop of Killala, the house was called Killala House; then it
came into possession of Lord Mountcashel and was changed to Mountcashel House. Later still, through Guinness ownership, it changed to
Iveagh House. Mrs. Delany was vastly partial to this residence. She writes
to her great crony, Mrs. Middleton: "A fine drum at Mountcashel's Palace
in the Green. Walls are hung handsomely with Damasks from France and
Italy, gold, rose and fiery crimson, all very Elegant, and the walls Swarm
with pictures brought from Italian visits. I was Favored with a Painted
Fan as a Keepsake."

The great drawing room at number 80 has one of the most glorious
ceilings in Europe. Spangle-coved, each diamond-shaped spangle is cen-
tered by a carved and lightly gilded artichoke. The color of the room is
four shades of tawny yellow, with bisque, beige, and oyster white. Richard
Castle built three more important houses. Two have been incorporated

into neighboring houses, and one, now a convent, has been completely altered. The two were Abercorn House and one for the Bishop of Synge. Castle acquired a number of sites, and, on speculation (which could not have been much of a risk in his case), built five large houses. Robert Emmet, patriot–poet, was born at number 24 St. Stephen's Green.

In Upper Merrion Street, stands Mornington House. A huge, high, rather plain-faced affair in a darker red brick than is generally seen in Dublin, it gains in aloof dignity by the power of proportion and the magnificent scale and placing of its nine large windows across the front. A feature of architecture, which ever since I was old enough to take in oddness of any kind has enthralled me tremendously, is the chimneys. There are three chimneys, high, narrow, and deep. Legions of chimney pots rise like an army with bayonets. Each time I pass Mornington House I stop, no matter how hurried I may be, and carefully count the chimney pots in each chimney. And still, after many years of counting, I do not believe that there are thirty-seven pots in one chimney and forty pots in each of the other two. Where, I wonder, do the flues start from? The effect is pretty impressive, anyhow. I just leave it at that.

The rooms in Mornington House are even more impressive than its incredible chimney pots. Never have I seen more arresting stucco decoration. Each room is lovely and infinitely distinguished. Six big reception rooms. Double drawing rooms, library, music room, two saloons and morning room, each in white, gray, and gilt. The hall is bisque and silver-gilt. The front drawing room ceiling is delicate in design, and yet sweeping in vitality. I cannot remember its counterpart anywhere. Young falcons fly across the ceiling, carrying in their beaks loosely bound garlands, more like vines of fruit, and roses. Baskets, modeled in three-quarter relief, are supported on the backs of falcons that have alighted for a second on a rose-entwined shell.

The staircase in Mornington House is wide, low of tread, and a pure wonder for the "grand entrance," as the mother of Arthur Wellesley, Duke of Wellington, knew all too well. The Beautiful Countess of Mornington, as she was called—the adjective being almost an added title—was renowned as "the glass of fashion and the mould of form" in her day.

In the dining room of this beautifully appointed house, there is a built-in sideboard of "Irish" Chippendale, fourteen feet long. At either end, a plinth carved as a phoenix supports a wine-cooler in the shape of a Roman centurion's helmet, all carved from Domingo mahogany and polished—one might say burnished—to the quality of red lacquer.

Belvedere House, number 9 Henrietta Street, now a convent, was a sensation when first built because its rooms were light and spacious. High ceilings had not been seen in Dublin's timber, clay-washed houses before the Belvedere appeared. After this came number 7 and number 8 Great Ship Street, with tremendous imagination expressed in the double doorway. Two arched entrances under one sweeping pediment. Stone consoles supporting the pediment and a wide band of rusticated stone, powerful in scale, forming a border around the whole. St. Vincent's Hospital has world famous stucco ceilings; the design of doves flying in flocks against piling clouds has been copied as well as may be in both painted decoration and plaster, legion times.

Charlemont House at the top of Rutland Square was built in the grand style for a man built by God in a far grander style, that smasher James Caulfield, first Earl of Charlemont. This residence fashioned of the "new" white stone from the quarries at Ardmulcan follows the best manner of Palladio in plan. For the high central oblong is flanked by two flexible oblongs, forming coach houses (colonnaded and topped by balusters), and each boasts a rusticated drive-in gate.

It was at a convivial dinner party of "bloods" to honor the opening of a new parliament, of which Buck Whaley was elected a member (1747–1760), that an incident took place which illustrates in full spate the rake-helly character of the redoubtable Buck. Having returned to Dublin but recently from a long stay in Paris where he had been regaled with all the fashionable vices, he remarked defiantly that Dublin seemed thin fare, in fact he was bored by his recent parliamentary appointment. Soon he would be off again. Someone asked him which city, far or near, would he choose to relieve his ennui. Without pausing in the act of forking food to his mouth, Buck Whaley answered, "Jerusalem." He then bet the skeptics, who thought he was only pulling their legs, that he would depart on the morn's morn. What's more, after staying for a lengthy visit he would return in, not out of, pocket. Bets were taken, extravagant sums, for it was a gambling age and Dublin was the very inner circle for prodigious wagers. In two years Buck Whaley returned from Jerusalem—after probably a good long stop in his favorite Paris bordellos as well—and collected his Dublin bets, claiming he was in profit to the extent of £7000.

Like so many profligate braggarts before him, monuments of attractiveness, Buck Whaley lost his fortune before middle age. He retired to a small property on the Isle of Man, his "tumultuous pleasures breeding not a moment's true happiness," gone forever, by his own confession.

Charlemont House was built by Sir William Chambers, noted English architect. Charlemont was a collector of lions in all the arts. Here were dined Goldsmith, Hogarth, Reynolds, Hudson, and Johnson.

The Rotunda, the Custom House, the Royal Exchange, the Four Courts, and the splendid Parliament House, designed by Sir Edward Lovett Pearce, Surveyor-General of Ireland, are all regarded by laymen visitors and authorities alike as masterpieces of architecture. The pillared façade of Trinity College was designed by Keen and Sanderson of London, but within the quadrangle by far the finest is the classic portico of the Dining Hall designed by Richard Castle. This is an edifice of which Andrea Palladio would have been immensely proud. Never, to my mind, did Castle follow more closely the teachings of the great Venetian architect. It was after building the elegant Printing Hall that Richard Cassels changed the spelling of his name to Castle.

The Lying-In Hospital at the foot of Rutland Hill is considered by many as Castle's finest building in Dublin. Thomas Ivory, an Irishman from Cork, gave to Dublin one of the finest buildings to grace the city: the Blue-Coat School and Hospital, erected by public subscription between 1774 and 1780 on the north side of the Liffey, on partial foundations of an ancient rabbit-warren of a hospital which had fallen, happily, into decay. The plan of this building is very like the great Villa Trissino at Meledo, a square central block, demilunes, embracing cubes. Three-story detached cubes form buildings like pavilions, each crowned with graceful cupolas. The tower rising from the central block is to my mind the most beautifully articulated of its kind I have ever seen. In fact, I can think of no other building as a whole I would rather own for a townhouse. To me it has everything. The sweep and airiness of the elliptical façade catches the breath in one's throat, like great music. Elegance of detail is marked and singularly simple withal. The plasterwork is by the Francini, and magnificent marble mantelpieces by the Italian Bossi, who carved the finest mantels in Dublin from 1785 to 1798.

A curious phenomenon occurred in the environs of this glorious building, for the stinkingest stews and dirtiest thieves' kitchens and whore-houses in all the city clustered about its fringes; such "whiskey traps" as Old Soaks Hole (later famous for beefsteaks and ale in 1822), the Dead Raven, Meg's Peg, Frat's Cellar, "Beg and Borrow, Steal and Sorrow," the worst plague hole of them all.

On the south bank of the river were eminently fashionable choco-late rooms, the finest being the Pearl Gardens, Ravensdale Arcade, Flow-ers and Feathers, the Royal George, and Regentsbridge Alcove.

Murder, rape, arson, and just plain and fancy pickpocketing throve in this region. Nights were ripped wide open by shrieks and the thud of running feet. The Watch, which was supposed to police Dublin in 1762, had a frantic time of it, according to a newspaper called *Tattle-All*, which relates:

> About twelve o'clock midnight, a woman was robbed and defiled in shame at Essex Gate, of seven shillings and her virtue, by two young genteelly fellows, primly dressed, one of whom wore powder, the other his own hair.
>
> Five villains were caught robbing plate and moneys from the house of Sir Richard Reynal of Ayspark [Ashpark]. All five will be executed near St. Stephen's Green.
>
> Pat Geoghan was stabbed in the groin in a brawl with Mary Betah, a bawd who had set fire to his lodgings in Aungier Street. Betah broke her leg in a fall down the stairs, all the other occupants were suffocated or robbed by Betah's pimp, Marty Callen, who will be executed on Friday in Pill Lane.

Very stirring times for the harried residents of the Liffey borders.

A Mrs. Elperiat, *maîtresse de luxe* to the gentry, obtained a splen-did house from an ardent old roué, in Dominick Street. She writes in her *Journal of Dublin Days*, which has been preserved in a private collection: "My new coach has Arrived. Vipers say it is above my Circumstance and Fortune, but I have a way above theirs to obtain what I Crave. My Draw-ing Room never darkens from sunset to sunrise, the ripest wit and the finest Leg in Dublin is made here."

A traveling Swiss, Anton Brücher, was shocked at the rank and fashion of Dublin. He says, "The finest houses in the classic taste enter-tained me. The owners did not. Dueling, sly wit, sharper than a rapier thrust, at my expense; over-rouged women, too much wine and gambling robbed me of sleep and pocket. The sport of horse racing has ruined the young gentry." Definitely a dud to try to entertain.

For Lord Bellamont, "that fantastic Earl," as Mrs. Delany called him, Richard Castle built a splendid tall house in Grafton Street. The building is now a public accountant's office. In this "wide lane," as it is inscribed on the architect's elevations, many magnificent houses were built that are now stores and commercial buildings, for Grafton is now the fashionable shopping street of Dublin. George Moreland said, "For Splendid Architecture, Riotous Living and Political Intrigue, such another Acre does not exist in Dublin."

Bellamont was excessively vain, immensely tall, flashing blue of eye, and wore his rich russet hair in a "love-mop" (lovelocks of the Charles II period), unpowdered. His insane delight in masquerade caused the "bloods" to call him *Bijou et Vernis*. Before his great townhouse was finished—indeed, scaffolds were still up in the entrance hall—Bellamont commissioned Sir Joshua Reynolds to paint his portrait to lend glory to posterity. The finished full-length portrait is remarkable. Bellamont is dressed in the regalia of the Order of the Bath, pale blue, cream, and rose, with a towering cream-plumed hat; the picture is most surely a *tour de force*. In the background one sees the unfinished hall of Bellamont House. If the Francini brothers ever wished to define *bravura* to the hilt, here it is.

Now we might, all in the lovely spring weather, take a walk around Dublin. Long wide street after street of tall, plain-faced, red brick Georgian houses. Here a black lacquer, fanlighted doorway. There a white painted door, along a bit farther a yellow or a gray or dark wine-red one. Deep flowerbox-cluttered areaways proclaim a pleasant kitchen. Against the pale turquoise-green sky, thousands of chimney pots seem to attract the sea gulls in from the Irish Sea, for they love to perch upon them. As we pass some of the houses, perhaps tenements now, a glimpse through an open doorway or window reveals a superb plaster ceiling. In another house the sweep of mahogany stair rail is like liquid fire as it ascends to the upper rooms of the once grand house. Lovely ironwork hems in grass plots or broken patches of hard earth. Tall iron torches may flank a Georgian doorway. Old violet and amber glass still winks from tiny paned windows in Smock Alley and Burrege Street. Fire and Famine Lane, where Peg Woffington lived, has old dormer windows with Dutch gables. Then the shimmering whiteness of the Law Courts, the Rotunda Hospital, and the spaciousness of the squares. I like best to walk abroad in Dublin, very early in the morning of a bright day, or at early evening in the winter.

The crystal-clear light, the variation of color playing across the old brick façades, the *clop-clop* of cab horses. A welcoming door opens, a trim maid takes the luggage, a luster chandelier sheds light on Chippendale chairs, flat against a painted wall. A lovely Dublin voice calls out: "And did you have a demented crossing, or was the old strip like a millpond?" So unique and so personal is the essence of Dublin that no one ever likens it to any other city in the world.

IRISH COUNTRY HOUSES

So pleased with his fine townhouse was the Duke of Leinster that it irked him, monstrously, to be kept waiting by Richard Castle—mixed up with his fawning clients and building-site schemes in Dublin—for three years before he could get on with his country place, Carton. True, there already was an old house standing in a vast demesne on the outskirts of Maynooth, in County Kildare. The house one sees today is actually a much enlarged version of the ancient "Carthyn," the castle of 1355 which had been only a drear stronghold and quartering for troops of the Geraldines.

The family used old towered and castellated Kilkea for a dwelling. The old portion of "Carthyn," or "The Carthyn" as the country people call it, is so carefully concealed that the magnificence of Carton completely banishes any idea of an older house existing. Lord Thomas FitzGerald, known as "Silken Thomas" because of the rich silk trappings of his horses, lived at Maynooth Castle, and when he was captured and beheaded at Tyburn by order of Henry VIII, hoary old Maynooth was surrendered to the British. This was 1553, but it sounded the death knell of the FitzGeralds until power and wealth flowed back into the family headed by Robert, nineteenth Earl of Kildare.

Even after Castle had finished the superb job, Carton, we now see, Leinster wanted to enlarge the façade, making the wings into demilunes, like those at Russborough. This idea, however, died aborning; he turned his creative mind toward his garden. It has always been a feature of the Irish demesne to lavish much care and, in some cases, boundless skill on the walled kitchen garden. At Carton the kitchen garden rivaled the ones at Versailles and Windsor, for it covered fifty acres of ground, with ducks and edible swans drifting upon the sheet of water.

A red Morocco leather sketchbook is preserved at Carton, left behind by Richard Castle. In it are three or four proposed ideas for remodeling and enlarging Carton. There are a number of sketches of other houses he had finished, was about to start work on, or, as with Hatt Park and Dunclenna, had not executed. Among the executed sketches are Castle Hume in County Fermanagh, Russborough in County Wicklow, Hortland in County Kildare, and Powerscourt in County Wicklow. In this book Castle has copied out a line that appeared in a lampooning rag, the kind that were the forerunners of the present-day tabloids. "Castle, the red-bull man, empties a flagon as fast as he can. He orders and orders, faster and faster. Woe and bedazzlement, wine is his master." However, a historian writing of him a few years after his death, says he was "Amiable, of high integrity, a past master of wit and forthright conversation, whose convivial habits kept him low in cash."

Castle's plan for Carton was to lengthen the main block of the house, add another story to the main building and the wings. Open colonnades would connect them. All this was carried out as Castle directed. The nine windows across the front are beautifully spaced, removing any hint of cold formality. Flanking these nine tall, square-topped windows are two

Venetian windows, on the second floor, and two oddly attractive bow windows with columns and an arched central window; these are topped by a marble balustrade which acts as a balcony to the Venetian windows. The wings contain six windows, across.

The interior of Carton is carefully considered. Each room is large, light, and the chestnut wood floors are glorious in color and sheen. Certainly Paolo and Filippo Francini spread themselves on the walls and ceilings in this house of the Italo-Irish Geraldines. Some of Castle's finest detail in stone is to be found in profusion at Carton. For example, on the wings of the garden front are two columned, pedimented niches, unquestionably as fine as any he ever did. A marble boy holding a dolphin (by P. Van Bauerscheit) stands in the niche on the right of the entrance, a boy with a turtle in the other niche.

Five miles of stone wall enclose the demesne of Carton. Four lodges give entrance to the grounds. Mrs. Delany wrote to Mrs. Middleton:

> A good meal awaited me last night at Carton where I arrived unseemly Late. The vileness of Irish Roads is not to be borne. My horses sank in bog-mud to the hocks, I vow. Chickens, fowls of divers kinds, five colors of bread, hot and cold. A quince tart, heavily creamed, and I drank clear China 'til bedtime. Great State is kept. Leinster in bad case because of gout, but the Duchess, rare fine, in hooped taffety.

The two paintings of the Duke and Duchess by Sir Joshua Reynolds hang in the saloon at Carton. Many consider that of the Duchess a veritable masterpiece. A small sketch of a woman in black hoops standing on a bridge poking at waterweeds with a long stick is one of the most engaging pictures in the house. It is by an unknown painter.

Caledon, in the County of Tyrone, is a bewildering house. Bewildering because the front presented to arriving visitors is a cold, formal, utterly handsome temple to Mars or Vulcan. One passes through the house, through a series of lofty imaginatively planned rooms, to emerge on an acre of *tapis vert*. Walk straight out, turn and look back toward the house. No temple to Mars here. Extravaganza! Fata Morgana! Here is a warmhearted, completely delightful country pavilion. White, as only white-painted stucco—with a generous dash of powdered oyster shells thrown in to give luminosity—can be. The whole effect from this view is rewarding after a long hot drive over the only truly wretched roads in the country.

I do not in any way mean to imply that the entrance front of Cale-

One Version of Palladio's Winged Façade.
Three Oblongs, Two Cubes, and Two Flexible Oblongs.

Three Oblongs, Four Flexible Oblongs.

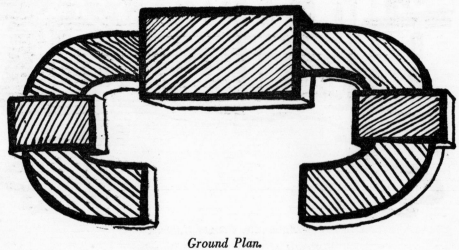

Ground Plan.

Two Cubes to Form Central Block. Two Flexible Oblongs and Two Oblongs.

Dunsandle, County Galway.
Result of Using Above Formation.

don is not extraordinarily fine, for it is John Nash at his best. The Ionic-columned portico was added by Nash in 1836, and permits a coach and six to drive under it with ease. It may be the really splendid colonnade on the garden front that so bewitches the beholder, for I have never seen one finer in detail, or better placed. In fact there are so many interesting and supremely different features at Caledon that I still think the word to describe it is "bewildering." The Georgian center block, with sculptured pediment (1779) is skirted, indeed surrounded, by the Nash additions, but they are only one story high, so in no way is the original house concealed. The curving waters of the Blackwater at Caledon form a natural mirror to reflect this white splendor. It is, in truth, as a friend wrote me after having seen the house one autumn day, "Most felicitously placed, meadow, stream and distant hill, serene."

One night when I saw the house from a low spot on the Kilgowlan Road, it was shattering white in the moonlight. A dark green-black sky spread behind it, and a rare lot of stars powdered the heavens. A long time I stood, looking. The deathless line of Rupert Brooke came to my mind: "High sat white Helen, lonely and serene, he had not remembered that she was so fair." One does not remember, when ranging the world, just how fair these remote houses are. It is a good thing to come back to them in moon or starshine, or on a bright or silver day. We squander our lives. Houses store their beauty and power. Take it out of its wrappings for admirers to see.

The interesting touches one finds at every hand in the two completely different façades of Caledon are threefold displayed when one enters the hall under the spreading portico. The semicircular entrance hall to the oval drawing room is classic in feeling, more Roman than Greek. A frieze of gilt figures is surmounted by a cornice, picked out in black, terra cotta, and yellow. One does not feel very much is left inside of the first Earl's house designed by Thomas Cooley, 1769. The library is a spectacular room of rising proportions, designed by Nash in 1812. An oblong room, it is dominated by the circular rotunda ceiling, which is, of course, the inside of one of the domes surmounting the wings at the end of the garden colonnade. The coving and diapered rosette decoration in each cove is strong in execution and luminous, being parchment color picked out in gilt.

James Alexander of Boom Hall, Londonderry (afterwards Earl of

Caledon), knew an imposing house when he saw one, for Boom Hall was that, even if it caused him to say, "Boom was huge, high ceilinged and drafty as the Cordeen Gap. But the grandeur of its sight, and the glitter of its hundred windows, caused all beholders to gasp." So did the beauties and odd turns in his new house cause men to gasp. Myself among them. One end of the 1779 block has a widely curving bow window, rising the full three stories. The rooms in this bow look out onto the famous white fuchsia walk. I am often asked in America why it is that Irish and English Palladian houses do not have wooden shutters. I expect the reason is not to spoil the beautiful detail that one so often finds in carved stone or plasterwork around windows. Shutters are an unnecessary detail, although I know houses—Christopher Wren houses for example—that have very handsome black, gray, white, or dark green solid shutters. But on Palladian houses, better not.

The two alcoved reception rooms at Caledon are delightful. Thomas Cooley either had not the second chance, or something like that, for he never approached the elegance of these rooms again. The boudoir with apple-green *chinoiserie* is a splendid room. The ceiling is extraordinarily different. Chocolate, scarlet, apple-green and tortoise-shell fans and festoons are skillfully painted, finer, I think, than the painted room at Rockingham, County Roscommon.

No other house in Ireland has so winning a name as Jigginstown, out on the Dublin–Naas Road. Strafford's massive Tudor house, long since collapsed, lies near Jigginstown, which is a long, low, red brick affair, with twenty to thirty foxhounds always lying asleep at fantastic angles in the white-pillared porch.

Richard Castle built only one brick country house, Ballyhaise in County Cavan, the seat of the Newburg family. This house has a grand sweep of stone steps, otherwise plain and comfortable, somewhat like the farmsteads built by Andrea Palladio in the hills around Padova. Brick for country houses fell into disuse with the opening of quarries like Ardbraccan whence came a stone of silvery gray, Golden Hill Quarry near Blessington, and pale creamy stone from Brookstown Quarry in County Clare. These quarries furnished practically all the stone to build the great houses scattered about the Irish countryside. Strokestown House has a remarkable plan, for at the four extremities of the crescent-shaped wings, which lie back to back, are placed the stables. These curved wings are called "curtain walls" in the old architectural documents. The "terrible" FitzBakers of Glanbogle in County Roscommon were the first persons to rip out the brick walls of their old (1622) house and insert elegant Palladian windows with white stone trim. Later stone coins were added at the corners; and inside (1700) an Italian journeyman painter ranging the back countries—and drear and remote they were at that date—painted a dining room for Agnes FitzBaker (called The Toothless), who is said to have ridden her horses bareback, and won, at the country races. The subject of the painting is Hell and Damnation.

At any rate, the FitzBaker *ménage*, however mad inclined, had imagination and taste. Very often at antique sales in Dublin, a particularly fine piece of brocade, or a Domingo mahogany table or commode will go under the hammer. Where from, I ask? The FitzBakers, is the reply. Either the old brick country houses were being pulled down to make way for stone mansions in the prevailing Palladian taste, or more thrifty persons (not an outstanding Irish trait, I may add) were washing the mellow brick walls with coats of gray, cream, or tawny-yellow stucco. Lashins, an old Queen Anne house in County Tipperary, was brought into fashionable focus by having the façade stuccoed and a pillared porch with broken pediment stuck onto the front painted pale blue and white. *There* was a fine Palladian dwelling. Phoebus Court was changed in much the same manner. This rickety Charles II house of the County Fermanagh Costigans was pointed up with a pedimented portico and twin cube wings displaying a Palladian window, flanking the main block.

On the night of September 10, 1750, the sky arching above the quiet little village of Cootehill, County Cavan, was ablaze with trillions of brilliant stars. Suddenly a Jovian skyrocket seemed to zoom across the gleaming firmament. Loungers at the village pub, and they looking heavenward, were struck all amazed. For the rocketing shower of stars fell all around an old stone castellated house called The Hill, wherein dwelt Charles Coote, and the watchers gave him up for dead. Dead and burned to cinders in the blazing shower of stars. But no, oh no, it would take more than a fiery shower, Jovian delivered or not, to extinguish so flamboyant, cocksure a creature as said Charles Coote. The stars missed The Hill and its owner by a mile. In fact, it is quite probable he thought this manifestation a sort of accolade, for at the same moment fire was scattering over County Cavan from above, a messenger on a spent horse was arriving at The Hill from Dublin, to acquaint Coote with the news that he had succeeded to vast estates. Before one knew where one was, he profited by the death of another cousin by inheriting the title and lands of Lord Colooney (County Sligo) and was made Knight of Bath, one of the most coveted honors in the British Isles. A parchment bearing the Royal Seal proclaimed that investiture should be hastened, and the ceremony was to be "in public and in pomp." That was needless advice. Anything to do with Lord Colooney, K.B., became, in his own mind, practically a public holiday. He was later created Earl of Bellamont and hastened to build a splendid Dublin house, then ordered Sir Joshua Reynolds to paint his portrait in full regalia, as I have already described.

Now, what was needed to emblazon the name of Bellamont indelibly on the minds of men was a grand country house. This forthwith Lord Bellamont proceeded to acquire. Now enters a tangle of conflicting statements as to just who designed Bellamont Forest. It is purported to be the work of Richard Castle, and most certainly no house in town or country resembles his clarity and simple dignity of Palladian style more sharply than this brick and stone cube. Some say the designs were drawn by an apprentice in Castle's Dublin office, one Donon Lynch, who did help him with Russborough and Summerhill (now destroyed), as well as Ballyhaise and Waterton. I firmly believe it was Castle who designed Bellamont Forest, for three reasons. First, the house is the nearest replica in all Ireland of the country villas of medium size designed by Andrea Palladio in the Venetia. Second, the bricks are laid close with little mortar showing, the edges and trim pointed up with stone. This is the manner in which the villas in Vicenza and along the Brenta were built by Palladio. Third is the fact that the house is four-square, presenting a carefully designed face on all sides, with a large winged window of superb scale in three of the sides at first-floor level. The central block at Russborough, Castle's masterpiece in Ireland, is nearly identical. A portico with columns of the Doric order support an entablature elaborately carved in bay leaves and crossed torches. The heavily molded pediment has a rather bold importance. A flight of shallow stone steps ascends to the first floor, this being raised on a rusticated basement.

Inside the house, all is rampageous, in character with its vain, unpredictable owner. It is said he moved the dining room four different times, rising once in the middle of dinner to shout to the butler to call all footmen and pages, for he must dine at the front of his house, not at the back. Another time when his father-in-law, the Duke of Leinster (Bellamont had previously married Lady Emily Mary Margareta FitzGerald), was asked to dine at Bellamont Forest, he was furiously indignant, on arriving, to be told by a lackey that there was no one to receive him and "no dinner ordered the night," for there was no dining room to serve it in. When Bellamont and his Countess arrived on the heels of this statement, he airily said that dining bored him; if the Duke wanted food he could go to the kitchens. The outcome of that would be entertaining to hear.

The one room in the house bearing evidence of extreme care taken by the owner to make it worthy of its adornment, to wit, the Reynolds portrait of the beplumed K.B., is the drawing room (first the dining room) wherein the plasterwork is extremely effective. Five huge paintings are set into frames of stuccowork, infinitely original in design. Flanking the door are the two Reynolds portraits of Lord and Lady Bellamont. He is the peacock, "in full plumage pied," she is charmingly dressed, but fades to unimportance beside her resplendent spouse. On a long wall at the left of the door a big oblong picture, Guercino's *Death of Dido*, is richly deep and smoldering in color. The situation of Bellamont Forest is one of its greatest advantages. Commanding a vista of two lakes and a winding river, the house seems to have alighted for a moment to rest upon a tree-strewn knoll. I saw it one day when massed white clouds behind its rose-red chimneys lent to the house the appearance of a Spanish galleon in full sail.

Mount Pallas in County Limerick was built for the Earl of Clare by a pupil of Richard Castle's who, oddly, signed himself simply *G.G.— 1790*, using the imprint of a small castle tower, which was the official device of Castle's pupils.

The large square house with detached pavilions is grandly proportioned. The high squared-off pediment is more an entablature, or closed balustrade. The columns seem to me a shade heavy and grandiose for the length of the house. The site is happy, however, being open and crowning a tree-fringed ridge with a high range of hills behind. Inside, two massively carved doorways give onto a circular hall from which rises a wide staircase, branching to left and right midway up the three-story stair well. It was at Mount Pallas that a joint—one might almost say wholesale— wedding took place in 1864. Four Bennet brothers married four Cariganna sisters in the huge drawing room, during such a downpour that the glass roof over the stair well crashed in and flooded out the assembled guests. Two of the brides caught pneumonia and died within a fortnight. A strange doom seems to haunt Mount Pallas. The last family to live there were the Nevins. After they departed the house withdrew within itself. It is still empty and lone.

Before I describe the most famous houses in Ireland designed by Richard Castle, Russborough and Powerscourt, I will give a brief résumé of four other houses of his that are noteworthy. Summerhill, County Meath, is no longer standing. At one time, however, this magnificent house in the Italian palazzo manner (only equaled by Powerscourt, County Wicklow) contained the outstanding collection of French and Italian pictures in Ireland. The remaining three to be briefly described are: Hazelwood, Calary; Roundwood, Offerlane; and Belinter, Navan. By actual count in 1938 there were two hundred and eighty-nine Georgian and Palladian houses still lived in, scattered over the springy turf of Ireland. This, of course, does not include the much older inhabited houses of Elizabethan, Charles II, and Queen Anne periods, or the ancient feudal castles the like of Killeen Castle, the seat of the Earls of Fingal, Dunsany Castle in County Meath, or half-derelict (but still sheltering its lords) Blanhaggy, off the coast of Donegal.

Hazelwood, Calary, in County Sligo, is a curious mixture of the fantastic that Palladio delighted in building, but always in the frescoed pavilion style. The house is two and a half stories, the lower rusticated. The stone is so dark in color that on dull days it appears black. The motif of the many kinds of shells used in cornice and entablatures further remind one of an Italian *casino marina*. Six wide-flung rooms to a floor create a most spacious effect. Floors throughout are yellow, green, and pink marble.

Roundwood, Offerlane, in Queen's County, is a simple square dwelling of Ardbraccan stone. The four huge chimneys sprouting tawny-yellow tile pots are rusticated, and a porthole indents each side, creating a most decorative effect. The façade is enriched by a generously proportioned Venetian window, a band of rustication following the outline of the window. The plasterwork inside Roundwood is not of any importance, because it was not carried out to Richard Castle's plan. A local artisan lent no imagination to his work. This often happens when "locals" are let loose in a house.

Belinter, Navan, County Meath (not to be confused with Ballinter, County Galway), is a big comfortable stone house, the first floor heavily rusticated in pitted "water-drip" effect. The columned façade (without pediment) is extremely massive in scale. The whole house is powerful without being overpowering. The Italian feeling for grandeur allied with simple spaces and huge conception of detail is marked in Belinter.

One of my special favorites is Kilboy House, County Tipperary. An infinitely gracious house in the grand manner, it is a misleading edifice, for at first glance the scale seems fairly small. A medium house. But this is not so, for Kilboy is large. Four stories and a superstructure, as at Powerscourt House, Dublin, allow for interesting placing of windows. Leeson of Dublin, the architect, is well known for his fine sense of placing windows to gain both light and the feeling of spacious planning. The entablature under the pediment is remarkable for its simple elegance. I have never seen one just like it. A wide band of dressed stone, with wide striations forming perpendicular troughs. A design so simple is seen usually in Greece, stemming from very early times. The rooms are high, and two are painted in the Italian manner with vistas of lake, grove, and mountain.

Pallas Hill, in County Tipperary, is a house of infinite moods. Crowning the ridge of a sloping rise, which is in reality the first foothill of Slievnamon, the Gaelic "Mountain of the Sleeping Woman," this gracious house commands one of the most spellbinding views in all Ireland.

The house has many features which ally it closely with the pavilion farmhouse type of building, so often designed by Palladio when he was left to his own devices. The main oblong has a "broken pediment" surmounting the cornice, extending across the entire length of the front. A huge marble urn, from the mouth of which spout carved flames, arrests the eye. This is in the ellipse caused by the break in the pediment molding. Two demilunes end twenty feet in front of the main block. A tall winged window, used as a door, pierces the end of each demilune. A half-circle cut-under porch has porthole niches above each door and window letting into the house. In these niches stand busts of Greek deities. In the black and yellow marble central hall a magnificent bust of Pallas Athena, helmeted and wearing her scaled aegis, tops a black marble pillar at the foot of the stairs. This was sent to the mother of Bay Middleton by the Empress

Elizabeth of Austria on one of her Italian visits, and gave the house its name.

In brilliant sunlight, Pallas Hill seems a house of gold, because of its wash of yellow paint. On gray days the yellow seems to turn to pearl. In moonlight, particles of crushed oyster shells in the paint point up the house to such luminous brilliance that it seems to be hewn from some sort of jade or quartz.

Drumcondra, County Dublin, is not a direct copy of Villa Maser at Asolo, for at this Irish house there are no beautifully painted dials of impressive circumference to record the sun and changes of moon and stars, as at Maser. It retains, however, the lovely long fluid line of façade. This pavilion might be called the garden house of the Countess of Charleville, for with a "green finger and a nod of approval from Demeter," she masses flowers both inside and out. The house is a garland.

In this house, as in many others in Ireland, one finds small but telling details such as finials at the corners of balustrades, or a marble ball, ivy wreathed. A loosely carved pineapple, symbol of hospitality the world over, or a fluted sea shell. A porthole window. Winged window pediments, and double coinstones. All these denote the Palladian touch, as no other motifs do.

Palladio excelled in designing doorways, wide, high, often flanked by columns, giving a sense of welcome, which after all is the principal function of a doorway to any house.

In Russborough we have everything. All the best of Vitruvius, Palladio, and Richard Castle. The site of the house is perfect to show to the best advantage the long masterly articulation of the frontage. For no other house in Ireland has so varied and interesting a façade. The pair of demilune colonnades, which swing in a long slow curve from the central cube, seem not to touch the two oblong wings extending parallel to the entrance front, but to hold them in line by suggestion, so lightly do they rest against them. These colonnades of eight Doric columns cannot be matched for soaring proportions and detail of cornice, finial urns and sculpture-filled niches, anywhere in Ireland.

In 1751, Joseph Leeson of Dublin was in Rome, later Venice. He drove in a huge painted coach along the Brenta Canal as guest of the Mocenigo. Here he saw for himself the same inspiring Palladian villas that had so captured the imagination of his friend Leinster, ten years before. If Leinster could build a vast Dublin house and extravagant Carton at Maynooth, he could top the two by building on his gently undulating fields near Blessington in County Wicklow such a spellbinder of a house that it would be the talk of Ireland, and farther, for years to come. All this came to pass, for when a visitor asks anyone in Dublin or Galway Old City (two extremities of the island), "What house should I see that will give me the greatest idea of Irish Palladian architecture?", the answer will invariably be, "If you want a feast, see Russborough."

On Leeson's return to Ireland, he set about his plans with enthusiasm and prodigality, two facets of his nature that gave him the nickname of "King" Russborough after he had been raised to the peerage as Baron Russborough in 1756. While in Italy, he had made the acquaintance of Count Ragona-Chizzole, a student of Greek marbles and Palladian architecture. Ragona-Chizzole possessed those two rare qualities, knowledgeable taste and feeling for tradition. When Leeson left Italy to return to Ireland, he commissioned the Conte to travel to Herculaneum, Sicily, Greece, and Dalmatia, to collect statues, marble, paintings, and brocaded damasks and embroideries for his new house.

For this reason, Russborough today is remarkable for the excellence of its statuary and marble fireplaces. The rich, live variety of the rococo stuccowork in the entrance hall and the first floor reception rooms is famed the world over.

It took many years to build Russborough. Some historians say ten years. We hear Bishop Barry say of the house, "Last evening I sat to meat in the unfinished dining room of Lord Milltown's Russborough [Leeson had been created Earl of Milltown in 1764], where the food was fair but comfort flew out of the unglazed windows as soon as darkness lowered." It would appear by this statement that Milltown had taken up residence in his house long before it was completely finished.

The initial cost of building "an elevated rise of sod, whereon to place the cellars of Russborough House" (from an old contract book pertaining to expenses incurred in building the house), for digging "ornimental" water (lagoons) and leveling pasturelands for lawns, was gigantic. Thirty thousand pounds is said to have been expended on this kind of spadework before a stone was laid to the walls. Even as rich a man as Leeson must have winced a trifle at this cost. But we learn that Lord Milltown spent £14,000 on importing Domingo mahogany for his doors and tabletops, so he never spared expense to obtain what he wanted. In the saloon one may still see doors, dados, parquet floors, as well as columned, pedimented architraves around windows and doors, all of glorious Domingo mahogany of a deep red-bronze color. In this room, original cut Genoese velvet of dark prune-red (1748) lines the walls. The effect of warm glowing color when this room is candlelit is one of mellow magnificence.

The drawing room is one burst of splendor in the height of rococo. So rich, in fact, is this miraculous Wicklow house in rococo plasterwork that it has been called "The Rococo Temple to Milltown's Pride."

A lampoon was hawked about the streets of Dublin concerning Lord Milltown's third marriage.

> Milltown weaned on pomp and pride,
> Takes to his bed a third young bride.
> He's buried two and thinks he's clever,
> Let's hope this one will live forever.

Oddly prophetic was this quatrain, for the third Countess of Milltown outlived her husband by sixty years, dying at Russborough in 1842 at the great age of one hundred years. Hale and intellectually undimmed, this lady was known as a great wit and supreme conversationalist to the end of her days. In her voluminous *Journal at Russborough* she says her husband once challenged Lord Tyrawley to a duel "with blunderbusses and slugs in a sawpit."

Before the arrival in Ireland of Richard Castle, there was practically no plasterwork to be seen in either town or country houses, not even the crudely bold crossbar and spangled ceilings of Elizabethan and Charles II period in England. With the arrival of Castle and his artisans, especially the Francini brothers, baroque and rococo panels and ceilings leaped into such full flower that then, as today, Irish plasterwork is regarded as highly as any in Europe. The most original and vivid is to be found at Russborough. It is known that the remarkably virile and literally foaming foliations that sweep up the staircase of this house are by one of the Francini; but Castle, and Bindon, whom he engaged to help him in building Russborough, used both Italian and Irish plasterworkers here, so it is not known just who was responsible for the majority of the work.

Castle was always immensely interested in mantelpieces. In this house he spread himself as never before or since, although the now destroyed mantelpieces at ill-starred Summerhill were exceptionally fine. In the square music room, the finest cube room in Ireland on every architectural count, the pale bisque Lantara marble mantel is completely entrancing. Across the top is a wide molding. Inset is a group molded in three-quarter round relief of Leda and the Swan, being mightily encouraged in the well-known amorous charade by a bouncing, extremely sophisticated Eros. All this takes place in a bosky dell, just as a full sun arises, casting warm rays upon the three participants.

The dove-gray Sicilian marble mantel in the library centers a superbly licentious head of Silenus, crowned in wreathed grapes.

In a cornice in the dining room the heads of hounds appear spaced five feet apart. In their mouths these hounds hold swags of bog-oak and ivy. Wherever one looks, within or without, at Russborough, the eye is regaled.

The house called Castlecoole in County Fermanagh is a strangely severe structure. More Hellenic museum than dwelling house, yet it has moments of undeniably superior detail, the kind of divine proportion and sweep that we associate with the best of Palladianism.

The north front is perfectly composed, and the south front is not far behind, except that it appears a shade bleak. The windows, completely unadorned by bandings or keystones, set flush with the plain face of the walls, have a tendency to stare one out of countenance, not wink companionably, or seem to nod, as do so many in Palladian houses.

Built of dun-gray Portland stone by James Wyatt in 1788 for Armar Lowery-Corry, first Earl of Belmore, the house suffered a disastrous fire in one wing which destroyed the dining room. This room now has plain walls and no paintings adorn them. In all other rooms the architectural features, the paintings, and Italian marblework are exceptionally fine.

No stranger spot in all Ireland could be found, it would seem, on which to erect this classic temple. Yet this Parthenon, this Vitruvian *museo*, is in no way incongruous to the rolling, oak-wooded landscape, astonishingly remote from all good roads and the haunts of men.

County Fermanagh is "auld ancient land," as the countrymen say, with a vengeance. Upper and Lower Lough Erne and the escaping River Erne water the County pleasantly. A quiet, peaceful—as peaceful as anywhere in chancy Ireland can be—farmscape lies all about the demesne of Castlecoole. In 1789 a brig, the *Martha*, was chartered at Portland to bring the huge blocks of "dressed and chipped at quarry" Portland stone to Ballyshannon, where Belmore had had a quay constructed to accommodate the "shedding" of his building materials arriving from England, Italy, and Haute-Savoie (spruce and chestnut wood). There they were warehoused until needed at the demesne of Castlecoole. Bullock carts were employed to take these blocks the eight miles to Lough Erne, then by boat to Enniskillen. Again the stone was transferred to waiting bullock carts to be hauled the last three miles over roads excruciating even to hardy bullocks.

Through towering beech groves, skirting Lough Coole (which has harbored, since 1700, immense flocks of gray lag-geese, the progenitors of the domestic goose), the Portland stone was carted. At last on Good Friday, 1792, Castlecoole was finished to the last chimney pot.

While the pleasant warmth of detail and grouping of main block, demilunes, and auxiliary wings, so dear to Palladio, is missing in the general severity of this house, there are a number of distinctly Palladian features. The west wing seems to have been designed almost as a separate pavilion, for it is definitely Palladian. Venetian windows flanked by niches, four Doric columns, fluted, supporting an entablature, and the top finished off by a stone balustrade.

Seen from across the wide lawn, Castlecoole reminds me of the gleaming Wilhelmshohe Palace at Kassel, now destroyed by R.A.F. bombing. That building, too, had the "perfect, cold marble brow."

The entrance hall and staircase at Castlecoole is outstanding because of its scale and beautifully handled marblework. For this important work one of the greatest workers in marble in any era was procured. Dominic Bartoli arrived at Castlecoole in July, 1794, to compose the yellow, streaked with brown, scagliola in the hallway, and the gray, black, and white scagliola pilasters in the oval saloon. This is a truly superb apartment. Against palest yellow walls, the white, gray, and black pilasters frame crimson satin curtains. Crimson-embroidered silk upholsters the gilt furniture, which was brought back from Italy by Lord Belmore on his yacht, the *Osprey*. The yacht was buffeted by raging storms, nearly wrecked in the Bay of Biscay, and it was thought for a time that this valuable cargo of Italian gilt furniture would have to be dumped overboard to lighten the yacht. Lord Belmore is said to have been adamant, professing rather to be swamped than yield his hard-come-by furniture to the waves. By dawn the storm had abated as well as Belmore's temper. Today we see the disputed cargo spread beautifully about one of the handsomest rooms in Ireland.

Castletown at Celbridge, County Kildare, is a large house of most pleasing aspect. Like a superb Junoesque woman, Castletown seems just right in size, for no one feature disturbs the symmetry of the whole.

Autumn, or at best late summer, is my favorite time to come upon Castletown. Backed by copper beeches, the house seems to take on a golden quality from reflecting in the large lily pond bordered by stooks of golden wheat. For all its formality of Palladio in his grandest manner, Castletown is like Marie Antoinette playing at farming at the Petit Trianon, aristocratic and smiling among its breeze-ruffled wheat.

A huge oblong block of luminous, silvery Ardbraccan stone, the house gleams to white heat in starlight and moonlight. Gold at noon, silver at midnight is this house. As often happens in Irish Palladian houses of architectural importance, the outstanding feature, at first glance, is the prodigious length of their fronts, the main block, either a long oblong or high cube given lightness and lift by prolonging the line in colonnades and continued wings. Castletown has all these features and is made memorable, architecturally, by this fact.

Castletown is said to have three hundred and sixty-five windows, one for every day in the year. At one time when the establishment was enjoying its heyday (roughly 1759–1821, Lady Louisa Conolly's tenure), a squad of four servants was employed to do nothing but wash the windows. It is told that by the time they had completed the entire complement of windows, they had to start all over again. It must have been, as Italians say, *aria di capo.*

Lady Louisa Conolly (nee Lennox, daughter of the Duke of Richmond) was an extraordinary character. Immensely charitable, witty, loving scandal for its own sake, and a notable trencherwoman, she ran her house almost as a hotel for her friends and acquaintances. Lady Caroline Damer, a frequent guest at Castletown, writes Lady Ann Conolly at Wentworth-Woodhouse: "Never was such activity or such good cheer. I eat too much, but such fine quality is all the food, I do not suffer, or start a pain. All is neat and clean, in spite of the vast rooms, and rackety servants."

CASTLETOWN, COUNTY KILKENNY. FRIEZE AND CEILING OF BLACK AND
WHITE LACQUER ROOM.

CASTLETOWN. MANTEL IN BLACK AND WHITE LACQUER ROOM.

The architects of this grand pile of Ardbraccan stone were Colonel Thomas Burg and Sir Edward Lovett Pearce. Speaker Thomas Conolly loved living in the grand style, and hospitality with its far-flung ramifications was practically his middle name. "I get what I want" was carved on his heart. Or so he is said to have told a friend who owned a pair of carriage horses he wanted. He had to wait ten years to acquire them, when the owner was on the verge of ruin through gambling. But he got them.

The front door of Castletown is massive and attracts the eye to the grandiose flight of steps in two terraces that ascends to its lintel. The whole façade is definitely reminiscent of the Palazzo Farnese by Bramante in Rome, excluding only the powerful cornice and enriched coinstones of that noble building.

The rooms on the ground floor at Castletown are planned *en suite* as in Italian palazzi, and are eminently worthy of the imagination and skill lavished on plasterwork and carved wood architraves and moldings.

The most stunning room is surely the great entrance hall. Great in many ways: in sweep, in scale, and in the impact of the painted panels inset among swags and floriated branches, which is particularly striking anywhere; but at Castletown it is used with signal effect.

The staircase is to my mind one of the three grandest in the world, the other two being the *scala grande* at Caserta near Naples and the one in the Palacio Madre Morio Pia in Toledo, Spain. All three have tremendous sweep, power of line and color.

The canvases inset at Castletown are varied in subject, from a brooding landscape by Frans Snyders, wherein three boarhounds bring down quarry that is nearly hidden by the writhing bodies of the hounds, to Bacchic revels by Lantini, a cousin of the Francini. A Mrs. Beresford wrote of a conversation with Sarah Siddons, describing a visit to Lady Louisa Conolly: "With Siddons, in regal form at the playhouse [Smock Alley] as Clorinda. We talked of her recitations at Castletown. She was full of the beauties of the house and called the staircase palatial."

The Long Gallery is a sumptuous apartment, one hundred feet in length. The coved ceiling with Francini plasterwork is rich, and the frieze paintings by Cipriani smolder in deep color, of imaginative mountain scenery.

Lady Louisa died in 1821 of an ague caught while living in a tent a few hundred yards from the portals of her great house. "For," she said, "I do not get any idea of the beauty of my house if I live in it. I get perspective and contemplation if I can gaze upon the house from a far off."

Headfort, in the springy turf of County Meath, rises three high stories and a generous attic above a built-up grass "mound" or terrace. This elevation tends to make the house look much higher than Robert Adam (who designed it) ever calculated it should. As there is no record of Adam ever visiting Ireland, Headfort, by far his most ambitious Irish house, must have been contracted for and built by either Thomas Cooley or Richard Charles, both Dublin architects. The date of building is 1770–1775. The Earl of Bective, for whom Headfort was built, was a famous archeologist in a day when few of this turn of mind were in evidence. That Lord Bective came by his interest rightly is shown in the fact that his demesne comprises and marches with some of the most historic land in Ireland. Kells of thrice ancient legend, and Tara's Halls are right in the

Clontibbert House, County Kilkenny.

meadows surrounding Headfort. Slane Castle and the Hill of Slane are close by, as well as that bewildering edifice known as St. Columkill's Cell, still an enigma to students of Ireland's Gaelic monuments.

Headfort is a long oblong, with two one-story wings carrying the line for one hundred feet on either side of the main block. A distinctive feature at Headfort is the wide deep area, enclosed by a stone balustrade, that runs the entire length of the house.

The garden front is enhanced by the witty topiary work practiced in clipping the box and yew into a "set-out" game of chess. The kitchen garden is equally noteworthy, for here the arcaded avenue of yew is dense and of the quality of folded agate-green velvet. This arcade is over two hundred years old.

The "eating hall" is in Robert Adams' most suave and elegant manner, the coved ceiling being exquisitely detailed in interwoven vines and draped swags in lightly molded plaster. In the saloon are six superbly carved and gilded rococo mirrors, conceived as a bridge, a flight of steps ascending at either side of the frame. A *chinoiserie* fence supporting airy pavilions forms the crown to this beautiful bizarre design.

Headfort, Castletown, Russborough, Bellamont Forest, Caledon, Castlecoole, Carton—all names to remember when Irish houses in the Palladian taste are discussed.

But still there is Richard Castle's largest house, Powerscourt, which I have reserved until last, because the magnitude of its beauties is enhanced by all the Palladian neighbors surrounding it.

Set in a landscape straight out of fable, in the heart of the Wicklow Mountains, this demesne of Viscount Powerscourt is equaled in variety and planning by only one other I know: the Gardens of Le Nôtre at Versailles.

A natural pond known locally by the engaging name of Juggy's Pond was the nucleus for these remarkable gardens, backed up by a curtain of dramatic perspective, Sugarloaf Mountain, "clothed in greenery and darkling shade."

Powerscourt House itself is from designs by Richard Castle. The house was started in 1736 as a long Palladian façade thrown up against an old fortified house of the Wingfields'.

The frontage at Powerscourt is prolonged to an extravagant degree by a series of walls, stables, and outbuildings for the home farm. The reach of the house is definitely that of a village in magnitude.

The main block is a pediment supported by six flat pilasters, topped by Doric capitals. A blind attic supported by volutes rises one story above the attic. Above the three arched windows between the pilasters are concave portholes containing portrait busts. The sheer exuberance of Irish baroque architecture, as expressed by a man like Richard Castle with his Continental training, is presented in resounding terms in this magnificent house.

The saloon, occupying the entire north front over the entrance hall, is a glorious room. The floor is composed of golden walnut parquetry in a design, immense in scale, of concentric circles. Ten columns of sienna yellow marble dress the sides of this apartment. The foliated Doric capitals are lightly gilded.

One would almost think the palazzi of Italy had been looted, so magnificent are the treasures from all parts of that country. Palazzo Zambecarri in Venice, Palazzo Gigi in Rome, and the Stradella in Bologna all contributed furniture to the glory of Powerscourt.

The ballroom, sixty by forty feet and forty feet high, is lighted by windows high in the wall. This design is freely adapted from Andrea Palladio's favorite Vitruvian atrio.

The country houses of Ireland vary in degree of size, comfort, and architectural stature or beauty as decidedly as do the counties in which the houses are situated. Almost any house larger than a farmhouse in the Vale of Aherlow in County Tipperary (a fertile, sweeping landscape of spacious whitewashed stone houses) is called by all and sundry the "great house." It is not only a term of differentiation and labeling, but of affection and local pride as well. For all villages are a shade touchy if the neighboring demesne or great house is not instantly known and admired. In France each village takes inordinate pride in its ancient (at least as late as the Napoleonic era) château, or *petit manoir* housing the leading family of the neighborhood. Ireland cherishes just as jealously its "great house." The goal of every growing village girl is "to go as parlormaid or 'all girl' to the great house, yer honor, sir," as she says when asked what she fancies to do in life. Usually this girl marries a footman or a groom from the stables. Now and again, as in occasions I know, she even marries the young squire.

Scattered about the undulating counties of Ireland there are many very moderate country houses that may have no great architectural flare, but some feature will distinguish them. A fanlighted front door. Arched chimneys indented with a keystoned porthole. A hexagonal cupola surmounted with a flying gold cupid as at Little Port House, a gay place of four rooms with brisk white hand-woven linen curtains in every room. Spring Hill, a small house on a daffodil-drifted hill in County Cork, which goes up for let a few months each year, and has would-be takers clawing each other's eyes out trying to get it.

FIRES OF BELTAINE

Every race of people scattered over the plains and mountains of this wide world has its legends. Very jealously these racial stories are guarded, cradled as it were in the hearts and minds of the people. Each country has a different name to define various phenomena, the like of eerie, elusive lights that appear in marshlands, along mountain trails, in the lonely reaches of bogs, and waver tauntingly among the tall grasses of plains and prairies.

In Delaware, Maryland, and the twin Carolinas, these lights are called marshfires. The far-flung Puszta, which seems to stretch the limits of the horizon, harbors mirage lights, piled castles, and towers reflected in misty water. The Czyskos call them candles of Fata Morgana. In the dark fastnesses of the Carpathian Mountains and all along the Dalmatian coast, the chief horror is the werewolf. The superstitious peasants wave little knots of dried garlic in front of them when they walk abroad at night. For the skittering lights they see in the fields and forest paths are werewolf-eyes, worse to encounter than the dread *occhio malo*, the evil eye of Italy, or in the Piedmont and Abruzzi *oltramontano*, "lights beyond the mountains."

In Cornwall, Devon, and Somerset, strange processions of smoky lights are seen at midnight, winding through moor and wold. Druid lights the farmfolk call them. In India the pale rose, violet, and blue lights that dance and shimmer through palace and temple gardens are called Peri-lights, for a centuries-old, captive Persian fairy princess who still divides herself into countless tiny flames, forever seeking escape from the laby-rinth of India.

In Ireland, riddled with legend, immediate and part of the daily round are the gloriously colored lights wavering in the western sky, lurk-ing in bogs or dark glens. They are called the fires of Beltaine. Sometimes one finds old countrymen and women in the far "back and beyond" of Counties Roscommon, Mayo, and Fermanagh, and they having only the Gaelic, who will speak of May-fires. For in the Gaelic hierarchy Beltaine is a sort of archangel, herald of spring. In all the shattering brilliance of armor composed of flashing colored lights, *Bealltuinn* appears in the man-ner of aurora borealis, off to the west at midnight on the last day of April, thus heralding the first of May.

The Irish, however, are not going to let this visitation of unearthly lights stop there. Because of the countless rivers, loughs, and hidden bog-pools webbing the island, the Gael prefers to believe that the reflections of this annual May Day display by Beltaine are caught and imprisoned in lough and bog-water. All during the year, therefore, particularly to herald a spell of clear days after storm, Beltaine lights or fires are seen beckoning the unwary to the fringes of brackish bog or bottomless lough.

In Ireland there is a dread fascination about the Beltaine lights. Just let an unquiet girl wander off and slip into a lough or inlet, for whatever reason. When her limp body is borne "away out of that," murmurs will eddy through the crowd of watchers. "Achone, the girleen, she's after treadin' too near the brink. Beltaine's fire wearied her rest."

In the West Country of Ireland stand many lonely, disheveled, forgotten houses, built in the "grand, wide days" of Ireland's prosperity, roughly between 1700 and 1808. Quiet, tired, withdrawn houses, often so lovely in proportion and sculptured detail it makes no matter that encroaching trees, underbrush, and strangling creepers have battered a cornice or chimney, or perhaps rotted a pediment until it sags crazily. Integrity of design and soundness of structure defies the elements, seems impervious to embracing flora and neglect.

Often one comes upon these hidden houses, crouching in the midst of demesnes so choked by rhododendron thickets, fifty feet in height, that the once whitewashed walls are frescoed by damp and mold, streaked in yellow, brown, and green, a veritable temple to mildew. To define just where these houses are situated, is difficult. To find out just why the houses were ever built in such inaccessible places, even from the owners, is to draw blank. Not that that signifies in itself, but I have often wondered, when closely studying the strong construction of heavy dressed stone, how materials were ever brought to these remote demesnes.

County Sligo; lovely Donegal of wide valleys and green pastured hills; Connemara, stark, like some Attic kingdom; County Galway, ever loved by me, having spent enchanted years among its beech groves and turf-crowned headlands; Little Mayo, reaching farther than one thinks. All harbor lost houses.

Some of these houses belong to friends of mine and are neglected for the reason that circumstances have caused the owners to live in foreign lands or in other parts of Ireland. One instance that is deeply moving concerns a woman who as a radiantly beautiful bride went to live in a Palladian house standing well away from the beaten track in County Galway. Near the Lough of Corrib it was. Not a huge house, fairly small in fact, as Irish Palladian houses go. But there was, from all the tales I have heard, an air of enchantment hovering about the place. This is very easy to believe, for even now when the place has a poignant air, enchantment is ever close. A kind of essence that causes one to remember in retrospect, at odd times, how lovely was the pattern of sunlight through carved balusters in the white-pillared hall, or the grace of the curving wings against the sheen of Lough Corrib water.

One day, after the lady had lived for a few years at Ballinter House, her husband had business away in Dublin. Leaving his wife in the house attended by a full complement of servants, the man set off with no qualms. Later that evening the lady strolled along the terrace that skirted the lough. There was no moon and a chill wind sprang up causing little white "horses" to cap the waves. As the lady stepped upon the portico to enter her house, a demented servingwoman from the Claddagh sprang out from the dark shadow of a column. With one lunge she hurled scalding water from a copper can full in the face of her mistress. What consternation prevailed in the household one may imagine. For months the lady lay only half alive. Finally she walked again upon the loughside terrace, but with a difference. The once lovely features of the lady of Ballinter were heavily veiled. Many years have passed. Her husband and two children died. Still she lives in Ballinter House, never appearing unveiled. Primrose satin frays to the like of fringe on painted Venetian chairs in the drawing room. Portraits of eighteenth century ancestors, painted by Reynolds and Gainsborough, darken through the years on the walls of the Adam dining room. Hounds have chewed huge holes in settees and needlework rugs. The house is woefully understaffed, but a sketchy kind of comfort manages to survive.

Always now the painted wooden shutters on the inside of the windows in all rooms are closed. For a visitor seldom enters the white hall. Now and again in summer a small regatta is held upon Lough Corrib, the finish line being just off the terrace of Ballinter House. Then the lady appears, veiled in yards of chiffon, to pour tea in the portico. This lends, for a few hours, a festive air to the shuttered house. For that is what Ballinter has become, a nearly forgotten house. Architecturally entrancing, it harbors tragedy. At Rosepenna in Donegal I once heard the occupant of Ballinter called "that old recluse, sunk in her sorrows." Both house and occupant are recluse. The Veiled Lady in the Shuttered House.

Dunsandle is not precisely a forgotten house, but so near as makes no matter. When the Daly family lived there in grandeur at the turn of the century, no other great house in County Galway showed so handsome a façade to guests from all parts assembled in the county for Galway Race

Week. Dunsandle was built in true Palladian style, a huge main block with colonnaded walls forming demilunes. From the end of these walls large two and a half story buildings extend right and left, parallel to the main façade, but set fifty feet in front of the entrance. Dunsandle has no portico, but a beautifully proportioned and embellished pediment surmounts the molded cornice at the roof line, centering three tall keystoned windows. One drives for miles through magnificent oak and beech groves after passing through the dilapidated pavilions at the gates. Only one of these lodges was lived in, the tender's family of ten children, all tattered and extravagantly handsome, crushing the life out of each other in trying to open rusty gates with a great show of strength. Gates that I observed could have been blown open with one good puff, so rickety was the delicate ironwork. As far as the eye could see on all sides, broken luxuriantly flowering rhododendron bushes stopped every vista with coral and crimson ramparts. This demesne is the very habitat of Beltaine fires, for legend garlands the place. Once many years ago, on the midnight hour of the first day of May, country people for miles around, even as far away as Galway City itself, thought Dunsandle was in flames, because of the fires of Beltaine. It appears the archangel was more brilliant on this particular May Day than ordinarily. So far-reaching in the arc of the heavens was his fire that the ponds in front of Dunsandle House reflected tenfold the red, green, and purple light, throwing it back onto the fawn stone façade in such strength that the many windows shone with an unearthly light. Until Dawn robbed Beltaine of his powers, people streamed towards Dunsandle demesne to help quench the blaze.

A charming, small, templelike house stands almost submerged in holly trees and transplanted Italian ilex bushes on an island in the Lough Arrow. County Sligo is well supplied with forgotten—in any case mislaid—houses, for absentee landlords (they who fled to England for what they fondly hoped was a better life during the Troubles) seem either to have died, away from their ancestral acres, or feel their remote County Sligo demesnes too meager, the houses too derelict to be lived in again.

And so the houses behind broken gates and deserted lodges dream away the years. Temple Arrow is a more delicately designed house than one usually sees, except rarely, in the west of Ireland. Palladian in style it is, surely. High and narrow, rather like Lucan House, rising almost sheer from the River Liffey and its gnarled willows in County Dublin. But

Garrow, County Donegal.

Temple Arrow is sturdy, else it would never have lasted so long, deserted except for a mouthing old craik of a caretaker, a hermit out of history.

"That auld timple," as the house is known to the countryside, was built by an Austrian in 1768. This man had married a daughter of one of the County Sligo gentry. The two retired to this island retreat where he proceeded to beat his wife to death. It was a sadistic, carefully planned campaign to liquidate an unwanted heiress-wife, and he enjoyed himself meanwhile to the full. Her cries of "Holp! Holp!" hardly carried across the waters of the lough. The Austrian is said to have told a tale, which was believed (at least until he had collected his late wife's heritage and departed for Europe), that his wife had been drowned during a sailing party. For forty years this exquisite house has stood empty except for the hermit in its cellars. At either end of the front, half hidden in climbing fuchsia, are twin garden houses that I would match for articulated beauty of design with any others in existence. Four delicately pillared Palladian windows form the sides. Wide winged windows, all shuttered in solid wood panels. Once these were painted with aquamarine scenes of *fêtes champêtres* on a pale yellow ground. Many are gone for firewood or fall to pieces from damp rot under one's touch. But three or four survived to tell their story when I was there in 1947. At one time stools were arranged in each window, and a marble table, now cracked and chipped, stood ready for food and wine in the middle of the floor. It would seem that cushions of aquamarine brocade were once flung on the windowseats, for I found long frayed tags of this silk still caught on nails along the edge of the rat-gnawed burlap covering. A few oars stood in the corner of one pavilion, and in the other a cheap paraffin lamp. Relics of picnic parties. Oddly, when Temple Arrow is seen from the Sligo–Dublin road across the mile of lough, the house seems gay and inhabited. The last rays of a setting sun slanted across the high pediment and the two domed pavilions when last I saw it. Lovely and lost. Perhaps some day someone will find it and give it the life it has never had.

Garrow is another cup of tea, altogether. A big rambunctious house rising like a great tenement on a hill in County Donegal. Built by a rake of purest ray serene. One wing burned during his tenure. Sir Neville French inherited a demesne of three thousand acres in County Donegal just as he was approaching his majority in 1740. In three short years he had built (some say Richard Castle was the architect) a big barracks of a house, nearly burned it to destruction over his head during a drinking bout, and lost every penny he owned at cards. Last heard of in 1746, he died in a debtors' prison in London. His estates, being entailed, had remained intact and went to a nephew. Until twenty years ago the house had been used as a retreat for fishing parties. Now the walls are cracking and one side has completely fallen in. Garrow reminded me, when I last visited the demesne, of many of the ruinous houses in Louisiana, along the treacherous Mississippi or the bayous. Stately porticos, roofless and moss-hung, each year casting Corinthian capitals and cornice moldings to the littered ground. Garrow has a quality of grandeur all its own. The circular steps leading to the gaping hall door are architecturally important, as is the *scala grande* at Drumlanrig (Dumfriesshire), or the wondrous stairs at Fontainebleau from which Napoleon Bonaparte bade good-by to the officers of his Grand Armée. Search the world, but you will never find a grander curve and rise of stone stairs in Palladian taste than these, curving upward to the tottering portico of Garrow House. In magnitude it rivals the *scala grande* at Malcontenta.

Yet these houses are so nearly forgotten except by searchers like myself, that they molder and fall utterly away, unseen.

Colnagh stands in the tragic wastes of Connemara, tragic because all about one lies the beauty of cloud-wreathed mountain, high-piled sky, and stretches of emerald and bronze bog, the very power of rock-strewn acres hushing the poverty and starveling children of the land. Colnagh is unusual in plan, pure Palladian in style, but almost a square keep and four truncated castle towers in mood. Yet, unlike many so-called Palladian houses in the north and west of Ireland, Colnagh is not just a Palladian façade thrown up in haste to be in style against an old stone fortress, the like of haunted Drumnacroagh, but a carefully considered arrangement of a hollow cube and four high demilunes.

As one approaches this large four-square structure, one is compelled to search the rock-hewn landscape to find a fellow building, outbuildings of some description. None appears. The first time I saw Colnagh years ago, a torrential rain swept the back of the house while the front was slanted in sunlight. *That* is Connemara. Against each of the four sides of the cube, forming walls about a courtyard, rises a three-story demilune with the remains of a splendid stone balustrade alternating with oblong entablatures on which are carved lines from *The Tempest:*

Beltara, County Sligo.

> I'll show thee every fertile inch o' th' island;
> And I will kiss thy foot: I prithee be my god.

And

> A most ridiculous monster, to make a wonder
> of a poor drunkard.

Now the gutted walls harbor the elements, never so violent or chancy as in Connemara. Colnagh is a cave of the winds with casks of soured wine in the cellars. A fringe of blowing grasses has taken transient root along the cornices.

Once this house was full of life and the laughter of men and women, for it is told that a ball was given in 1860 to entertain members of Queen Victoria's suite, she resting at Queenstown on her yacht *Victoria and Albert*. A Mrs. Ardree, a sort of latter-day Mrs. Delany (perhaps of the same family for her maiden name was Granville, and Mrs. Delany was born Mary Granville), wrote to Lady Errolton:

> Dancing at Colnagh, that Temple of the Winds, continued the whole night long. Such a gathering of local gentry and Dublin Swells has scarce graced the wilds of Connemara since the day of The O'Haughtby. Why Charles [presumably Charles Courtney, her cousin] persists in acquiring this windy monster of a house, the Saints alone can guess. The pink satin curtains at all windows are handsome, fringed deeply in silver, and thousands of bog-roses entwine the stair-rail in the court.

A fire, probably set by tinkers, destroyed the furnishings of Colnagh in 1891. As a plan it is unique, and someone would profit by copying it entire.

The Tinkers' House is a haunt of Hecate, Bedlam *in excelsis*. Actually the house, within a dark woodland belt in County Fermanagh, is called Ballycortee. But no owner has occupied it for thirty years, being absentee in England and the property in litigation. The people of the roads, immemorial wanderers as well as tinkers, have used the huge deserted rooms to hold carnivals and celebrate the midnight fireworks of Beltaine. So far they have not burned the place to a charred heap, or at least riven walls the like of Colnagh. But give them time. A caretaker was found one misty morning, his chest ripped open from chin to navel. All the "Godless bloodletters," as the old woman at Barteemore who told me the story called them, had fled the countryside. No man has accepted the job of caretaker since. The three-story central hall, pillared in sets of four

engaged Corinthian columns, is magnificent, as is the stairway which rises
from the center to branch to right and left, then turn back upon itself to
join a gallery running around the entire hall. The pediments over the six
doors giving into reception rooms on the ground floor are draped with
carved swags of fruit worthy of Grinling Gibbons. Once this hall was
marbleized in three grays and black touched with gold, in the Italian
manner. Lighted by four huge porthole windows in a shallow dome, it is
still a superb room. The floors throughout the house are beautiful and
noteworthy, probably laid by local craftsmen. Immense chevrons of chestnut wood, shading in all browns, compose the floor. Once highly polished,
the floor would reflect a chair its entire length in the richly russet depths
of the boards. Now encrustations of bird-droppings and the refuse of
tinkers' banquets smudge and dim the luster of chestnut chevrons. A few
pieces of heavy furniture remain, pushed back against the walls, as if
scorned by the tinkers; solid Domingo mahogany, and French walnut
tables and commodes. The plan of Ballycortee is simple. A central block,
from which at right angles project two long colonnaded wings. A high
Palladian window with richly carved keystones and a swag of carved fruit
decorates the central arch of the window. One could, with a fair amount
of money, great patience, and a deep feeling for really splendid craftsmanship, reclaim Ballycortee. Time stays his hand, waiting.

Clinticket is a clown of a house, or three houses to be exact. For
no possible reason that one can fathom (little can be obtained from locals,
for they shrug questions off their shoulders), three identical houses were
built in 1790 by a man named Dabney from Clifden in Connemara. No
one has ever lived in any of the three, or so I heard. I learned that one
fact, and that only, from Johnny the Post, and he on his daily round driving his cob near the row of houses. No porticos, but three identical pediments, each pierced by a porthole window sprouting winged keystones.
The arrangement of windows is very fine, for, tall and wide, they dress
the plain façades of the houses. This could not have been a class of housing scheme, or detached villa arrangement, because a demesne wall encloses the fifty or sixty acres comprising a garden, now overgrown, and the
usual complement of gates with a pair of gate lodges fronting the Clifden
road. One odd feature is that all the floors in the downstairs rooms, six to
each house, are poured cement, like a modern garage—apparently of far
more recent date than the houses. One house was struck by lightning a few

years ago, curiously enough on the night of April 30. This happening was "good red meat" to the Irish countryman, of course. He says, "Would ye think now that Beltaine, in his high wrath, 'ud clip the one shebang, and slight the other two?"

BOOK III

ENGLAND

INIGO
JONES:
VITRUVIUS BRITANNICUS

Down the windy arches of Time—receding almost to an echo when battles were clashing, ringing out clarion clear when the sweets of

Peace lay upon the land—the cry from the battlements, "The King is dead, long live the King!" has caused the eyes of men to look ahead toward something new in life. When the Elizabethan age sank upon its brocaded velvet cushions and expired in a whirlpool of gold galloon and wired lace, a new style appeared as if by magic upon the English scene. The style of the *classique masque,* the *fête champêtre,* the *farandole.* Dress, court manners, dancing, entertainment in aristocratic houses, and most of all architecture, took a turn to the right, the road to open meadows shaded by clumps of trimmed trees, woodland pools, the long vista through vales disclosing far mountain peaks, and the gay habit of eating out of doors. All this happened when James I, dawdling son of Mary Queen of Scots, ascended the throne of England.

For years a quiet sort of man called Inigo Jones, enraptured of poetry and the theater, had traveled on the continent of Europe. He had studied in Italy, had visited Vicenza and contemplated the wonders of Teatro Olimpico. He had gaped like any bewildered traveler at the "double" palazzi in Venice, double by courtesy of water, the real and the reflected. So clear were both in the crystal moonlight that one scarcely knew which way was right side up. Rome had held Inigo Jones in thrall, as that arched and columned city has so many artists before and since. And then he came to Denmark. There, opportunity, full panoplied, awaited him in the sparkling person of the young gifted amateur, Christian IV of Denmark. This was indeed a happy meeting, for Jones was employed by the King to design masques and theatrical entertainments of all kinds for the court.

The length of his first visit is disputed; some say five or six years, others no more than two. This does not really matter, because we do know that during this stay at the Danish court, Jones did not design any castles or buildings for the simple reason that he had not yet become an architect. In fact, at this time his entire enthusiasm was the theater. One of Jones' most extolled masques for King Christian's delight was Greek in theme. This alfresco entertainment was acted in the light of furiously burning torches borne to and fro by turbaned and plumed lackeys, blackened to the like of Negroes and flamboyantly dressed in vermilion, yellow, and silver. The motif of the masque was the pursuit of wretched Actaeon by his own hounds, after he had surprised Diana at her bath among the mossy rocks of pine-dark Phellius. So realistic and so vivid in action was this masque, starting with the scene of Actaeon discovering Diana surrounded by her shrieking nymphs, ending with the defeat of the antlered hunter, that the court was thrilled to shouting applause. It is said that the originality of production displayed by Inigo Jones at this time won him a permanent theater, built by royal bounty. A painted proscenium, gilded and sparkling with powdered mica, was moved to different parts of the wooded river meadow where the masque was played. Within this glittering frame the vignette of action was mimed.

Soon after his new theater was built in the environs of Copenhagen, Jones was asked by the newly sceptered King James to return to England. Here the excellent Anne of Denmark took Jones under her wing and saw to it that all the good things going at court were shared with him. He soon became Surveyor to Henry, Prince of Wales, and his duties as *primo meccanico della teatro* gave him scope for his favorite mechanical effects.

This surveyorship was not of long duration, for the sensitive, intelligent prince died untimely. After the elaborate funeral, all managed by Inigo Jones in resounding style, Jones again left England for Italy. This trip must have been of consuming interest to him for he filled many sketchbooks with details which we see later in his most successful buildings. In the library of Worcester College, Oxford, are preserved these sketchbooks and a well-thumbed copy of Palladio's *Architettura*. Many dates and notes made while in Rome, Tivoli, Venice, Naples, and Vicenza are of absorbing interest.

Inigo Jones strayed, leisurely, entranced, through a country still gleaming with the treasures we see today cracking at the seams, the paint dimmed or peeled away, the sculpture stained and in fragments. Sansovino was dead only thirty years. Vignola was scarcely cold in his granite sarcophagus; Caprarola, his most magnificent work, was still resounding to Farnese laughter. Palladio, who was so worshiped by Inigo Jones, was dead certainly, but never had a man left as much behind him, still pulsing so vividly with his essence that one expected him to appear from under a portico momentarily.

Indeed these were great days—1614–1621—to be alive, young, fairly quivering with invention, and in Italy. Palma Giovane might walk in front of you across a humped bridge, a fabulously eccentric Venetian courtesan on either arm, for he was the painter who immortalized them, in lacquered pattens, puffed breeches, jeweled stomachers worth fortunes, and piled coiffures bleached with urine. Scamozzi, nearing old age, but still surprisingly active, would have invited Jones to a festa at his great house on the Brenta. At this festa would appear, no doubt, the incredibly lovely Isabella Andreini who immortalized the character of Colombina in Commedia dell' Arte, and provoked, by her red-gold beauty, a duel between hot young bloods, nightly.

Inigo Jones visited at length Mantua, Modena, Tuscany, Firenze, Bologna, and Parma. Everywhere he sketched and took notes. Suddenly, after one last look at the Palladian villas along the Brenta, Inigo Jones returned to England and for the second time was offered the post of Surveyor General to King James.

By this time, as he says in his notes, "I am Italian, in thought, in heart, and in my applauding interest in the Vitruvian architecture of that lovely land."

As the years progressed, and one after another of Inigo Jones' buildings and great houses (both townhouses and those reposing in the countryside) rose, had their being, and took the place most of them now occupy in the panorama of posterity, this man was likened to Vitruvius. He was called, perforce, by his pupil Webb, "Inigo Jones, Vitruvius Britannicus."

Born at Smithfield, son of a cloth merchant, in 1573, Inigo Jones was a Londoner by birth, however much he adopted Italian ways and art, and started to study the mechanics of the theater at an early age. It is interesting to find that in his day there was only static scenery, if any at all. Usually, very much in the manner of the classic Chinese theater of today, a given scene is suggested, even described by a narrator, and members of the audience must create illusion on their own. After the second return to the court of King James, Inigo Jones introduced movable stage scenery for the first time on record.

In 1614, after devoting ten years to designing scenery, Inigo Jones was forty years old. He felt it high time to start a really active career as an architect, if ever. Not that he would drop the theater entirely, it was too deeply seated in his nature to love the dramatic sweep, the moving of lighted color; but only as an adjunct to his architecture.

Ben Jonson's *Masque of Blackness*, a boldly imaginative piece, had called forth huzzas from court and townsmen alike. The brilliance of

Inigo Jones' costuming and settings had started the town talking. A contemporary writes of this piece:

> . . . the like, for glad color and contrived invention, has not been seen in London before. Extravagance in light and shade followed one the other in red, purple, and mother'd pearl. A black shell opened upon a silver world we knew not of. In happenings of magic, my mind lost count untill all disappeared in smoke. A mighty carnival of pretend.

All the time he was occupied with architectural studies and problems in draftsmanship, Jones was designing both plays and masques. For Fletcher's enchanting pastoral, *The Faithful Shepherdess,* Inigo Jones designed scenery so delicately colored that it set a mode of dress for ladies and gallants at court which lasted for ten years. Barbara Villiers, Duchess of Cleveland, was painted by Sir Peter Lely. "I am," she wrote, "painted by dear Lely as Fletcher's pastoral maid, the King [Charles II] preferring it." And if ever a woman set the style it was the divine Castlemaine.

So extravagant did costuming become when masquers appeared that courtiers vied with one another to outshine rival or neighbor. Feuds ensued, jealousy ran rampant, and men were more the peacocks than even the extraordinarily elaborate male dress of the period demanded. Finally such heights of folly in dress ensued that Inigo Jones designed a masque where all participants must appear in plain habits. With this decree—bolstered by the King—only four cavaliers from the famous Court of the Cavaliers appeared at rehearsal. Soon after this Jones devoted his time mainly to architecture.

The greatest work of Inigo Jones in London is surely the Banqueting House at Whitehall. This superbly articulated building embraces all that is finest in Palladian teaching, with a great deal of Jones' inventive skill to round out a perfect whole. The ceiling of this house (the great room) was painted by Peter Paul Rubens. The house was built during the later days of the reign of James I and used by him for splendid banquets, which have been visually preserved in a series of aquatints painted by Ralph Webb. The contemplated palace of Whitehall, which was to have been built but never was because of a depleted exchequer, remains rather a mystery in that the plans are supposed to have been drawn by Inigo Jones, and then stolen. He wrote later that he knew the culprit, but never disclosed the name.

Next in importance within the London picture is the severely classic

The Queen's House
Greenwich-on-Thames

building of white stone known as the Queen's House, at Greenwich. Here we have lofty balustraded walls and immensely sweeping colonnades. We have a long room so masterfully designed in the finest Palladian taste that there is nothing in England quite so grand in detail. The long room I speak of has been variously named. Banqueting room, drawing room, long gallery, whichever it is, the fact remains that no other plasterwork or scagliola in existence is finer.

Verde antico, in a richly silver-green, pale yellow marble and soft rusty-pink *broccatello*, has been used for the backgrounds to throw into relief the tall panels of rapturously entwined dolphins with cupids astride, said to have been set up to symbolize the marriage of the Princess Royal to William, Prince of Orange, in 1734.

The Palladian shell motif decorates the cornice in this room that becomes a veritable *sala di marina* with all its maritime detail. The architectural doorcases, which engage fluted pilasters, Corinthian capped, and strongly molded pediments, are reminiscent of Palladio at Villa Piovene. In both places these elegant carvings seem eminently suitable, though Greenwich is a royal palace and Piovene a spacious farmhouse.

The entrance staircase leading to the pillared terrace at the Queen's House has a fascinating history regarding its design. It appears that when Inigo Jones was in Italy he made a drawing of the great Villa Poggio a Caiano by Sangallo, which consists of a huge oblong block with a doubly curved entrance staircase of great power. Two bridgelike colonnades connect this building to oblong wings jutting at right angles from the main house. This plan, coupled with Scamozzi's Villa Capelli alla Brenta, form, for the better part, the Queen's House.

When Inigo Jones was invited to come to Wilton, the Salisbury seat of the Earl of Pembroke, to design a façade incorporating a gatehouse designed many years before by Holbein, he went, reluctantly, accompanied by his pupil and nephew Webb. Reluctantly, because Jones saw no interest or profit artistically in refurbishing so old a house, however grand and distinguished its lineage. Little did he know that this work at Pembroke's Wilton House, including the Palladian casino in the garden, would remain to this day his finest country house; the double cube room is considered one of the three architecturally inspiring rooms in the world.

The Inigo Jones façade at Wilton is simple but so marvelously proportioned that the architect could rest upon the laurels tossed to him on this work alone.

Of the long garden front at Wilton, Inigo Jones said in a letter to Lord Sulgrave, "I deem my work at Wilton to be my eternal signature. The garden face alone is my portrait, as fine a fragment of I. Jones to foist upon posterity, as ever was my features by Van Dyke."

This portrait alluded to is very fine indeed, for it shows Jones in his sixty-first year full of health and spirits. His long fair hair falls in ringlets upon a pair of strong, broad shoulders. There seems to be no gray in his hair or the beard and pointed mustache (in the Cavalier style), which give to the rather long face a most distinguished look. For a man assuredly past middle age he wears an astonishingly youthful look.

Inigo Jones loved color. By that I mean he had the faculty to suggest in line and mass the stark impact one senses in a fine full color harmony. The two pavilion-like towers at Wilton, with heavy, powerful stringpieces and high pedimented windows, fronted on the ground floor by marble balusters, sings with *chiaroscuro,* and in the sunlight of a fair English summer is dappled the like of a pied tapestry. Webb, who was a good deal of a cynic, said, "Wilton has as many faces as a wanton mistress, with a different character to each face." This is true, for no less than five architects, "each the fullest in talent of his time," left their mark upon the face of this immense house. The first known was Salomon de Caus, then Holbein, then Inigo Jones. Later Wyatt, who it seems so displeased Lord Pembroke that he deemed him "worse, far worse than fire or flood, ruining my house by tinkering." The Manège, or riding school, was built by V.D. 1775. More than that about the architect is not known. There was an Austrian horseman-architect traveling in England about this time, mightily interested in all the phases of *Haute Ecole*. His name was Vincente Dracönner. The chances are this is the man. The building is worthy of note for the manner of *intaglio profondo* brickwork, almost a brick rustico. This is unique and handsome. The window and door trim is ivory-white stone. Horses' heads act as keystones, and two rampant stallions, front hoofs flailing, manes rippling in the wind, crouch upon the pediment over the arched entrance gate.

The Palladian bridge by Morris, spanning two converging rivers, the Nadder and the Wylye, is a gem in line and lift, and has been copied many times, as at Stowe by William Kent and at Prior Park by Wood.

De Foldeau, a French architect who traveled in England in 1769, compiled a book on Palladiana in Britain after his return to France. He alludes in rapturous terms to Wilton, saying in part, "A titan, sumptuous house, nobly planned by numerous minds. The lasting memory taken away is of the work of Inigo Jones, poet, painter, architect, and gentleman."

In the fame of Sir Christopher Wren it is churches that set the pattern. Still, the man might easily live in hallowed fame for one perfect building alone, the Orangery at Kensington Palace. It is the very signature of Wren, and a masterpiece of graceful movement in stone. Palladio stalks through this temple to "tea and orange flowers, where," said Queen Anne, "I learned to make light lace."

Sir Christopher Wren built almost entirely in or in the environs of London, so in one way and another, by fire, flood, and enemy bombing, a great many of his lovely brick and marble or silvery Parr-stone houses and churches have been destroyed. St. Paul's Cathedral seems to lead a charmed life, and at this moment is far more beautiful and heart-lifting than it ever was before when a clutter of oddly incongruous rattletrap buildings clawed at the gleaming pillars of this church. Now one may stand ten blocks away and feast the eye upon a great edifice.

Few buildings in any land have the soaring quality of this masterpiece of Wren's. Of over fifty known churches built by Wren, only a handful are left standing, and, if standing, are probably gutted to the point where total demolition is the only answer. Emmanuel College, Cambridge, is probably the most nearly Palladian of Wren's buildings; the pedimented, cupola-crowned main block flanked by colonnaded wings is in the Vitruvian ideal. The gaiety of richly modeled swags of fruit that sway between the Corinthian-capped columns of the portico would most certainly have delighted both Vitruvius and Palladio.

Nether Lypiatt, a manor house drowsing the years away behind a high urn-crested wall in Gloucestershire, is one of Wren's few country houses. But a fine example of elegant severity it is. The tall, coinstoned chimneys alone are noteworthy. It is a relatively small house, but spaciously planned. One often wishes Wren had designed more houses for country building.

In 1664 he visited Rome and held lengthy conversations with the incomparable Bernini, then an old embittered man. However, he is said to have brightened noticeably in the warmth of admiration evinced by the young Englishman for his work. He gave Christopher Wren a small alabaster model of his Apollo and Daphne fountain in the Farnese Casino. A splendid memento to last one's lifetime. And a long lifetime it was. Wren was found one evening, fallen upon his dinner table, dead. He clutched a pomander that had been given him for his ninety-first birthday.

Sir John Vanbrugh swings into the Restoration picture as architect and dramatist, epicure and beau gallant extraordinary. "A lewd fellow, but of such spirit and warm address, generosity personified, that we forgave the blush he brought to our partner's cheek, as she readily seemed to do." Thus spoke Lord Lyttleton after an opening night of *The Relapse*, Vanbrugh's best theater piece.

Of his houses, Sarah Marlborough complained to Queen Anne that they were "stone cliffs, cloud-climbing; unafraid," wherein "I catch each draught, wishing only to wring its neck, and so survive." He built for the greater glory of architecture, and away with the unfortunate persons who were to live in his houses. But few men in any of the arts have ever been so staggeringly successful in what their mind conceived, and what their eye later perceived, when the given plan was finished. It always seems that the palaces—for that is what his buildings are—to the very last superstructure and battlemented chimney, are more fabulous in reality than on paper, which is very seldom so even when the greatest genius is at work.

Vanbrugh's three tremendous gestures in masonry are Blenheim Palace for the Marlboroughs, in the forest of Woodstock, Castle Howard in the Yorkshire wolds, and Seaton Delaval on the stark Northumbrian shale, more craggy than any seashore has a right to be. Then Kimbolton Castle, Huntingdonshire, sharply red and white, smart as a guardsman's dress uniform, but sprawling and ungainly as a dwelling house. Gilling Castle, Yorkshire, built around a quadrangle. Grimsthorp, built "for pomp and Ancaster, one and the same," as a London lampoon read. The proud Earls of Ancaster gave Vanbrugh carte blanche and he retaliated with a truly imperial palace of a house. The tremendous entrance hall fills the eye, and members of the family in life-size array seem to step in painted splendor from their niches into the upper air of the three-story apartment.

About Grimsthorp Castle there is the shade of fearsomeness one

GATE HOUSE
KELTON PARK

senses in all of Vanbrugh's grandiose houses. He was immensely fortunate to find clients who were so desirous of a Vitruvian or Palladian background before which to strut their lives in pomp and circumstance, that he could go ahead, all out, and do his monumental best.

Eastbury fairly booms with grandeur. So many flambeaux were needed to light a company of gentlemen through the tortuous corridors from dining room to cocking-pit (the mains were held in the vaulted cellars) that one participant tells us, "the torches flamed and smoked like the caverns of Hell, spitting pitch, untill the feathers of our birds were singed."

Marble floors in gigantic patterns of black, white, and pink, as in the great hall at Grimsthorp, or red sandstone and sienna yellow marble at Eastbury, were like a signature to Vanbrugh. Soaring stone chimneys, like stacked piles of military trophies, as at Blenheim, were the order of his day. "A prodigious tall man, well harnesed against paunch, and richly turned out in satin, velvet and spangled lace" is the way one of his actors in *The Provok'd Wife* describes Vanbrugh. Whether this is a stage costume or private apparel, one wonders. In the Kit-Kat portrait by Sir Godfrey Kneller, Vanbrugh appears in a mightily curled wig but a plain velvet coat.

At Castle Howard he peacocked it, perhaps to be in keeping with the atmosphere of the *Sleeping Beauty in the Wood* and *Prince Charming*, which he had created for Lord Carlisle. Thirty flunkies in powder and silk hose lined the flamboyant staircase when a grand ball was given, it is said, and two huge bearded men "in wadded coats and fur caps, *a la Russe*, brought in twelve-foot logs for the hall fireplaces."

No more flabbergasting effect has ever been devised by an architect than the four-story hall at Castle Howard. The sweep of walls and staircase seems to be borne up on clouds. Silk banners hung from gilt poles sway and billow from a breeze—"unholy draughts," Sarah Marlborough continually complained of at Blenheim—we do not feel, so far below. The scrolls and foliations in creamy marble which wreathe cornice and mantel are echoed in the Corinthian caps of pillars of enormous circumference. Life must be fairly grim in these vast understaffed houses these unsure days. Built for "pomp and pleasures pied, silken smiles, unease to hide," wrote Charles II in one of his ballads. That was the mood of these romantic palaces. Plenty of unease now, it is well that smiles can hide it.

The Temple in the park at Castle Howard is in a way a reminder of the Casinissima at Caprarola. Not that this Temple is like it in architecture, though both are set high on a stone terrace and are of gray stone, but the approach up a grandly mounting flight of balustraded stone steps is very like. Both are a retreat for solitude or dalliance, away from but within hailing distance of the parent house.

The Temple is built in almost exact plan of Villa Rotonda, in miniature. Four-square in block. Four pillared, pedimented porticos, surmounted by urns here, instead of statues as at Rotonda. Demeter and Persephone in twice life-size flank the east entrance, and a dome with lantern cupola surmounts the whole. A beautifully articulated *bijou*, lovely to look at, to hide away in for an hour, otherwise utterly useless, a gigantic vase set in a sward of green.

James Gibbs hit London and the snobbish shires with a cold slap. He was a Scot, coldly precise in manner, but so great an artist in manipulating stone that he holds high place as a master of the rococo. He employed Venetian craftsmen, workers in stucco, and wood-carvers, foreigners exclusively, for, he said, "I ask for style and freedom of curved line. When I want a double volute, I do not wish to say more than that I want it. I *get* it from my Italians." And that is as it should be. From that manner of thought-transmission between architect and craftsman comes the great decoration of the world.

The Senate House, Cambridge, is one of Gibbs' finest buildings. The splendid use of fluted columns, capped in the Corinthian order, alternating with engaged flat pilasters between the arched or segmental windows, gives a most lovely rhythm to the façade.

Next in importance is Canons Park, Edgeware, the countryseat of "the gorgeous Duke of Chandos," as this handsomest man in England—certainly all female historians named him that—was called. It is oddly prophetic these days to find half the houses in London with any pretense to grandeur harboring some exquisite bit of long-demolished Canons, for some of these houses are demolished in turn. A staircase rail in a house in Cavendish Square. The fine portico at Hendon Hall. These once graced Canons.

Sudbrook near Petersham was a *tour de force*. The best of every art represented to the hilt. Bagutti, lately from work at the Queen's House, Greenwich, did the stucco garlands in the hall. Laguerre and Stillo painted the ceilings. Bellucci painted the dining-room walls in fading vistas and receding architecture.

Ditchley, and Sutton Scarsdale, now only a wraith of draggled stone and gaping windows, empty and staring upon a changing world, are such woefully contrasted houses. Ditchley lives and flourishes in beauty; Sutton Scarsdale, once a wonder of the age, is dead and rotting, but unburied.

The Octagon is a fantasy of Gibbs'. Built as a pendency to Orleans House, Twickenham, it was prepared for Caroline of Ansbach, when Princess of Wales. But she put off her visit for two years, "owing to a gout, and a pain unmentionable," as her lady-in-waiting wrote to James Johnson, owner of Orleans House.

The house is golden "flat brick," thin and rough textured. The pilasters are rose brick and the architraves and cornices are of "white granite"—probably Portland stone—and black marble. Sheer Palladian in concept, this house remains a unique relic of the stress put upon royal progresses, however untrustworthy the plans, which so often miscarried.

The Cherry House at Somerset Water is another of Gibbs' baroque or rococo masterpieces in the small. For he loved to work in almost doll-house size. In fact he made many dollhouses for the royal children. The Cherry House is destroyed to make way for huts in distressed areas, but Mrs. Deerford transferred the domed cherry-painted ceiling by Bellucci to Ireland for her Flower House, so that it survives in lovely color.

William Kent set a style of luxury in equipage, furniture, "follies," palaces, and sumptuous stables, second to no one, not even Sir John Vanbrugh. Of all his work my favorite is the oddly fashioned pavilion at Badminton Park known as Worcester Lodge. His Horse Guards in London is like a faceted jewel in perfection of balance and mass, but a singular charm, a heart-warming grace, clings about Worcester Lodge that defies description. A tall building, its first two stories are rusticated in deeply pitted stone, as if a waterfall had run over it for centuries. A massive doorway, through which a coach-and-four can pass, is surmounted by a high Venetian window letting onto a balcony. A banqueting room, white as jade, has a marble octagon table in the center and white *chinoiserie* chairs and carved and painted panels. The room is white. Stark, startling, luminous white, the kind I can never get enough of, and never have, unless I turn in and paint it myself. The impact of dark larch-green satin damask, with a design of saddles, bridles, spurs, and whips, is the last word. The obelisk-roofed gatehouses that flank the Lodge lend great style, the like of attendant dragoons to a mounted monarch on parade.

BADMINTON

MEREWORTH CASTLE
AND THE LONG VISTA

Whe Colin Campbell built Mereworth Castle for the Honorable John Fane in the oak and beech plantations of Kent, he was forced to surmount many obstacles. Not the least among them was the hue and cry attending the banquet observing the coming-of-age celebrations for Mountjoy Fane. After the port had gone round, a great roll of papers mounted upon linen was laid upon the polished board. John Fane with a flourish removed the cord that bound the roll. "Here, gentlemen, is my new house. Campbell erects this Palladian villa in the park of Mereworth." And erect the house he did. Never deviating a jot from the original plan, which is inspired, to a degree seldom encountered elsewhere in architecture, by the Rotonda near Vicenza. While the plans for Colin Campbell's favorite project proceeded apace, a veritable storm of protest, even ridicule, swirled about the heads of John Fane and Campbell.

"Why in God's name proceed to pour the Fane patrimony into this sieve of folly, a draughty barracks in which no Englishman could possibly live?" "The fogs and bitter channel winds will soon drive Fane out of his four whistling porticos." These and more scurrilous remarks were contributed freely by friends and foes alike. Campbell retorted to these tongue-waggers that the adaptation of the architectural mood of one country to that of another had been tried many times before with marked success. If the English manner of living did not conform to Italian standards, then the Englishman must change his habits, and not adapt his houses to them. Mereworth made no pretense of being an English manor designed by an English architect for an Englishman. If a connoisseur of the arts wished to fill his galleries with paintings representative of the great masters, he ranged the world and brought back from Spain, Italy, Holland, or France the most splendid pictures he could find. Why then, contended Campbell, could not the Renaissance architecture of Italy rise to glorify the lovely countryside of Kent? Exception is always intriguing, doubly so when the exception is sumptuous. For sumptuous is the word best to describe Mereworth Castle as it stands.

Once the desired site for the building of Mereworth had been chosen, a veritable labor of Hercules presented itself. The famed "leafy glades of Kent" were here encountered with a vengeance. Nearly a year passed, it is said, before a cleared space of sufficient area allowed Campbell to commence actual building. Beech trees, centuries old and of enormous girth, as well as giant oaks and tall ash, had to fall before the ax of scores of woodcutters. Cisterns, wells, and endless tunnels for sanitary purposes—unlike the sketchily contrived sanitation of eighteenth century Italy—were dug. Finally in the spring of 1721, the deep wide moat, from the center of which the square block of the house was to rise, was finished. "An hundred spades, mattocks, point-bars, and axes were laid aside, the shouts of men rose into the air. A lusty Paean of Triumph, that at last their efforts to clear the silent forest were to be crowned with a Temple, a bosky Habitate," wrote Mildmay in his journal. But the spades and mattocks were not thrown aside for long. After clearing nearly ten acres for immediate terraces, walks, and gardens around the house, the wood-cutters were again hard at work clearing the "rides," four in number, which were to extend in long straight ribbons of cropped green turf and leafy branches from each of the four porticos as far as the eye could see.

Mereworth was the first Palladian villa to be built in, one might almost say transported to, England. Just so was the "long vista," so dear to the heart of Italian architects and gardeners, first to appear in breath-taking style at Mereworth. True, there had been rides cut through the forests and parks of England before this. Many Tudor and Elizabethan houses featured long rides for huntsmen. But purely ornamental vistas (for example, Wanstead, in Essex, demolished in 1822) terminated by a graceful *temple d'amour* were first revealed to delighted English eyes at Mereworth.

Certainly no other house ever settled into a landscape so felici-tously. All tends to expand in rural beauty. Woods and garden comple-ment the pearl-colored Portland stone walls. The soaring dignity of the porticos and the lanterned dome seem like immense and lovely sculpture set in waving greenery. Two pavilions and two loggias are removed just far enough away from the main structure to have strict identity but in no way confuse the outline of a silhouette so individual as that of Mereworth looming against trees and sky.

It is a great pity the moat was ever filled in, for the scale of the broad steps leading to the porticos, as well as the sweep of Ionic columns and swag-draped pediment, would hold magic if seen doubly reflected in still water.

According to a letter written by Colin Campbell, the house was "roofed in the Autumn, and the first fires blazed on marble hearths on Boxing Day, *Anno 1723.*" This mention of blazing fires brings to mind an item of construction that has always interested me. In Colin Campbell's *Vitruvius Britannicus,* he sets forth with enthusiasm his method of equip-ping a house with chimney places, twenty in number, while pretending not one chimney exists. Only the sight of blue smoke curling skyward from the central lanthorn surmounting the rotunda reveals the ingeniously hidden flues.

Many innovations reared hitherto unknown heads all during the building of Mereworth. The whole project, from clearing the dense forest to the setting of the last Italian urn on its plinth or terrace balustrade, was like a Donnybrook Fair for the curious countryside. It is told that whenever the weather was fine, no matter which season, interested watchers embracing all classes made holiday in the vast clearing of Mereworth Park. Finally, what with the appearance of the inevitable thieving gypsies, Fane placed guards as sort of outposts, and no one was allowed to enter the clearing except those who had business with Campbell. For many months the forest aisles rang with the shouts of the draggers, drivers of the "stone-boats" used to transport the huge blocks of silvery Portland stone from the quarry to where the walls of Mereworth were slowly rising to confront the Kentish scene. How startled must the birds and small forest creatures have been, they whose lifetime had been spent in solitude and foraging for food. Now the clank and rattle of chains, the clamor and din attendant on the passing of men and horses, rang through shadowy glades. In short, a "conceit," an "absurdity in any case," a "folly paramount,"—to give the house a few of the names incurred by unimaginative observers—was slowly taking shape. The finest of its kind in England, then or now. For, with all its apparent unsuitability to the English climate, as well as the fact that it broke all rules of what constituted the country-seat of an English gentleman, Mereworth was greeted on all sides as a masterpiece, an edifice of "extremest beauty and pleasures uncounted," as Horace Walpole said in one of his numerous letters extolling the advantages of the house.

I am nearly won from Gothic by the elegance of Westmoreland's Italian villa. Art and proud vistas abound. A range of woodland runs up a hill behind the house, all seems like an Albano landscape, broke here and there by temples, a triumphal arch, urns and ponds. The chimneys collect in the dome uniting in one flue. A rarity in England, and not to be advised. However, this house is only the beginning. Where will this Palladian motif end?

Well may Walpole have wondered. Where indeed would houses in the Palladian style end? The end is not yet. For down the years since the architect's death his style has penetrated to nearly every corner of the earth, either copied as faithfully as Mereworth was from Rotonda, or in wings, porticos, and windows, in less ambitious houses.

The approach to Mereworth Castle is auspicious, giving more than

just a hint of the splendid rooms within the house. The first time I saw
Mereworth was on a late summer day. I walked slowly along the driveway leading to the north portico, so massively welcoming, rising from the
wide shallow steps that extend clear across the six Ionic columns dressing
the front. To left and right the flanking pavilions displayed porticos,
smaller but in exact design as are those of the main house. All buildings
were dramatically accented by the black-green cedars that spread low
writhing branches on every side. Approaching evening cast shadows of
branches across the sculptured pediment and traced lines of black, like the
festoons in a gigantic spider's web, over lawn and terrace. Not a sound
broke the silence of evening. No bark or whine from kennels. No horse
whinnied in the stables, which I could see just behind a screen of cedars.
No bird called to its mate in the greenwood. No breeze stirred the trees.
I stood in the midst of stillness. Was this the Sleeping Wood? And then
all at once a garden gate opened as a hand clicked the latch. A pony cart
sped sharply past me, the piebald pony hurrying to his evening oats. A
peafowl split the air with its shattering cry. And a lady in a white dress
appeared under the portico to greet me. The drowsing house had wakened.
For years the picture of this great house, carved in silence, held in my
mind's eye.

On my next visit to Mereworth, I took an embattled afternoon
walk up the driveway from the gatelodge to the north portico. The day was
one of the "English particulars," so often encountered in early February.
I had decided to take the dogs for a walk before tea time. When I looked
out into the park about three o'clock, it seemed a dank, heavily gray day
of dripping trees and gusts of rain, but no more than that. The kind of
day I am very used to in Ireland. So off we started. As usual, if terriers
are of the dog pack, they lead off. True to form, Airedale and Sealyham
shot into the beechwood, first crack out of the bag. For an hour or more we
ranged the rides and came out upon the bridlepath that skirts the park
wall on the inside. All at once thunder rolled, the kind of sudden un-
seasonable thunder one gets during the transition from winter to spring
in a temperate climate. The heavens burst, the four winds let go their
hoarded squalls. I ran, literally for my life, under the crashing branches
of ancient trees. Drenched dogs raced on all sides, barking hysterically.
We made the broad driveway, where once I had walked in the utter stillness of a summer evening. Today rain lashed to fury by the shrieking

wind. Broken branches lay all about and continued to break away from the trunks with a grinding sound. By now the dogs had outstripped me, and doubtless gained the warmth and safety of the kennels.

And then I stopped, for an extraordinary sight, one of overpowering beauty, forced me to halt, no matter how torrential the rain. Through a rift in the lead-gray sky a fragment of sunset shone forth. The entire west portico of Mereworth was etched against the wet cedars in liquid gold. The brilliance seemed alive. It was magnificent. For a moment I felt as if Andrea Palladio himself had lifted a dun curtain at the edge of the world, the better to see how his great design fared. For a matter of minutes only did every line and curve of the west façade shimmer in glorious sunset, then the curtain of night dropped, the wind sank to a growl, and rain lessened in fury. As I ran up the steps under the north pediment, I couldn't wait to paint what I had seen. Mereworth never lets one down: gray day, day of demented weather, hot sun of noon, or wreathed in the mists of autumn; four-square, garlanded in carved stone, Mereworth justifies the myriad talents lavished on its fashioning.

Outside, the impression one gets of Mereworth is silvery gray of Portland stone, dark, richly green cedars, the paler dusty green of beeches, and burnished clear green of oak. Over all, the sky changes from blue to gray or is streaked with scarves of brilliant color from Kentish sunsets. But the main effect is muted.

Not so inside, here the effect is splendidly rich and varied. The painted ceilings, displayed in most of the reception rooms, are by various Italian painters, Artari and others working in England with Bagutti, whose facile stuccowork throughout Mereworth is amazing in conception and detail. Never does the man repeat himself. Never does he try to ram overembellishment home to gain powerful effect, as is often seen, particularly in the plasterwork of Frenchmen of the period. All Bagutti's designs flow around a central motif. Like vines of leaves and berries growing over a stone wall along a country lane, the central theme is richly powerful, then the tendrils wander off, becoming more delicate, but forming a lovely frame for the central figure. In the portrait heads that appear ensconced in curving shells above the doors in the superbly lofty hall, Bagutti is at his best.

On a summer day anyone standing in the center of the circular hall at Mereworth can look away through porticos to a vista north to south

Mereworth Portico

218

or east to west, with nothing to halt the eye between. It is a grand sight entirely, and prompted a traveling Irishman, indeed a possessor of wide lands himself, to write:

> No prospect in England has delighted me so fine as the vistas at Lord Westmoreland's Italian house in Kent. A wealth of flowers and trees extend on all sides as far as the eye reaches, at least my quizzing glass tells me so. The pavilions mimic the house, and are gaily painted within. All stuccowork at Mereworth is the finest ever I beheld. Ireland will gain by importing this stuccodor to its shores. Did I not live in an ancient abbey, and no gold about to change my position, I would build a house in the stately Palladian mood. Alas and woe, I am ragged and strangled by debts.

Once in Italy I saw a fantastic effigy of Jove. In glistening white Capo di Monte, it was, I expect, designed to be used to decorate the center of a table. The seated figure of Jove was twenty inches high. A rocky base to the broken column on which the God of Olympus sat was surrounded by a narrow lagoon of water. Across this, four bridges extended and little ladders were raised so that the lesser gods and goddesses might clamber about Jove, begging the eternal favors which legend tells us made up Olympian conversation. These figurines, Adonis, Ceres, Juno, Eros, Hermes, and the rest, were only five or six inches in height. Juno sat on the Jovian shoulder whispering into his ear. Athene stood upon one knee, as if in doubt what her request would be. Eros perched happily among the hyacinthian curls of Godhead. And so on. One deity poised halfway down a ladder, as if undecided whether to explore the outlying table or not. A more charming conceit would be hard to find. I remember thinking when I saw this group in softly glowing porcelain that the whole reminded me of Mereworth. The grandeur of Jove was the house. All the figurines were the people who had lived there, constantly coming and going through the years. But always returning to the many pleasures offered by the gardens and the terraces, summer days under the massive porticos, autumn and winter nights before a fire in the long painted galleries.

Lady Fairfax, widow of the colonial Governor of Virginia, built a house near Charlottesville beside a mountain prospect, girdled by a river. Sycamore trees cast shade across the wide lawns when she took China tea under a painted silk marquee. She called her house "Salubria" for "this light salubrious air, this dappled sward," of Donne's. So Mereworth is, a most salubrious house.

SEATON DELAVAL, BEAUTIFUL AND DAMNED

One evening a few years ago, a schooner on which I was one of a party lay idling off the bleak and jagged coast of Northumberland. Twilight had lowered early, for the time of year was early October. We had set out from a small fishing village a few miles farther up the coast shortly after noon, but an oily swell rolling diagonally across our bow had hindered the schooner mightily. We had made no appreciable progress for the last two hours, and much as we all disliked the idea, the prospect of an unquiet night, anchored in the small harbor dimly seen to port, loomed large. A decision was reached; there was nothing for it, apparently, but to put in at the choppy, triangular bay where one or two pale lights winked a feeble sign of life. The day had been overcast but no rain—so often encountered in driving fury along this hagridden coast-line—had materialized, a few sharp pelts in midafternoon having blown out to sea. But a curious miasma, a witch-fog, seemed draped ominously about the masthead. Visibility was rapidly worsening.

All at once a sharp whistle shrilled in the damp air; the short nerve-wracking blasts seemed to come from a spot behind the dim harbor lights. Then, as if a curtain had risen on a scene from *Walpurgis Nacht im Brocken*, a sight to behold lay before us. Yellow, orange, and vivid vermilion tongues of flame appeared to writhe out of heaps of black rock. A terrifying hissing, as from a thousand adders, rode the air. No wind disturbed this incredible picture, for the flames, seeming to mount higher and higher as we watched, rose like raging pillars, drowning the color of the sky, by contrast. This livid splendor turned the heavens to onyx, throwing into bold relief a most amazing edifice, an upflung portico, immense in scale, sprouting widespread arms of stone. Towered and battlemented, this fabulous structure silhouetted against the ring of fire in such a way that the mass of mortared stone showed now purple black, now bronze red, flicked meanwhile by wavering veins of fire. No need for me to ask what this citadel of flame was. Instinctively I knew, recalling stories I had heard since early youth. Seaton Delaval, magnificent and damned.

The story is recorded that in a London club one night, in the year 1702, the architect–dramatist, Sir John Vanbrugh, heard on arriving at the door of the gaming room an altercation among the assembled players. Not wishing to become embroiled in an argument which in no way concerned him, he was managing to give the gaming room a wide berth when the door leading to the stairway flew open and the vastly drunken person of Admiral Delaval was catapulted into Sir John's arms. The upshot of this sudden, rather embarrassing meeting between England's foremost architect and the wildly eccentric and dissipated head of the "fantastic Delavals," to give them only one of the many sobriquets hung upon them down the years, was a long inspired friendship; but, more to the point, Delaval evinced an admiration so deep, so sympathetic and intelligent regarding Vanbrugh's architectural powers that he commissioned him to build carte blanche a veritable monument to Vitruvian architecture on the wind-wracked coast of Northumberland.

For that is what Seaton Delaval most surely is, a monument. An enormous piece of sculpture. A stone "set-piece," the epitome of its grandiose era. Superbly dramatic then, unbelievably dramatic now. Torn by its constant battle with all the fury of sea-born storms, riven by a devastating fire within its walls in 1822, the vast pile stands battered but intact among its acres of withered grasses. A lichened stone trophy emblazoning the arms in the pediment and evoking in every soaring arch the pride of the long-dead Delavals.

On every count in the human calendar, this large family was as compelling of attention, as flamboyant in appearance, as their house. The three generations preceding the redoubtable Admiral were particularly noted for constant financial straits, beauty of person, and sudden deaths. Indeed, a quatrain was hawked about the streets of London after the death of the Admiral's father by apoplexy in a coach crossing Newmarket Heath. Two lines were:

> Delavals don't die in Bed
> Delavals just drop down Dead.

Annals pertaining to the exact number of children fathered by Admiral Delaval vary. Birth certificates are either destroyed or—more probably, considering the laxness of the times, the remoteness of Delaval's house in Northumberland, and the disheveled manner of life among the clan—never recorded at all. We know of five children, three boys and two girls, all outrageously handsome, debauched, and spendthrift. Then stories are told of the escapades of numerous nephews and nieces of the Admiral, sons and daughters of Sir Francis Delaval, whose reputation was as blazing as the pillars of fire which now surround his blasted house.

One disapproving chronicler of the period says, "Sir Francis outstrips in license his outrageous progenitors. No rout or drum is safe from becoming carnal if he is among the guests. A Lothario of the first fashion, he turns his Northumbrian house into a bear-garden to entertain his hilarious and impecunious cronies." Soon after this, the Furies beckoned Sir Francis to their side. As he was returning one night from a drinking bout at a neighboring house, his horse plunged down a ravine. A few days later the broken bodies of Sir Francis Delaval and his horse were found.

It would seem, tracing the vivid, unconventional lives of members of this family, that they were damned from birth. Any house harboring them was damned as well. Probably, considering the splendor of her portraits, "Almeria" was the most beautiful of all the family born at Seaton Delaval. Her fantastically long and luxuriant red-gold hair she always wore unbound. No confining ribbon or rope of pearls, as was the prevailing fashion at the time, hindered this wondrous mane, day or night. Even when she rode about the wastes of Northumbria as a girl, and after she became Countess of Tyrconnel and rode madly across the Irish bogs, her hair, streaming behind her when in motion and sweeping her horse's rump when still, was a banner on the wind. A story is told in Ireland that seems in the true Delaval vein.

Lady Tyrconnel appeared one evening on the terrace of her house dressed for entertaining at dinner a Chief Justice of the Four Courts from Dublin. The evening being warm and no breeze stirring, Lady Tyrconnel was dressed in a flowing gown of black and gold gauze. When she had seated herself across from her guest, footmen entered the terrace bearing platters of food. The meal proceeded. It seemed to all at table as if a blanket of humid mist crawled up the valley, for as dinner progressed the heat became intolerable. The Chief Justice pulled a large silk square from the pocket of his skirted coat and raised his hand to mop his perspiring face. Suddenly his hand paused, the handkerchief hung in midair. With eyes popping from their sockets, he gazed at his hostess. Lady Tyrconnel had dressed herself that night in true Delaval tradition. Her flowing skirt of black gauze was just that, a skirt and nothing more. The fichu that had partly concealed her shoulders she whipped off and used to fan herself, displaying as perfect a torso and bosom as the honorable Justice had ever hoped to see. Completely unaware that exposing herself at the dinner table, naked from the waist up, was unusual, the beauty of the Delavals grasped her flowing hair and twisted it into a Psyche knot, thus both baring and cooling her superb shoulders. Many are the stories told of Lady Tyrconnel. Far too many to relate here. However, one other shows her caliber, her pride and arrogance, which would not be brooked.

At a ball given in a castle a good few miles from her own Clonaggart, the Countess overheard a slurring reference to her wild mode of life, uttered by a squireen from hell-and-beyond in County Tyrone. It is within reason to suppose that aspersions, even insults, heard constantly uttered against her family or herself, would pass unheeded. Otherwise she would have spent her life in defense. Apparently this particular jibe, uttered by a man she considered a poor fish, flicked her on the raw. But she appeared not to notice and bided her time. The guests departed, Lady Tyrconnel among them. Knowing that the squireen had ridden off on his horse an hour or so before, she ordered her coachman to drive slowly until the crossroads were reached. Here she got down and, after borrowing the coachman's whip, ordered him to drive home alone. The picture evoked at this point is surely in the maddest Delaval tradition: a rocky back-country road, a tall woman whose flowing hair shone like copper in the moonlight. Long skirts tucked up so as not to hinder her stride, she probably mulled over in her mind just how she would deal with this boor once she caught sight of him.

Up the long, grass-grown driveway. In at the front door. Silence in the lower rooms of the house. In keeping with her mood, she probably took the stairs three at a time, for it is known that "Almeria," as some infatuated poet had named her, was a tall, strongly built woman. Perhaps a few doors had to be flung wide before she found the room her quarry was sleeping in. Once she discovered him, we can well imagine the rest. It is told to this day in the pubs in Tyrone and Tyrell's Pass that, cursing like a dragoon, Lady Tyrconnel thrashed the unfortunate squireen to within an inch of his life. Apparently awakened suddenly from a drunken sleep, he made no effort to defend himself against the tiger-strong woman. It is told as well that Lady Tyrconnel stalked out of the house, commanded a horse be provided for her, and when a frightened groom brought it, leaped into the saddle and galloped off to Clonaggart Castle, her bright hair tangled but streaming in the wind.

By some strange alchemy, the stark Northumbrian shore, the beautiful unruly family of Delaval, and the romantic pile of masonry, Seaton Delaval, all fuse into a magical legend. All this was a legend while the Admiral and his children were yet alive, a circumstance seldom true.

On a blustering cold winter day, certainly the most inappropriate season one can imagine to walk the grounds running parallel to the sea off Northumbria, Sir John Vanbrugh and Admiral Delaval planned the great house that was to affront the winds, harbor the most fascinating, violent, and profligate race in the North of England, and end its days cracked by decay and blackened by the smoke of encircling collieries, a Valhalla for rooks and bats.

The house rises sheer from the flattened top of a hill on a bold shore. The forecourt in front of the portico is bounded on two sides by flanking wings three hundred feet long, each with its pedimented façade. The floor of the court is like the Champ des Mars, and as desolate. In fact desolation drapes the place like a gorgeous funereal pall. So complete is the mood of magnificent decay, that one waits, wary, poised for anything to happen, like the crescendo in Greek tragedy.

Now the belt of towering oaks that once grouped behind the house has been shattered by the tunnels of the surrounding collieries. Constant hacking at the roots of these fine trees has left the surrounding acres bare. Once the outbuildings and long arcaded stables were as fine as the house. The same flare for scale and address that still gives Seaton Delaval such sublime arrogance was noticeable in all dependent buildings. Today a small-gauge railroad, used to transfer slag to the many high-peaked mounds bulking like a range of miniature saw-toothed mountains to the west of Seaton Delaval, wanders across arid land that was once the park.

The huge main block is three high stories rising from a twenty-foot basement. Surmounting the groups of three engaged columns flanking the entrance door, is a superstructure, a kind of gigantic penthouse. A pediment of richly sculptured stone surmounts this penthouse and is one of the most exciting triangles of carved trophies I have ever seen. The arms of Delaval are surrounded by all the spoils of war. War when it was a contest of arms dictated by the tradition of chivalry. Crossed cannon, fringed banners, helmets crested in flowing plumes. Drums, trumpets, corded and tasseled. Spears, swords, halberds and body armor, the like worn by Roman conquerors, emblazoned with Medusa's vipered head or a rampant stag. A mélange of pure wonder.

The stonework at Seaton Delaval is remarkable for its grand style. All is massive. All is deeply incised, *intaglio profondo*, as Vitruvius wrote. This setting of stones with wide, deep channels between gives tremendous character to the whole building, causing as well a strangely beautiful texture, even now when the house seems, on dark days at least, cold and blank. Seaton Delaval nearly defies description, for it has so many moods. On sunny days of summer, an air of ordinary neglect rides the portico. One feels that only a matter of a short time and lots of moving figures up and down its wide steps will bring the whole picture instantly to life. On days of storm and shrieking wind, it is a tower in Bedlam, battered rooks twitching in death-throes along the cornice shelves, having failed to breast the wind. At night, and the furnaces in the collieries spewing red flame, Seaton Delaval takes on a savage splendor. It is a pagan altar across which livid flame-light shudders, sinks, and dies in the shadows.

Another unpremeditated mood, one of rather bewildered gentleness, gripped the grim hulk one day in spring. I had been stopping with friends at a house a few miles to the east of Seaton Delaval. Never wanting to pass so close to one of my favorite houses without stopping, I had the car driven into the grassy court in front of the steps.

A lovely soft spring morning it was, the sky a limpid robin's-egg blue. As I looked toward the portico, a few panes of glass winked sardonically, but what held me enthralled was the shimmer of white on the broad scarred steps. Four or five long straggling branches of early plum-blossoms lay entangled like a delicate lattice. A few branches were flung hastily into the empty doorway. What was this? Had Seaton Delaval become a temple to Flora in its old age? The delicacy of the gossamer petals and thin brown branches of plum against the dark gray lichened stone of this cavernous old house was unique. Children from the smoky colliery regions had, I expect, built a snowy tent in the shadow of a mountain.

There are three rooms only on the first floor of Seaton Delaval, two flanking the entrance hall at the front, and one across the entire house at the back or garden side. What vista this room once had may be judged by Lady Amherst's writing to her son:

> How I find myself in this ill-omened house of Delaval, I know not. At least no one of the breed is at home. The house overpowers and sets the anger rising, for waste is all about. I cannot gainsay, however, that the prospect from the garden-front windows is fine. Bordered alleys and pleached walls abound. Pools for lilies and carp entrance the eye. No roses grow, for the winds off the sea preclude their blossoming. The blue satin parlour is handsome and the dining room impressive, though the walls and furniture are scarred to ruin by riotous living by that scoundrel Francis, and the lust-mongers he entertains.

Lady Amherst would get a shock if she chanced to look out of the garden-room windows of Seaton Delaval today. Gone into limbo are the pleached alleys and rippling carp ponds. A few hundred yards from the house are a level crossing and a signalman's hut, rising behind this is a ring of blackened slag heaps.

One of the most arresting moments when one wanders around

ruinous Seaton Delaval is the sight of the long line of arches in perspective, of the wings embracing the forecourt. A triumph of diminuendo, seeming more than any other fragment at this timeless barracks to etch the signature of Vanbrugh, who, with his exuberant ideas of what a house should be, built for the ages.

All windows are crowned by winged keystones, massive in scale, and the entire Ionic portico, grim as it appears, is wonderfully simple in detail. Every stone tells. Every window and architrave is a clear picture in the hugely proportioned mass. Vitruvius, Palladio, and Vanbrugh walk hand in hand, surely, in the complete design.

Inside the house the rooms lie moribund. Far more sense of disaster pervades the interior than the scarred façade. This is, of course, due to the devastating fire that occurred in 1822. It transpires that a member of the family residing in the house lighted a fire, the January day being intensely cold. The room in question was the library to the right of the pillared hall. Jackdaws and rooks had built nests in the chimney, and the leaping flames soon caught the rubbish that goes into the building of birds' nests. For hours an exposed beam smoldered, finally a part of the ceiling dropped embers onto the rotting silk banners arranged in battle array at cornice height. So intense was the heat from the blazing roof that the lead corbels posed as finials on the eaves, as well as the ornamental drain pipes, melted and streamed in molten showers down the outer walls. Far out at sea, sailors told afterward, the blazing towers were visible.

Although crowds gathered to gaze in wonder at so marvelous a spectacle, none raised a hand to quench the fire. Down through the rooms where Francis Delaval had held his orgies and played his outrageous practical jokes, the flames ate their way. Red and green and yellow brocade seared on the walls of as many rooms. The pride of the house, Vercelli's sportive ceiling whereon Bacchus drained a boar's skin of purple wine, rained down on the marble floor in black ash. In the hall the galaxy of allegorical ladies, Music, Painting, Geography, Sculpture, Architecture, and Astronomy in their sheltering niches under the cornice, were partially saved, some lost their satin and galloon draperies to flame and smoke, but a worse fate awaited them from rain and wind before the house was roofed over twenty years later. So outraged have these ladies become through ill-usage that they now gaze down at visitors in rancor, minus ears, noses, and one, half her torso.

The litter drifting in heaps across the rose, black, and moss-green marble floors must be kicked aside as one wanders through the echoing rooms. For Echo rules supreme in this vaulted house. Footsteps gain in sound and stature tenfold. To walk the length of the garden saloon is to become one of Lord Dunsany's Gods of the Mountain, of awful import. A pebble tossed into the cornices sends pigeons and bats helter-skelter to another room. The mighty Empress Galla Placidia, when she took in marriage the King of the Goths, caused a monolith of black marble, topped by her insignia of an eagle in full flight, to be erected on a hill near her fortress-castle at Forli, or *Forum Livii* as the Romans called it. The eagle has fallen and lies broken in the waving grasses of a Romagna farm, but the monolith stands, hung with vines, unharmed by the centuries. This was a monument to power and pride of name. So have many monuments been built. Triumphal arches, palaces, churches. Down the centuries man has ever had an urge to saddle posterity with a monument to his ego. Some, like the House of Usher, fall, some seem impervious to pursuing disaster and to time. Some are worthy to stand for centuries, some would never be missed were they to crumble to dust tomorrow.

As a sheer breath-taking monument to architecture in the great tradition, of a magnificence we will never see again, the seat of the mad Delavals, defiant between the sea and the Great North Road in Northumberland, will defy time.

LORD BURLINGTON
AND THE PALLADIANS

And now the curtain rises upon unparalleled activity. The sound of fanfare winds upon the English breeze. A long vista of pale marble porticos is disclosed, diminishing through the vale of Middlesex, through borough and village, into farmland and sea-washed shire. A brilliant throng bearing gold and crimson banners approaches, streaming towards London. All is sound and singing, tumult and shouting. Headed by Anglo-Irish Richard Boyle, Earl of Burlington, the Palladians are approaching.

And a fine vigorous army of enthusiastic dilettantes, architects, artists, and craftsmen it was. Heretofore only a handful of houses in the full Palladian style had risen to bewilder wind-swept gapers, who shouted derision and worse at the open galleries and fog-draped porticos of Italian pleasure houses in an alien—certainly climatically—land. Fine to look at, of course, these temples to Vesta, Hermes, Mars, and Poseidon, but only the daft would want to live in them. And then for some unexplained reason—only that human nature in general is daft—Chiswick House struck the public fancy.

Set a short way out of London on Thames side, an old house named Belchiswick was occupied at one time by the ill-starred Duke of

231

Monmouth, renegade son of Charles II. Wonderful gardens sloping down
to the river had been the feature of the ancient gabled house when Monmouth lived there and met, clandestinely, Sophia Mary Montagu. But to
no lasting happiness, for by royal conniving he was married in haste to
Anna Buccleuch, a "hard, proud piece," as Sophia Mary called her. Old
Belchiswick set the scene for Lord Burlington's fine pavilion house. Unlike so many of this style, built out of hand just to be in the swim, Chiswick materialized in the midst of rose bowers, vine-hung caryatids, and
balustraded terraces, all found. Chiswick House, as Burlington called his
new "toy"—for he was wont to describe the results of his ceaseless architectural activities as "delightful toys"—dominated the entire countryside
when it was first built. Today, rather dilapidated among cheap boxlike
houses and shops, it still carries the air of eighteenth century elegance
and grace, dominating the scene as surely as it has dominated domestic
architecture for nearly three centuries. For remember Villa Rotonda was
mother to Chiswick.

Richard, third Earl of Burlington, was his own architect. It was
in fact the splendid result he attained from this house that won him the
title "Architect Earl." Flitcroft put Burlington's ideas into practical working order, and William Kent designed some of the decoration in the cube
rooms and most of the magnificent furniture.

This house was not meant, ever, to be a permanent dwelling;
rather, it was intended as a sumptuous retreat for a patron of all the arts,
a connoisseur whose collections of books (rare and superbly bound),
coins lying upon ecclesiastical velvet trays, statuary, and paintings were
first in the kingdom.

Hard by, behind a garden wall, stood old Belchiswick, which
Burlington had inherited; so Chiswick House, or Villa, as appears on some
of Kent's sketches, was never the official family seat. Years later when the
Cavendish family had inherited the villa, the beautiful Georgiana, Duchess
of Devonshire, spent a great deal of time there. A painting, only a sketch—
but what a vivid one—was painted by Sir Joshua Reynolds showing
Georgiana seated, surrounded by her admiring court of "élégantes, lit-
térateurs and social somebodies," as Mrs. Middleton wrote to her friend
Mary Delany, on the terrace of the sweeping but intricately designed steps
leading to the six-columned portico. The Duchess wears a "country sack"
of rose muslin, a wide apple-green sash, a tremendous chip hat, danger-

ously and marvelously atilt, and she is hulling strawberries. What a perfect place to do one's hulling.

After the Cavendishes had taken over Chiswick, they found it "small, ill-fitted to dine a company, and generally run down," as a letter to Wyatt discloses. He was asked to remodel the house to make it tenable, and, I presume, ducal.

Wyatt, let it be said in his favor, deplored the task of enlarging so perfect a gem of architecture. But he did as his ducal patron wished, but not very cleverly. His heart was not in it. Two cube wings connect with the main block by low ineffectual galleries, huddled and mean. A labyrinthian tunnel connects each wing with the miniature pavilion, in a depressing manner. Never was greater pity than that the *chef-d'oeuvre* of a man of superb imaginative taste like the Earl of Burlington should have been so mangled, for no good reason. An appeal is now on foot to remove the Wyatt wings entirely, thereby restoring to the advancing generation a building only sixty-five feet square, which is as nearly perfect in scale and proportion as anyone will ever see.

Burlington House in Piccadilly is a village, not a house. When one attends the annual Royal Academy show of paintings, one is amazed at the magnitude of this "Titan's lair," this "great old monster of a house," as my chauffeur in Ireland calls any number of houses where I visit. ("Ye needn't direct me, I know it's that great old monster of a house be the Klinshally road.")

Built by the Architect Earl, or so much remodeled from a series of older buildings that the result was to amaze all London, the house caused fury among a platoon of workmen who were not paid for nearly a year after Burlington was ensconced in his palace. This house dwarfed any other. Lord Verney snorted, on meeting Burlington one day in Piccadilly, "Your London house comprises all London." Servants were quartered in separate tenements abutting on what is now Cork Street. So violently noisy was this arrogant crew of spoiled retainers that the neighbors complained to the major-domo of the household. He sneeringly accused them of prime insolence, whereupon a riot ensued and many heads were bashed in and eyes gouged out. It is said that for days after the white and gold corridors and Palladian reception rooms of Burlington House resembled a field hospital, and when His Grace rang for a lackey, the bandaged appearance of all retainers caused him to retire to Chiswick until the staff at Burlington House had recovered from its battling.

Lord Burlington has been called "the Prince of the Dilettanti," and to some purpose, though by his many fine achievements in the arts I would say he was an extremely accomplished one. William Kent, when he returned from Italy in his thirty-fourth year, became a partner, one might say, with Burlington. Certainly one sees the two names linked many times; for example, in collaboration at Chiswick and alterations at Burlington House where Kent had a suite of rooms placed at his disposal.

William Kent was talented far beyond most men, in an age when men like Vanbrugh combined playwriting in the grand style with designing such resounding monuments as Seaton Delaval, Castle Howard, and Blenheim. Kent was a portrait-painter of skill, his furniture ranks second to none in magnificence of scale and sumptuous detail—like the four Rousham armchairs with mermaids combing their seaweed hair, astride ramping dolphins, forming arms and front legs, all in one piece, carved, gilded, and painted.

At Raynham Hall—haunted by the famous White Lady of Raynham who descends the stair, moaning or smiling, according to how the Townsend fortunes fare—Kent painted a spirited staircase decoration for Lord Townsend, and at Esher Park a dark smoldering piece of scenery which has tremendous sweep of design.

He designed Devonshire House in London (now demolished), a house that for many years was a criterion of all that was glorious in stucco, painted decoration in the grandest of the grand manner, and superb furniture to dress such magnificence. Kent designed whole rooms of carefully considered chairs, banquettes, settees, tables, writing desks, and consoles in the most formal style.

At Rousham, in Oxfordshire, Kent became the presiding genius to General Dormer, a man of exquisite appreciation. Here Kent swept all before him and brought the decorations of this house to the highest possible taste. It was at Rousham that Kent perfected his "Rousham blue" that was to become so famous. A clear sparkling blue, like the luminous sapphire one sees in Italy in the cloaks folded about the shoulders of *quattro-cento* madonnas.

Holkham, The Horse Guards, Houghton Hall, and Badminton: what a rising song to Palladian architecture that quartet of names inspires.

The Horse Guards is a triumph of flat surfaces and grandly designed masses and attendant pavilions. Holkham is a great country house which could as easily stand beside a city square, and by the same token The Horse Guards might just as easily be a country house lying long and lazy in a beech-ringed park in Dorsetshire. A yellow coach-and-four with two chestnuts, and two black-pointed gray wheelers should swing up to its entrance porch. What a sight that would be! Badminton has the most sumptuous length of line of any cupola-topped house in England. The central mass depends on just this exciting lift to balance the long flow of succeeding wings. The great range of frontage that so distinguishes Badminton is composed of nine distinct buildings and six roof-line levels, thereby lending most pleasing variety to an edifice in the highest and most exciting tradition of Palladio, as interpreted by William Kent.

The collection of buildings—again the roof levels are delightful—when Badminton is seen from the west, across and reflected in the large pear-shaped Horse Pond, is unique. For a moment one believes an entirely new house has somehow elbowed its way into the picture. Of course, history is so rampant on every hand at Badminton that long-gone but memorable events we read about at school fairly crackle on all sides.

Is that Henry Beaufort, Duke of Somerset, great-grandson of devious John of Gaunt, arriving bloodstained from the War of the Roses? It could be, right enough, for he skulked home in terror, palsied with an ague, or fear, or both, which never left him, never.

There is a remarkable painting of the "Ruined Earl" of Worcester, who was "shipwrecked, and all his fortune, in the *Royal Stuart* sinking." Raglan, his beautiful house, fell into a desuetude from which no hand could raise it. "The stones wept, all spirit dead."

When the incomparable Canaletto painted three versions of Badminton for the third Duke of Beaufort, he had such superb mastery of lineal composition that his huge canvases give a far more comprehensive even breath-taking sense of the scope of Kent's design than any latter-day photograph has ever done.

No artist but Canaletto could have painted Badminton so sympathetically, for he was, in effect, painting a palazzo in his own Italy. Near Padova it might be. Or near Meledo. Or Starella alla Brenta. Own brother is this stunning house to Palazzo del Strà. Both were built by admirers of Andrea Palladio. Both are richly powerful in feeling.

Badminton has always been a temple to horsemanship. For the Somersets have, since their line began, been famous in the sport of fox-hunting, racing, and *Haute Ecole*. The Beaufort hounds have long been one of the legendary packs in the shires. The blue livery of the hunt, pointed with buff facings, has an eighteenth century air.

In the entrance hall at Badminton there is a life-size painting, about twelve by sixteen feet, of an Arab stallion called Badour. The cream-gray horse is by Wooten and is painted with spirit and strong racial points. The plaster decorations in this room are delightful and noteworthy. Panels, oblong and cube shaped, form a frieze. Foxes hold in their jaws the ends of a rope which is used to tie, in a loosely decorative manner, a mélange of trophy. Whips, spurs, spades, hunting-horns, bows and arrows, all gear for hunting the fox and roebuck.

Houghton has splendor. Splendor on all counts. No other house in England is so ornate. One thinks immediately of the fabulous baroque palaces of the Brandenburg Electors or Herrenhausen. Perhaps this is partly due to the work of Rysbrack, who worked in Saxony where he had fled from his native Belgium as a boy to escape political persecution. After a few years he wandered to England and there engaged in sculpture in many houses for Kent and Colin Campbell. Houghton is actually designed by three architects: Campbell, Ripley, and Kent. But it is the work of Kent that is memorable. Nowhere can the match of Kent's furniture for Houghton be found. It is, in my opinion, and the opinion of countless others, unsurpassed.

The Genoese cut velvet on many of the chairs is beyond compare. Yellow on dark burgundy. Veronese green on white. Crimson on pale gray. Black on primrose. Claret on pale saffron, with gold and silver threads. Pink on silver damask. Black on turquoise. And so the colors flow. Room after room seems more alluring than its neighbor, until dusk comes down, candles are lighted, and the silver, copper, and gilt threads cunningly worked in the damasks and velvets wink in the candlelight. In sunlight or the soft glow of candles, Houghton quickens the pulse.

When Godmersham Park was built for Thomas Brodnax in the hopfields of Kent, the Palladians must have rejoiced. For this house—actually a completely remodeled former seat of the May family—was to strike a clarion note for the elegance and style possible in a medium-size house. Through the years Godmersham has been a criterion for the fastidious. In an age when Gargantuan houses, the like of Wentworth-Wood-house, Holkham Hall, Heveningham, Houghton, Badminton, and Wan-stead House (demolished) were "all the crack," it is refreshing to find this fairly small, eminently distinguished edifice so highly regarded. That the architect is unknown makes the house all the more intriguing. An air of mystery keeps interest alive.

Robert Morris, who worked at Wilton House, may have been em-ployed by Brodnax, but the fine hand of William Kent seems more likely. Certainly the impressive hall, in the very first rank of Palladian style, was designed by Kent. Three oval windows, so effective in the façade, light the upper reaches of the hall. A masterly decoration in freely drawn plaster incorporates all three windows in a frieze.

In all Europe there is no more lovely portico than at Crichel, the "white wonder of the Sturts of Dorset," as Bubb Doddington called the house. Some porticos are handsome and fulfill completely the reason for which the soaring columns were built, to offer a dignified approach. But at Crichel, it is when one sits at table within the portico and looks out and away across the park that the true beauty of this lofty room invades one's consciousness. I have sat at lunch or dinner many times in an Eng-lish summer when the late Lord Alington was alive, and marveled that a room—walls containing statuary-filled niches, doors, and pedimented windows embrace three sides—could be so satisfying when it is really an open loggia, and whitest of white yet full of the subtle color of reflected light and shadow.

Wyatt did this house. To me, it is far his most inspired work.

Throughout the house the coved ceilings are miracles of delicate tracery in plaster, with combinations of color I have never seen elsewhere. Pale mauve, lime green, and gray. Rose, beige, brown, saffron, and black. Venetian pink, beige, russet, indigo blue. Malachite, sienna yellow, black, and pale hyacinth blue. There are three Crichels: Long, Little, and More. More Crichel is the loveliest of the houses.

Kirtlington shouts "Palladio!" through cupped hands. The archi-traved windows are splendid, and the Domingo mahogany doors set in wide plaster moldings are reminiscent of Palazzo Colleoni in Vicenza. Smith was the designer of Kirtlington, in conjunction with J. Sanderson. Smith we know from Chevening, Houghton, and Lyle Abbey. The plan of all these is generally the same. A main block has corridors lower than the wings it connects. Each wing is surmounted by a cupola. Engaged columns of Doric order support a pediment with the tympanum sculptured in flower garlands or trophy.

Sutton Scarsdale and Thames Park, as well as the opulent Rokeby and Stonleigh Abbey, are by Smith. He was prolific and much in demand. An "adamant Vitruvian," Viscount Wenman called him.

A crackling page of English history is that of the Cokes of Holkham. A wondrous fine family, in a wondrous fine house. As far as we can find out, Sir Edward Coke founded the family, as such. He was in full flower during the reign of Elizabeth Tudor, acting as her Attorney General and later as Lord Chief Justice of England under James I. During this last tenure, Sir Edward acquired the vast lands of Holkham and Burnham Overy in Norfolk.

In 1712 at the stripling age of fifteen, Thomas Coke, son of Sir Edward, set out to make the Grand Tour of Europe. He was accompanied by a princely retinue: a "governor" who rejoiced in the resounding name of Hercules Fontenoy Bracegirdle, a tutor, four postilions, a valet, four linkboys—or as some documents say, "front-runners"—and a retinue of two coaches, "one lightsome, one heavy," and five "baggage carts." Few Englishmen traveled so richly.

The tour included France, Italy, and Austria with a year spent in the Electoral Courts of Brandenburg, Hesse-Darmstadt, and Hanover. All during this resplendent tour, Coke was busy collecting statuary, books— his library at Holkham was famous for rare folios of scenes by Piranesi and of Vitruvian triumphs in Rome—as well as cut velvets and damask from the looms of Barri and Geliccili in Genoa. His tutors watched over his purchases at first, but he soon outstripped them by leagues in taste and knowledge, astounding in a man so young.

In Rome he met an Englishman making drawings, as Palladio had done before him, of Vitruvian ruins and early Renaissance palaces. William Kent was his name. A few years later he was asked to design a countryseat to perpetuate the glory of the Cokes and house the rare treasures brought back by Thomas Coke from his travels. He told Kent: "My dear joy are my books. Make my library a rival of the Vatican."

Few men survive in posterity for simply building a house, however grand. Coke of Holkham, later Earl of Leicester, has turned the trick, for Holkham is so extraordinary a house on all counts that its founder will always be remembered. One reason Holkham is unique in a country of vast, extravagantly planned country houses is that both Coke and Kent planned it primarily for the treasures it was to house; a treasure house of the arts first, a dwelling house afterward. In 1734 the cellars were dug. It is said that a building, curious for those days, was erected a half-mile from the site chosen for the house, a sort of hangar. In this tarpaulin-covered shell was housed £400,000 worth of treasure, guarded day and night by a platoon of soldiers.

Holkham follows very much the Palladian plan of an oblong 120 feet long, with a gallery flanking it, and an oblong wing adjoining at either end. In short, an Italian palace from the brain of, first, Vitruvius, and later Andrea Palladio in the hills of Meledo, via William Kent. The house is built of Peterstone brick, which the winds of the sea close by have weathered to a silvery beige. The entrance hall is one of the most famous rooms in the world. Thomas Coke stood spellbound in the atrio of the full-scale temple of justice model built of cardboard, painted, for a festa in Rome. A painted piece of scenery, nothing more. But hugely evocative. He cried, "I will build it of marble!" He did.

Spellbinding is the word. Entirely of alabaster and marble, the rise of fluted marble columns with gilded Doric capitals fills the eye as few architectural gestures do anywhere. As so frequently happens, houses of the magnitude of Holkham take so long in the building that the owners die before they can enjoy the pleasures of the dream. This happened to Thomas Coke. His nephew, a noted sportsman, known as Coke of Norfolk, succeeded to this vast estate. Cock-fighting, fox-hunting, rough shooting, and fishing the numerous streams in the vicinity filled his mind. The library amassed by his studious uncle lay dormant, behind locked doors. Hospitality waxed as never before. Activity in the huge vaulted kitchen is said to have assumed such proportions that ten cooks held sway during the hunting season. Lord Gore called his visits to Holkham "such riots of food and folly as spend my purse and health. But these I would not forego, for love of my pleasant Coke." His close friend Charles James Fox said, "He is pure ornament to this realm. A firm friend and a sportsman to whom the very foxes bow and the birds halt for his shots." Coke was offered six peerages during his life, but refused them all, fearing the creation would involve him in politics, which he loathed. To William Pitt the younger on the occasion of refusing an earldom, he said, "I resent being called from my cocking-main or my shoots to vilify my opponents; I'd rather rid my farm of vermin with beagles."

A house called Ston Easton, standing in the apple orchards of lovely Somerset, commands attention. Not only for its simple dignified Palladian façade, but for the reason that it contains a room so impeccably proportioned and decorated—both architecturally and in the inspired furnishings—that though it meant traveling many miles to view it one would be mightily rewarded. In the manner of Kent and Ware, it is said to have been built from elevations "from a book, copied out close and detailed."

The saloon seems to me, when I stand within its portals my eyes sweeping over the countless beauties of stucco, grisaille, and carved architraves, to be one of the few thoroughly satisfying rooms within my knowledge. When I have left Ston Easton, weeks, months, years later, I recall the impact of gray against Venetian red, accented by gilt and black; then I know it is one of the big five of the rooms I have seen. I once had a house near Rome, a pavilion far from a frequented road. In this house, when I took it for let, was a big bare room. Within six months it was bare no longer. It was the talk of the Roman season. I had done it over, as nearly as I could, to evoke the Palladian saloon at Ston Easton.

A wide frieze carries completely around the room under the molded cornice. This has richly relieved shells and swags of fruit, white against a background of Venetian red. Gray are the walls, black and gilt the furniture, upholstered in rose-red damask, and the grisaille panels are framed in white stucco ornamentation of great beauty of detail. The entrance door and overmantel are treated as a columned portico with a magnificent pediment of carved fruit and vines.

Wanstead, in Essex, considered by many as Colin Campbell's most supreme Palladian gesture, contained the famous olive-green and gold-leaf ballroom, where an entertainment that was the sensation of society was held the night before the house was razed. The guests, who had been asked to come dressed in brilliant scarlet, were not told of this until they were on the point of departure. So Wanstead went out of this world in a scarlet blaze of finery.

Giacomo Leoni was the only Italian member of the Palladians in England. A protégé of Lord Burlington, he enjoyed attention both to his person and his talents. Besides having his book on Andrea Palladio mag-

nificently produced by Burlington, he designed, carte blanche, **Lyme Hall.**
The portico of this huge Italian villa reminds one enormously of **Villa**
Malcontenta della Brenta. Carved sheaves of rushes in the pediment **are**
free and deeply incised.

Leoni's most renowned works are his additions to Moor Park, which
contains some of the finest stuccowork in England, as well as vast painted
walls by Thornhill and Amigoni. The pedimented windows are vast **in**
scale.

Isaac Ware comes into the Palladian picture in England but briefly.
His work is as thin and vitiated as his person is said to have been. His
nose dripped eternally and he spizzled through his teeth when talking.
Fox called Ware "a pusillanimous piece of manikin." Ware's linen **was**
dirty, his staircases narrow deathtraps, but his beautifully proportioned
rooms cleanse his memory.

Ware designed Wrotham Park near Chicksands in Bedfordshire,
but it has never signified as a great house. Most of his London houses **have**
met disastrous fates, by demolition, blitz, and the like. In Soho Square **are**
a few fine façades still. Ware was a cockney born within hearing of **Bow**
Bells. It is fitting that his best houses should have risen to beautify **the**
London scene. He had no feeling for the splendid country house.

Flitcroft, on the other hand, had so much feeling for country houses
that he built Wentworth-Woodhouse, the largest house in England, **six** hundred feet long. If I called Burlington House in London a village, I should
then call Wentworth a city. No other house I know is so full of anachro-
nisms and blunders of proportion as this sprawling pile. Yet by the **very**
preponderance of sculptured masonry, Wentworth-Woodhouse presents a
breath-taking appearance. A pun has been thrown at the façade of Wentworth by George IV who visited there. "Built by Böth? [German archi-
tect] Why Both-er?"

It has been said that Böth had a hand in the original designs. **The**
famous Whistlejacket Room is unique, for the life-size painting, by Stubbs,
of Lord Rockingham's golden stallion, Whistlejacket, dominates a white
stucco and green Genoese velvet apartment of unbridled splendor. In the
dining room of Wentworth there is a large collection of Stubbs' paintings
of mares and foals bred at Wentworth Stud, which is remarkable and
beautiful of its kind. Open-faced coal pockets and mine shafts now march
to the very portico of this foundering house. Smirched by coal dust and

shored up in places, this banner to Fitzwilliam pride awaits a fate that no one can predict.

Carr built houses in York in the Palladian taste, but they are of no great moment. The brothers Wood of Bath, however, are of another kidney. Bath rose in grandeur and remains now, in spite of brutal treatment in the bombing of Great Britain, a wondrous city to behold.

So graciously does Bath rest upon its semicircular hill, a verdant valley spread at its feet, that no other city, anywhere, is comparable. Bath stands proudly within her crescents, singularly alone.

Wood the elder used for his buildings a mauve-white local stone that is very subtle. In sunshine it is glittering white with deep violet shadows. In moonlight the walls take on a rose-violet hue. The two Woods followed the Palladian movement strictly. In fact, so little did either one deviate from firm classical teaching that one wishes for a shade more imagination in their work. Wood the elder showed more freedom in his interiors than his exteriors. The Crescents, the Circuses, the Paragon, give Bath a cachet unparalleled. The culmination is, of course, the Royal Crescent, which sweeps in an immense half-circle or pillared majesty until the senses reel. Shades of Sarah Siddons, Georgiana Spencer (Duchess of Devonshire), Mrs. Middleton, Beau Brummell, The Bracegirdle, The Beautiful Lady Blessington, all seem to glide in and out of the pedimented doorways today, "furnishing the town with wonder," as Sheridan wrote.

A few private houses survive and are, to me, memorable. Titanbarrow, in Bathford, is a delightful house; the pediment, rising above Corinthian-capped columns, bears three extraordinarily vital pineapples, carved with much swank.

Batheaston claims Eagle House, built in 1729 by John Wood. This house has more character to the square inch than one can imagine. I should love to live for a time at Eagle House. Built of warm rose brick, it is pointed up with Bath stone and has massive chimneys. Seeming to have lighted in transit on the apex of the small pediment surmounting a niche is an eagle, wings spread to fly away again to heights above the clouds.

Rosewell House is pure Italian rococo. Caryatid pilasters support the window moldings. Two male, two female, depicting the four seasons. When looking at this house, one feels the warm Italian air eddying about, for the essence of Verona or Padova emerges entire. John Strahan is said to have designed this house on his return from a Grand Tour in 1735.

The Palladians had their fling as regally and completely as **any** other group of persons within history. To England, Ireland, Scotland, even Wales, though few instances are found in these wildly beautiful mountains, they gave a magnificent and lasting heritage. The end was **not** yet, for the Adams came trumpeting along. A bit more delicate in conception. A shade more effete. Classicism fined down, as it were. **James** Wyatt rose to almost unimagined fame. Henry Holland enjoyed **the** friendship and patronage of the Prince Regent. John Nash shone in Holland's reflected glory. The fusing of ideas, of taste, of an epoch, between the Palladians and the Regency was handled in expert style by Robert Adam.

ROBERT ADAM AND THE CHANGING FACE OF LONDON

When the Palladians retired to rest from their labors, within the walls of their templelike mansions, no letup in building great country houses occurred. Robert Adam, late out of Scotland, rode into the lists full armed with a number of splendid designs for houses, which he forthwith set about erecting for fastidious patrons. Syon House rose in the rustling reaches of Ilesworth, proud and architecturally impressive behind tall gateposts upon the top of which raging lions seem eternally to forbid entrance to this rural stronghold of the Dukes of Northumberland. Kedleston in Derbyshire, Saltram, Brocket Hall, all are supreme examples of the subtle elegance and graceful tailoring of stone and stucco as Robert Adam of the four Scottish brothers would have it. There were four sons born to William Adam who built Hopetoun. Of these the only names we hear in the architectural world are Robert and James. James assisted his brother in London more than in building big country houses.

To me Syon House is a dream. Once one has wandered through the rooms of Syon and departed, memories like those of a dream occur at odd times. Memories of up-sweeping line. Of gilded figures out of legend and Greek myths, standing against lapis lazuli walls. Walk out of Syon, but you do not wholly leave this gravely beautiful house. It marches ever with you.

Explaining in minute detail all his ideas on architecture in his book, *Ruins of the Palace of the Emperor Diocletian at Spalatro in Dalmatia*, published in 1764, Adam contrived to introduce severe classical forms into decoration for walls, ceilings, furniture, even to the hardware used, until a complete whole in "Adam Style" resulted. I believe that the unity of idea resultant in his work can scarcely be paralleled by any other architect. He employed the best artists and craftsmen of his time. Angelica Kauffmann, whose painted decorations I do not altogether admire, and Antonio Pietro Zucchi often painted walls, ceilings, and furniture—usually medallions—for Adam.

Robert Adam, painstaking in assembling his houses, required that exteriors, interiors, furniture, and liveries for servants must harmonize. So deeply did the Adam style impinge upon the imagination of the discerning, that imitators of his work have multiplied down the years since his death. Robert Adam was the first architect to use an entire row of buildings to create one flowing motif. Adelphi Terrace in London is probably the most notable example I can think of to illustrate this point. He devised many graceful schemes for housing in the lovely but woefully overcrowded city of Bath. The University of Edinburgh is one of his chief works. But it was the great country houses situated in spreading parks wherein his genius lay.

Kedleston remains one of the glories to English architecture and its creator Robert Adam, alike. As we find so often true, it is the vast entrance hall of Kedleston that both fills and astounds the eye, first off, by the magnitude of its scale and the imagination that conceived it.

The Alabaster Hall it is called. Twelve fluted columns rise twenty-six feet to a wide cornice in which winged griffons disport among papyrus fans, gold, highly burnished—as is all Adam gilt—against lapis lazuli. The high coved ceiling in the Alabaster Hall is strong in line, but immensely delicate in detail so that in a dim light one has to strain the eyes a bit to see that urns of flowers on tripods alternate with slender flowering trees, all bound into panels by a trailing vine motif.

Brettington and Paine is written large on a number of the elevations for Kedleston. There is always controversy about these houses, because sometimes three or more architects and designers of furniture, stucco, and the attendant details which make the finished house, work singly or together. It seems apparent to me that nearly all the interior of Kedleston was done by Robert Adam. His inimitable touch, at once so firm and so delicate, is all about the place.

The coldly formal aspect of the Alabaster Hall called forth all sorts of abuse, jibes, and even catcalls. A drunken guest at an evening party punched the noses of all the Greek sculptured figures in the niches, and broke the bones in his hand in the fracas. Dr. Johnson called it "a dank sepulchre, fit only for a test of Samson's strength." A Mrs. Arbuthnot fell down on the slippery marble floor and had to be generously recompensed with a fine jewel. Mrs. Delany writes in her *Daily Round Journal:* "What Confusion at Kedleston. A Lady cracked her head slipping on the Dais [probably erected for chairs of state] when presented. I doubt not she survives, for a Costly Brooch was pressed upon her as a Keepsake." Mrs. Delany seems to have had a keepsake complex, for she is constantly referring to them in her letters.

No other house in England seems to recall the great Renaissance palaces in Italy, with red and purplish brown brocade-hung walls and gilded gesso doors and architraves, as much as some of the state rooms at Kedleston.

Adam was fortunate to live in the same era as Thomas Chippendale, for the two masters worked amazingly well together, each complementing the other and bringing out his best points. The ebullient curtains and sweeping pelmets conceived by Chippendale were used to the very hilt by Adam in some of his finest rooms. Some of these were a full production in themselves. At Harewood House, in coal-pitted Yorkshire, this fact is well established, for the crimson and gold pelmet in the Adam saloon is as important and full-looped as an Electoral Box at the Opera House in Dresden when the Bibiena contrived the ballet and the *grande entrée.*

No lovelier house was ever designed for a touted beauty than number 19 Grosvenor Square—the numbers are now changed and this house blown half asunder by enemy bombs—near famous old Derby House. Miss Boonton was from Yorkshire. Her place in county society was suspect to London rank and fashion, but to the bloods in search of a fortune with which to ward off the daily irks of life, her purse was not. What Miss Boonton had to offer was much. A deliciously pretty face and sumptuous figure, all accompanied by masses of money. "Old Boonton" was a cloth-merchant, whose family had always held high place in the profitable wool trade. Gossips said the elderly red-faced man who established Miss Boonton in her charming house was not her father, but her protector. The lady tossed her shining curls and laughed. London. What a mind!

Robert Adam outdid himself. A four-story house of rose brick, pointed in Portland stone. A white and gold and lapis-blue entrance hall, a green and silver and sepia dining room, a saloon and boudoir of rare delicacy decorated in vines painted by Vioni of Venice, and pearl-collared sphinxes acting as free-standing caryatids to support the window pediments.

It is told that after a gay drum at her house, Miss Boonton would ask a few cronies to remain behind to talk over the party, usually the best part of her entertainments. One evening a great deal of champagne had been drunk and a playful youth, madly in love with Miss Boonton, conceived the idea of surreptitiously removing her double string of pearls and hanging them around the neck of one of the chokered sphinxes. When the hue and cry of robbery had passed, he would retrieve the pearls and earn his adored one's gratitude, and the gods knew what other favors. All went well until the smitten young man, having taken a few more glasses of wine to give him courage, forgot which sphinx he had collared in Miss Boonton's pearls. She had meanwhile discovered her loss, and her screams rang through Grosvenor Square with awful shrillness. At last the frantic youth remembered and grasped at the pearls too hard; the gut broke and spilled them upon the carpet every which way. Days later the lady visited the young man in gaol and effected his release, on condition that he play no more tricks.

Records show that the mysterious Miss Boonton lived in great style in Holland as Baronne Letérier. One of the last portraits by Gainsborough is of this lady painted after her marriage to Letérier. It is called *Lady with a Muff* and shows a brilliant-eyed woman of stirring beauty, winter clad. Her brown velvet hat is awave with blue-gray plumes, and she has thrust her hands into a muff of soft gray fur.

Carpets were almost an obsession with Robert Adam. One of the rarest heritages left by him are the legion beautiful rugs and large circular and octagonal carpets designed by him and expertly executed by Thomas Moore. The glorious gold, red, and green rug, forty feet in circumference, in the dining room at Holkham is epic in needlework. The design of immense floriated scrolls with a twisted ribbon border is remindful of carpets at Osterley Park, where the pink and gold Tapestry Room is to be found. Adam designed tapestries (executed by Gobelin) and rug and chair coverings of flower-strewn petit point for this room. Certainly this warmly glowing room is as complete as the imagination of one superlatively gifted artist could make it. The pink, crimson, and gold dining room at Osterley with Adam's lovely lyre-backed chairs is a room to cherish in any age.

Hepplewhite came into the stream of artisans towards the end of Adam's and Chippendale's career. But there are instances where Hepplewhite's attenuated chairs and settees were used by Adam. For example at Bowood. To me, Bowood, stunning house though it is inside and out, means stables. For the Bowood stables, not designed but remodeled very successfully by Adam, are more perfectly appointed for thoroughbred horses than most houses are for human beings. The stewards' room in the main block of the stables, with its four corner cupboards, features in carved wood the puff-cheeked winds, North, South, East, and West. Whether the horses notice the freedom and spirit in the carving of these elements, I do not know. Horses always appreciate being well housed. So I expect they do.

Chinoiserie was vastly becoming to the style of room called Adam. Mirrors in particular reached the heights of ornamentation, often fantastically intricate in carving of staircases, cascades, rocky islands crowned with palm trees, and pagodas containing singing birds from Dresden. The famous mirrors at Crichel are the finest I have ever seen in the Adam-*chinoiserie* style. Twelve feet tall, gilded, and resoundingly carved *con brio*, these mirrors are part of the architectural motif of the drawing room, complementing in design the Genoese cut-velvet curtains.

In my New York flat I have a tall Venetian mirror, very much in the style I mention. Ever since I bought it in Venice many years ago it has virtually governed my life. The wall it hangs on must be at least sixteen feet in height. I raised the roof of the room where this mirror hangs— literally raised it—five feet when I designed the alterations of the flat from scratch. Greyhounds of *sette-cento* Venice crouch upon the fern-wreathed pediment of this mirror. What gives it distinction, a delightful *Commedia dell' Arte* touch, is the fact that the tails of the greyhounds are floriated and cascade down the sides of the mirror in garlands.

When drawing his elevations for interiors, Robert Adam apparently enjoyed himself as much as Andrea Palladio appeared to, and in much the same vein. Adam drew fanciful annotations and fragments of design on the margins of his huge sheets of "pale olive buff" paper, as he called the rag-paper sheets, made especially for him. The Adam drawings for Saltram are entrancing. The long, magnificently varied and composed façade of the building attracts me no end. The two oblong stable blocks with curtain walls and great domed gates, deeply rusticated, give tremendous style to the frontage. Stables always do. At Russborough in Ireland it is the stables and massive gates—a pair of them, flanking the front— leading to the paddocks that give more than a hint of the treasured thoroughbreds craning from loose-boxes for sugar or an apple. The gate arches act as finials. Saltram elevations bear a card painted in *trompe l'oeil*. Attached to a compass by a shaded ribbon, it reads in flowing script: *The Rt. Hon. Lady Katherine Parker, at Saltram.* The drawing was dedicated, as a souvenir, to the daughter of Lord Morley.

An extremely interesting fragment of drawing was once shown to me in Ireland. It concerned the proposed staircase in Headfort, County Meath; the interior of this house is among the finest works of Robert Adam. This particular staircase hall was modified and greatly simplified, I think not for the better. However, the drawing was made on an old piece of parchment paper, which in smeared and faded ink contained an elevation of Chevening, in Kent, the work I believe of Inigo Jones. I am intrigued to know why Adam was using this sheet at his fashionable John Street office. Scrawled in one corner of Adam's proposed plan is *Adelphi, 1772.* At Chevening the morally unstable Lady Ann Palmer-cum-Fitzroy,

The Evolution of a Country House by Robert Adam, Using the Principles of Andrea Palladio, Is Demonstrated by These Four Sketches.

daughter of Charles II and Barbara Villiers, rampaged her life to tatters. Here, much like La Malcontenta, she was remanded in duress vile.

Adam once wrote to Moore, who made his carpets: "Chatsworth is a fair house, better within than without. Why is Tallman not better known?" Why indeed? William Tallman is seldom even mentioned though he designed one of the grandest ducal houses in England, Chatsworth in Derbyshire. Here the Cavendishes live surrounded by their legion art treasures, one of the most valuable private collections in Europe. Tallman built a charming pavilion on a lake at Drynam, then we hear no more of him.

On went the years. The Regency acclaimed Wyatt for Heaton Park, and his Irish houses. Heveningham Hall in Dorset set Wyatt very high in the notice of the Regent, because of the ravishingly painted saloon, by the brush of Biagio Rebecca. Henry Holland built Carlton House behind its Ionic screen to keep at bay the smoldering venom of an angry populace. The hated Regent planned a new ball, having just buried the one of the night before, and sneered behind the blowing draperies. Sir John Soane conceived the Bank of England as a mighty bulwark. His dream came true. A house was built in a green dell outside London for Lady Blessington. Thomas Turlby, her footman, designed it. It was a fiasco and she never lived in it. Turlby then went to work for John Nash. Now came "Nash's tissue-paper London." Flimsy white colonnades wound in and out along the Serpentine and the Regent's Park.

The great days of England's architecture waned. Inigo Jones, Sir Christopher Wren, Sir John Vanbrugh, Colin Campbell, Robert Adam, Sir William Chambers, have left more than enough style and dignity in architecture to inspire all who see it for a long time to come.

WILLIAM ADAM:
VITRUVIUS SCOTICUS

The seventeenth century may be said to have burst upon Scotland with a display of architectural fireworks. The Scottish nobles found themselves far richer in actual coin of the realm than they had been for two hundred years. Many were richer than at any time since the clans had emerged, claymore in hand, from the mists of antiquity. This affluence was due greatly to the secularization of ecclesiastical properties at the Reformation. Trade mounted. Export of wool and hides improved many pockets. The buying and selling of real estate in Edinburgh, Glasgow, and the far-flung environs of both teeming cities filled hitherto woefully empty exchequers. A few built townhouses. Witness stately Melville House in Edinburgh, the residence of Admiral Duncan, hero of Camperdown. It was made of the finest "laid stone, dressed and delivered before, chipped to talley after, and paid for on completion," as the building book tells you. Or Baron Ord's huge house in Queen Street, Edinburgh, which reached its prime in the Regency, though it was begun many years before, when massive almost fortress construction was used by Scottish builders for town and country houses, alike.

It is in the "Great country houses of the Yesters and the Hopes" (as William Adam wrote his son Robert, admonishing him against aggrandizement, which he contended ruined many otherwise fine houses) that we find the most sudden, deliberate *volte-face* concerning the shedding of the old and the adopting of the new, in erecting stone and stucco countryseats.

William Adam speaks of the Hopes, a rich and politically powerful French family, who came to Scotland as advisers to Madelaine, first wife of James V, in 1537. The family, for all their prominence in Army circles as well as administrators of Scottish law, were never particularly well housed until 1697, when an enormous house, long and ornate of frontage, was begun by Sir William Bruce for his patron, the Earl of Hopetoun. This sweeping spread of masonry is four stories and a generous attic in height, crowned with a stone balustrade supporting a veritable panache of handsomely varied urns. A few of the old die-hard Highland chieftains snorted at what they termed "paste-pot, lace-paper" architecture, silly, destructible, and downright sybaritic. Give them a gaunt, towering, battlemented fortress-castle complete with portcullis and workable drawbridge. Somewhere within its walls a warm snuggery could be found to house women and bairns. But if an Englishman's house was his castle, then surely a Scot's house was his peel tower, or fortified keep.

No—this "Scottish Palladian" house for the proud Hopes would not do at all. But it did. Many fine large houses began to take form in the Lowlands. Yester House, Winton House, Haddo House, and Drum. All these are beautifully lived in today by owners who are proud of the fine houses built by their forefathers, and happy to show an interested visitor about.

Even if Hopetoun House, flung out on the shore of Firth of Forth in West Lothian, had not had two long pavilion-like wings connected to the house by colonnaded demilunes in the manner of Russborough and Castletown in Ireland, it would have been a singularly well-proportioned house. But the additions designed by William Adam which appreciably lengthen the frontage, swinging around to embrace the forecourt, add a sense of lightness to the whole mass that is both delicate and powerful at the same time; delicacy and powerful lines fuse, as in the conformation of a thoroughbred race horse.

Hopetoun has great style, an elegance of mood, well sustained in every line and detail. One feels that neither architect left so much as a hidden basement window to chance. When William Adam added the two wings to the William Bruce center block a few years after it was built, his admiration was so great for the work of his colleague that he went all out in designing his cupola-topped pavilions. He never again—to the minds of many authorities—touched the clarity of proportion, in the best Palladian tradition, that he reached when enriching the façade of Hopetoun House.

For all its classicism of Doric colonnades, pedimented windows, urn-topped balustrades, and lantern-shaped cupolas, Hopetoun is primarily a Scottish house, no doubt at all of that. A massive calm broods over the many-windowed front, backed by the heavily foliaged oaks of East Lothian. There is a unity of mood in the placing of so important a house athwart the wide reaches of restless water, for Firth of Forth is never quiet. Wooded hills gaze back at Hopetoun from the far shore. Fishing fleets are constantly "riding out and driving back, breasting the choppy water," as Robert Burns wrote of this firth. A typical Scottish scene.

The interior of Hopetoun House is very grand, but not as impressive as one might expect, considering the sweep of the outside. The rooms seem rather narrow, legion halls and wide corridors intersecting the plan at every turn. The plaster ceilings, especially those in the ballroom, are good of the period. The widely varied collection of French and Italian paintings, many of early and late Renaissance, seem to be far the greatest treasures of the house.

Winton House, East Lothian, enjoys a striking location, silhouetted against the sky. More French than Italian in feeling, it is still of classic mood, and no finer windows, tall, wide, and well spaced, are to be found in Scotland. William Wallace, the builder of the façade, which is thrown up against a far older building, emerged from obscurity to build Winton. A suite of rooms, now called "King Charles' Gallery," was entirely decorated to honor the visit of Charles I in 1633. So successful was his stay at "cheerfull Winton, where," he wrote, "I picked plums and raced my spaniels," that in admiration for its owner he sent him a portrait by Van Dyck. It is thought by many that Sir Walter Scott in writing *The Bride of Lammermoor* had Winton in mind when evoking Ravenswood. The great staircase at Winton House is tremendous in its sweep, recalling some of the early Renaissance châteaux in Touraine.

Of Yester House one could speak reams. There is a gaiety to the lilt of its roof line, both in the main house, very spaciously accommodating nine windows across, and in the two pavilions flanking the center, pedimented above four flat Ionic columns. The central part, three windows wide, rises two stories above the long oblong that is the main block. William Adam designed this house with one eye, it would seem, on some of the lyrical Dutch country houses, Grundorp and the white tile Bentinck houses near The Hague. As well, I have seen many houses in the environs of Dresden and Potsdam with the same bell-cast roofs and entablatures embracing swags and flower-filled urns above tall fanlighted windows. The garden side of Yester is particularly pleasing, for one gets the best view of the house from this side. The detached pavilions have a flight of steps leading to terraced walks, and the central block has a curiously pleasant air of a "flowerhouse," not only because it embraces a wide blossoming acre, but also because a terraced garden room is let into the basement under the pediment on this side.

The high tiled roof contains, six across, dormers that are sunk into the roof; the tops of the small-paned windows are flush with the roof line, the bottoms rest on a wide window sill.

The interior of Yester House is in the very flower of Palladianism. Many authorities are of the opinion that the drawing room at Yester is the finest Palladian room in Scotland. The room is immensely lofty. The ceiling is fourteen feet from the cornice to the central panel, the sides rake in a suave curve. The plasterwork (anonymous) is particularly free and richly conceived. The four corners of the coved panel contain urns from which stalks of wheat and fernleaves describe flowing curves. Doves and smaller birds flit among the fronds. The whole has a great sense of sparkle and liveliness.

In this saloon are ten huge paintings, which actually form a mural decoration, although each is a separate motif on its own. They are framed in wide plaster molding and deeply incised in a design of ferns. The scenes represent romantic ruins in the classic taste and are beautifully rich and varied in color. In 1761, a French painter named Delacour painted these panels for the exact spaces in which they now hang.

Yester House occupies the site of an older house. From its terraces one sees ancient Yester Castle, made famous in Scott's *Marmion*. This grim old tower of ivy and lichened stone was built in 1267 by Sir Hugo de Gifford. Accredited to be a wizard, Sir Hugo terrified everyone, even the most arrogant and stalwart border laird. He lived on the wild reaches of Hopes Water in studious solitude.

Two magnificent Waterford glass chandeliers of truly bewildering scale and delicacy grace the saloon at Yester. The stairway is sweeping and pleasant to mount or descend, for the treads are wide and shallow. Palladio propounded to his apprentices the Vitruvian axiom regarding stairs:

Let the rise be gentle, stairs are not ladders. Let the tread be wide, lest sandle toes betray the unwary, and blundering footsteps ensue. The body motion when ascending a flight of stairs should be that of breasting a slight rise of ground where the path is smooth. When descending a staircase, the motion should be as if stepping lightly down from one cloud to another.

Mellerstain House gains greatly in importance by the thickly wooded heights from which a spreading parkland drops gently away to a large sedgy lake and a panorama out of fable, the distant violet-bronze of the Cheviot Hills. A long house of semifeudal castellated style, it is built in three sides of a quadrangle. The house, which is fairly old, belonged to Sir Patrick Hume, later Lord Polwarth, and was "dressed with additions," as a contemporary of Robert Adam wrote, about 1775. What Adam really did was to design a big, square, four-story house—one story and attic higher than the two earlier ones—to act as a center to a pair of three-story stone houses that had been built fifty years before. The finest exterior feature of Mellerstain House is the extraordinarily long reach of the double level terraces that extend for five hundred feet in two tiers in front of the house. Intersected by curving steps, balustraded in finely turned granite, the urn-embellished terraces give tremendous style and importance to the severe frontage, displaying seventeen windows across.

The richly wooded broadlands of Berwickshire and Roxborough— Mellerstain is on the border—contain many fine houses, feudal and eighteenth century, but none has quite the baronial air encountered when approaching "great Mellerstain, Haddington's pride," as Scott called the house.

Marching in unison with the splendid coved saloon at Yester House is the library at Mellerstain. Robert Adam outdid himself, in Scotland at least, when he designed this room. The proportions are noble, the plasterwork inspired, and the carved pilasters and cornice moldings of the tall bookcases that dress three walls of the room he has never bettered. A series of panels in the form of a frieze shows armored warriors and spear-bearing amazons apparently in parley, for the amazons use their spears as staves, and the helmeted warriors lift their visors and lean upon their shields. The figures gain in power because they are white against an *aubergine* background. The room is fifty by twenty feet and sixteen feet in height. The freedom of design in the plasterwork of the ceiling is enhanced no end by inserting painted plaques of woodland scenes and heads of Roman emperors and empresses among the white foliations.

Drum House, situated in a vast park in verdant Midlothian, seems to have assumed the state of parenthood to half the houses of England and Virginia—particularly after 1789, when the great wave of Georgian architecture swept both countries—in the same manner that Villa Malcontenta and Villa Rotonda did in Italy, Ireland, and England seventy-five years before.

Character seems to me the best word to describe Scottish houses with any pretense to Palladianism. Whether it is severely classical Hopetoun House or dark, deceitful Craigiggin in Morayshire. Always there is some strong note of waywardness in the design, which sets the house aside in one's memory, to be taken out of the mind's pigeonhole in retrospect and examined closely. For example, there is one of the most delightful of all wayward houses, Craigiggin, where a bland highwayman lived.

One comes upon this old gray house of harled stone in a most unexpected manner. After passing through the village of Cardo, the road winds downhill through a silent wood of oaks. Presently a wide stone "pack bridge" presents itself and after one crosses and turns to the right, there lies Craigiggin in a dark lonely valley. The main block of the house is palpably a late seventeenth century addition to an earlier fortress. It is a classical three-story oblong, brown, gray, and striped in white harl lines, caused by lime whitening the mortar between the stones and spattering over into "pancakes." A heavy balustrade dresses the top story, with pedimented windows and a Palladian window, used as a door, piercing the center front. What gives the tremendous character is a high peel tower, ornamented at the four corners with candle-snuffer turrets. Feudalism *versus* Classicism in one remote old Scottish house.

Gordonstoun, in Morayshire, is in part—two parts to be exact—feudal. There is a beautifully proportioned three-story and attic central block, so fully harled as to appear white spotted in dark polka dots. From the driveway front, seen from the road through fine double gate pillars crowned with covered urns, one observes only the Palladian façade, displaying tall, well-spaced windows and an arrangement of engaged Doric columns supporting a pediment. But once the grouped trees are passed, two old castellated wings with high peaked dormers and massive twisted chimneys appear.

When Adam Black and J. J. Robinson, Edinburgh publishers, brought out the large and handsome volume, *Vitruvius Scoticus*, by William Adam, the year was 1726. This might be said to be the middle years of the Palladian reign in architecture in the British Isles. William Kent, Lord Burlington, Colin Campbell, the Venetian Leoni, and others styled the Palladians, had held the reins since 1715. After William Adam died and bequeathed his voluminous mantle to his two sons, a lighter touch than the powerful, grandiose Palladian style (the true Vitruvian) came slowly into focus. Known as "Adam," as simple as that, this style endured supreme, until ten years preceding the coronation of George IV of England. This conceited, flamboyant prince, whose escapades and extravagances gave a name, the Regency, to modes and furniture, architecture and behavior for twenty-five years, left a heritage in decoration that is by far the best thing he ever did. Light, graceful, and luminous in color, Regency houses and furniture are considered collectors' items in the markets of the world today.

When William Adam designed Drum House, he built, in effect, Villa Trissino at Meledo or Villa Cornaro at Piombino Desi. In fact a generous fusing of the two. The central block of Drum House is entirely rustico, while the intermediary wings, two stories in height, which join the three-story pendant cube wings to the main house, are treated to rustico trim around the windows. This, with deeply indented coinstones, is the same treatment given the windows in the cubes. A fine Palladian window, extremely high and generously arched, surmounts the segmental pediment of the entrance door. When Drum was first built, it was sneered at by the country people round about Gilmerton, but when word began to drift in that such fine houses as Balveny House, Banffshire, and Tindwall, Belhaven, Dumfries House, Seggiedin—very like Caledon in County Tyrone, Ireland—Haddo House, and Craigiehall, were the order of the day, the tune of derision changed immediately. Drum House was then eulogized in song and story. "Drum, Drum, Gilmerton's Pride" was used as a clan song.

Haddo House is so beautifully articulated that it is, I think, the master stroke of William Adam when he occupied his mind in designing this Scottish countryseat in the grand manner of Palladio. In *Vitruvius Scoticus*, Adam dwells at length and lovingly on his initial conception of the house, and his delight when it was "roofed and chimneyed, fires lighted and a carpet laid upon the stair," which apparently denoted a house ready for occupancy.

Adam designed another house to march with the Haddo House park in Aberdeenshire. This house never got beyond the carefully limned elevation stage. It was to be called Penarkie. Later we see the elevations used in a somewhat reduced manner for Newhall, East Lothian. Five units comprise Newhall, the same as Haddo: a main oblong, two demilunes, and two cube pavilions. Two dependencies, one flanking each pavilion, elongate the appearance of the frontage to considerable length. Two rusticated plinths bearing urns with pineapple tops define the entrance to a garden path at the side of each pavilion.

Hamilton Hall House has been used time and again in England and Virginia. One frequently encounters this high, square, immensely dignified house on old grants along the eastern shore of Maryland. It is not the usual type of Midlothian architecture, breaking away from the ancient fortified, towerlike building. Adam in his *Vitruvius Scoticus* discourses on the use of the high-peaked roof topped by wide chimneys as a relief from the flat-topped Palladian attic roof line.

Lord Milton's House, as a small square building in Edinburgh is known, is very definitely reminiscent of the charming Villa Molin near Padova. This is one of Palladio's smallest and at the same time most perfect villas. It is three windows across, and the lower floor windows are treated with heavily rusticated stones in the form of a winged border.

Pediments over the windows display an enriched keystone with double wings. A wide molding forms a stringpiece between first and second floors. The house is only two stories high. This type of townhouse has been used in various forms, many elaborate, some exceedingly plain, in the Georgian squares in Edinburgh.

Georges Square—erstwhile Great Square—contains whole rows of stone houses built on the plan of Lord Milton's House. Alternating with this plan will be large four-story houses like the stone house at number 13 Georges Square. Craigmiller stone, an odd violet-gray in color with now and again a blood-red stone harboring quartz crystals, will catch and shoot off stars of light in lamplight or in the rays of the moon. The chimneys of these houses are extravagantly high, and sprout tall red clay chimney pots.

As a relief from the rather dun appearance of this quarter of Edinburgh before the square was completed in 1785 by a "Master Builder of Aristocratic Domiciles of Forthrightness and Substantiality," as Michel Naysmith advertised himself, the new inhabitants proceeded to give gay dinner parties and balls. In fact, so rowdy did some of the parties become that the eccentric Mr. Sym, Writer to the Signet, hired half a dozen street urchins to throw pails of water on the steps of number 27, which was occupied by a young and dashing Captain Colvin. The night in January being intensely cold, the water would freeze almost immediately, and departing riotous guests would get their well-deserved comeuppance, or so Mr. Sym hoped. By some ill chance the boys mistook the house, and threw water on the steps of number 26 where the dignified, literate Hugh Erskin, son of Lord Buchan, resided. He too, it appears, was entertaining a party of friends on this same January night, but friends of a very different sort from those dancing at Captain Colvin's. The story is told that Sym and his bravos gathered in the shadow of a tree to await proceedings. These came with a vengeance. Ladies and gentlemen alike emerged from the brilliantly lighted doorway of number 26 Great Square, took a flying leap, sailed through the freezing air, and landed bottom side up in the gutter. Breeches ripped, displaying judicial behinds, while lace pantalettes belled like beckoning banners in the wind. After this little fracas the Square is said to have quieted considerably.

Number 25 was the home of Sir Walter Scott for many years. This house is four stories, of Craigmiller stone, coinstoned in Dundas granite, which is also used for the Doric columns supporting the molding of a lofty entrance porch. In Sir Walter's study at the back of the house, the mantelpiece is of white alabaster carved in running stag design. Around the edge of the mantel he used to write names for his literary characters, which he would choose at will, and wipe off with a damp rag when the list became confused.

To William Adam and his two sons, Scotland owes much for having placed her in the front rank of dignified and elegant architecture, largely through his compiling *Vitruvius Scoticus*.

CRAIGDRUE - MORAYSHIRE
SCOTLAND

BOOK. IV

CONTINENT OF
EUROPE.

THE CONTINENT
OF EUROPE

With the exception of a few large villas and houses of the palace type, Palladian style in Europe confined itself during the seventeenth and eighteenth centuries to hunting-lodges, or forest retreats, for the endless amours of the aristocracy. The various courts of France, Germany, Czarist Russia (particularly under Catherine II), Hungary, and the Grand Ducal and Electoral Courts of Hanover, Baden, Westphalia, Württemberg, Hesse-Darmstadt, and Saxony, borrowed Palladian mannerisms as avidly

as a harvester garners wheat. But the outline of simple stately elevations
and Doric porticos is so blurred by baroque incrustations that the basic
idea of Vitruvian architecture loses identity to a great extent in tortuous
scrolls and emblazoned cartouches.

A few lovely, rather plain-faced houses adhering strictly to Palladio's ideal are to be found in Scandinavian countries. Sweden and Norway show many white-pillared and pedimented country houses, set far
back from frequented roads, sharply relieved or accented by curved belts
of spruce and richly dark pine trees. This pointing up of classic white
porticos with evergreens or other trees is used wherever Palladian houses
are to be found. In Italy it is cypress. In Ireland, the nearly black, spiky
yew. England plants a crown or copse of mighty oak, beech, or sweeping
Lebanon cedar, to flank the wings. In Virginia it is thickly foliaged English
oak and sycamore of the luminous white bark. The ancient box bushes that
drift like waves of a dark sea about the entrance steps of Georgian and
Palladian houses south of the Mason-Dixon line harbor the morning dew
and the hot sun of noon in pungent green depths. In Hungary, rhododendron bushes mass in crimson, pink, and white splendor along driveways,
ending in clipped banks at the entrance.

I first saw the gigantic hunting-lodge, Caserta, when I was ten
years old. Never have I been known since to ask anyone *what* a given
building is. When I alighted from a *carrozza quattro cavalli*, a coach like
a long surrey drawn by four starveling horses, which used to ply between
Naples and Caserta la Torre I was so flabbergasted by the overpowering
barracks of this pink and yellow Palazzo del Re, that I shouted, *"What* is
it?" My father told me it was the largest house in the world. I believed
him. I even believed him when he went further into detail and said it had
been built originally as a shooting box for the giggling *buffone*—Neapoli-
tans called Ferdinand far more scathing names than this—King Ferdinand
IV of Naples and the Two Sicilies. As it turned out later, when I had
grown up and was living in Rome, I went into the dossier of fabulous
Caserta more deeply. In order to make clear to anyone who has not seen
this pile of marble, which is cluttered by as many rooms as a rabbit war-
ren, I must cite statistics. Usually dull fare, statistics, but this time full of
color.

About twelve miles outside of Naples lies a small incredibly dusty
village called Caserta la Torre. In ancient days, before Caserta was built,

THE FABULOUS GALAXY OF TROJANS. GARDEN FRONT, TROJA PALACE, PRAGUE.

a lonely stone tower marked the spot of a crossroads here. From the top of this tower a forester could spy the herds of deer that were quarry for the huntsman who made this spot a rendezvous. La Torre, this clutch of huts surrounding the tower was called. One day a hunt was arranged for Ferdinand IV. The hunt met at the crossroads of La Torre. So successful was the day's sport that Il Sogghignare (the giggler) commanded his chief huntsman to clear a wide space for a hunting-lodge. Ten years in the process of building, a vast edifice arose upon a plot of ground with nothing to distinguish it, except that it was a remount for the hunt and it possessed a gushing fountain which proved to be nearly bottomless.

Caserta is constructed of travertine marble: contrasting creamy white, rusty pink, and beige-yellow from quarries at Capua. Four court-yards of enormous size form outlets to sprawling catacombs for kitchens, stables, offices, guardrooms, and coach houses underneath the building. Facing the preposterously ornate park gates, a frontage of eight hundred and thirty feet confronts the visitor. The lodge is pillared and porticoed, swag-draped and curlicued to the last inch. I am sure I am not the only one, child or adult, who has cried at first sight of Caserta, *"What* is it?"

A majestic grand staircase ascends from the center of the middle court to the *piano nobile,* which in this place is the third floor, under a towering rotunda. On the first landing of this wide staircase Ferdinand of the Bourbons, as he liked to style himself, used to dine in state, attired in magnificent, gold-embroidered hunting attire, his velvet tricorne aburst with pheasant plumage. A portrait, twice life-size, of Ferdinand and two of his sons, dressed in the most vivid and flamboyant hunting clothes, seems to leap from the wall of one of the twenty-four reception rooms.

Every room at Caserta is elaborate to a point of frenzy, no matter what its use. Even two suites of rooms for the changing of the guard are miracles of gilding, frescos, stuccos, and carved wooden ceilings. One wishes ardently for a drearily bare hall bedroom just for contrast.

The scale at Caserta tends always to be larger than life size. It takes a really noble height to make one noticeable in any of the rooms. In the "false" gardens, where perspective is forced to the point that even statues and temples are in dollhouse size, the terraced cascade emptying into a star-shaped lagoon is, to quote Lord Nelson's letter to Romney, "fantastic, absurd, frightening, and gleeful." Nelson used to picnic on the brink of this cascade with his "adored Goddess," Emma Hamilton, who was boon companion to Marie Caroline, Queen of Naples and daughter of imperious Marie Thérèse of Austria. Nelson's use of the word "frightening" probably alludes to the vicious marble boarhounds, as large as leopards, engaged in tearing Actaeon to pieces, mounted, by way of diverting sculpture, on a rocky island in the pool.

Above the entrance gates a trophy of hunting-gear, antlered stags, incongruous body armor, and plumed Roman helmets, proclaims to the world that this place is *Casa Caccia del Re Ferdinand IV*. No "hunting-house" was ever grander.

An Irish traveler named Darley wrote to Horace Walpole: "Descending from my coach at the Gates of Royal Caserta, I was instantly choked by the white dust of the vile Neapolitan roads, churned to clouds by lackeys, foot-boys, postilions, and the wheels of every class of horse-drawn vehicle, which from dawn to dawn dash to and fro between Naples and this Bedlam in Marble." Sir William Hamilton wrote: "Caserta beggars description. Palladian in conception and plan, all is obscured by icing of Baroque sugar and tarnished gilt. Life within is strident and unreal."

Two Palladian villas of moderate size are all but lost to view in France. One, called Château Colombier, at or not far from Nancy, has been badly mauled in the process of enlarging to accommodate succeeding generations of children. When last I saw Colombier, it resembled nothing so much as a Gargantuan nursery, one hundred thousand diapers floating straight out from every window, in the high wind.

Villa Porto at Deauville remains chastely silent, all passion spent, for when Gaby Deslys was the toast of France, she stayed in the villa for her holidays. The walls buckled in the high pressure of her entertainments. Here she indulged her whim of gilding lilies and roses, literally, then winding them and the vase with her world-famous pearls. Now the villa is closed, though I believe it is still owned by an Italian family.

Villa Porto at Deauville follows the usual plan of a central cube block, pillared. A long flight of steps climbs to a high first floor. Two wings, set ten feet back, flank the pediment, but are as high—three stories —as the main block. One rather different note at Villa Porto strikes the eye. The two wings are lightly rusticated, but the central cube is not. The high entrance hall is decorated elaborately in stucco; the ceilings in dining room and salon are painted by French artists, in the Empire taste.

I asked various French authorities on architecture what accounts for the lack of interest in Palladian taste in France during the life of Andrea Palladio and down succeeding years. They generally agreed on the fact that the French mind is far more interested in diminutive detail and the carefully controlled scroll and volute, than in the grand sweep of line and simple bare wall spaces we see in Palladio's Vitruvian houses.

After turreted castles came the early French Renaissance. Elaborate detail in carved stone became the rage and with the advent of Le Roi Soleil, and his Château de Chambord, the real French note was cast. Louis XV and Louis XVI varied the theme, each more delicately, but never disturbed the main stem, the French Renaissance. Whenever an architect, either from fatigue or lack of any forthcoming ideas, absently left a broad simple wall space between windows, he quickly remedied this fault by filling the space with carved cupids, roses, swags of knotted silk, birds, and fruit.

Not until the Napoleonic era did this change. Then various Roman templelike buildings were constructed in Paris, and some châteaux with delicately columned porticos appeared in the carefully clipped woods surrounding Paris. The Greek Revival, it was called.

The Hermitage near St. Petersburg is an instance where Palladian architecture was followed pretty closely, although I have always felt it resembled more directly some of the grandiose houses along the Mississippi, up-river from New Orleans. Deserted wind-wracked Belle Grove, for example, or mist-wrapped Blanche Isle.

What a superb ring of license is evoked by the tale of a banquet that took place one night in the porphyry and gold dining room at Hermitage. Empress Catherine had gathered together a brilliant group of foreign visitors, diplomats, and traveling milords. Comte de Ségur, who had, so near as made no matter, captured the volatile affections of the "Semiramis of the North" (as Voltaire called Catherine), was in crimson velvet evidence. Baron Güellert, a handsome young Belgian, and Prince de Ligne of the acid tongue and towering height, all awaited the surprise they knew was forthcoming.

At Catherine's right sprawled Prince Grigori Orlov, drunk and nearly disorderly, his white wig sprinkled with dust of diamonds. Catherine had each glass filled to the brim and, clapping her hands, summoned a lackey to fetch forward the costliest garment the world has ever known.

A golden coat for her lover, Orlov. Many men have had gold-brocaded coats, but this one was different. Catherine, completely infatuated by her "Adonis-Apollo," as she had commanded to be carved upon his statue, draped over his shoulders a garment that was to shock not only Russia, but the world at large for wanton extravagance. Valued at four million rubles, it was a gift for value received. The lining was pure gold thread woven to represent a deed, signed by Catherine, to a million acres of land, and all contained therein including power of life and death over fifty thousand serfs, male and female. The Palladian Hermitage, built for a hunting-lodge, had certainly proved to be the "Orlov luck."

In the grounds of Hermitage was kept the incredible sledge built for Catherine II to her own design. The sledge, truly a Greek temple on runners, contained a drawing room, a large bedroom, and a dining room. Drawn by thirty horses, six abreast, this entourage must surely have been a breath-taking sight. The bed occupied by the Northern Semiramis and her current lover was by all accounts the acme. Countess Skavronsky, niece of Potemkin, for years a sort of confidante-in-waiting to the Empress, says, "So huge a bed resembled the Ark. Gilded stags' antlers, hung profusely with diamond and emerald drops to mimic frozen crystals, formed a canopy. The bed swung on chains of gold and silver links, all heavily jeweled, diversely. Swaying gently with every lurch of the swiftly moving sleigh, I must often re-arrange the gold silk coverlets which were heavy from the sable and ermine lining." Hundreds of outriders bearing flaming torches preceded all this pageantry when Catherine traveled by night, which she liked to do. At every horse-change, mounted landowners from castles in the vicinity waited by roaring bonfires, bearing gifts of stallions, rare wines, and furs for "Mother Catherine," a title of affection which, oddly, for so ardent an *amoureuse*, she liked.

The Margrave of Bayreuth had his architect, Hans Fött, design a theater in the strict Palladian taste to commemorate the twentieth wedding anniversary of Margrave and Margravine. A white marble dream of tall fluted columns, Corinthian capped, rises on the lip of a *lac sauvage* where the wild fowl gather to breed. The foyer of this theater has alternating panels of indigo blue and pale yellow marble. The curtains in foyer and boxes are silver satin, embroidered with flocks of wild white geese in full flight.

At Dröttningholm, a theater, also in Palladian taste, has a most enchanting façade, like a classic toy palace in a darkling wood. This pure-white, dull-finished tile edifice has a black roof. One enters a long alley through gateposts whereon bronze Mercuries accompany majestic, friendly looking lions.

When the auditorium at the Dröttningholm Castle theater was finished in July, 1766, Carlo Bibiena designed the settings and costumes for a Royal Presentation performance. The ballets chosen were *Le Château Enchanté* and *Le Temple de Cythère*. A series of arched colonnades arranged in the true Bibiena diminuendo set the stage for both ballets. Only props were changed. Roses, roses everywhere. A Swedish friend gave me an *aquarelle*, signed by Carlo Bibiena, of this pink, wine-red, and yellow scene. In it, rose-swathed columns pierce the clouds.

It is the theater at the Castle of Gripsholm where Swedish Palladian comes into its own with a terrific fanfare. The auditorium is semicircular, engaging fourteen gold-fluted columns with black and gold Doric capitals. A magnificently conceived rotunda, semicircular as well, surmounts a wide entablature style of cornice. This displays alternate masks of Comedy and Tragedy in black marble, with swags of the same color swinging between. Gabriel patterned this theater after Palladio's Vicenza plans for a private theater at Villa Trissino. Carlo Bibiena designed scenery for the ballet *La Belle au Bois Dormant*, danced here by La Pericoli, the darkly flashing *donna fatale* of Italian ballet, by her own admission.

Scattered about Sweden are many small or medium-size country houses of immense charm and quiet dignity. White as Swedish winter are these Palladian houses. Often the roof is black or indigo-blue tile. Inside, the use of white lacquered Swedish baroque furniture, a cross between the Queen Anne period and Dresdener, repeats itself in grave or gay patterns. In a way it is odd that in northern countries like Norway, Denmark, and Sweden, the most elegant drawing rooms feature white chairs upholstered in gray, white, or cool green or blue leather or damask. But the heat from white porcelain stoves dispels any feeling of cold. As a Swedish housewife says, "It looks so clean."

In 1930, I designed a country house for a Norwegian friend who lived near Stavanger. The house was built without so much as a doorhandle in my original plan being changed. I painted two rooms, a music room and a large entrance hall. For design I fused a Palladian villa at Caldogno, near Padova, with the style of a big simple Norwegian manorhouse. The coved ceilings were carved wood, by native craftsmen. One was painted deep larch-green. One claret. One bronze, gold, and silver, marbleized. Another malachite. Floors were spruce. A lovely gray-mauve color. And then, just before the owner and his two young boys took the front door off its hinges and ate their first meal on it (an ancient Norse custom), the Nazi Messerschmitts blew this house and all in it to hell.

In the Tuscan hilltown of Lucca a small Palladian house stands, quietly retired, in a *cul-de-sac*. It is not large. Only eight rooms, four to a floor. It was built in 1578 by Andrea Palladio, who took personal supervision, for his son Leonido married a daughter of the Baddi family. Palazzo Baddi it is called; Filippo Baddi for whom it was built came from the *primo nobile* of Tuscany. Of fawn-colored stone quarried in the vicin-

Imprisoned Electress

ity, a sienna yellow marble curtain-façade lends tremendous style to this perfect little house. Small though Palazzo Baddi is, there is the grand air of a larger house embracing it. San-Souci in Potsdam is not unlike it, nor is the Hermitage, nor Petit Trianon. All are small, compact, but alluring in a most personal manner. The cut-under room over the pillared entrance door is spacious and painted pale aquamarine blue with drifting white clouds and pale silver-gilt stars. In the cleft of the broken pediment a unicorn lies at ease on a tasseled marble cushion, eye cocked for a chance virgin approaching. Languid caryatids—paired-off nymphs and fauns—support broken pediments over windows. Certainly languor holds sway.

There is a black and silver-gilt lacquer room at the right of the portico on the first floor. I know of only two other such rooms. One is in the Palladian Villa Manfredi outside of Padova. The other room in this style is of fearsome import, for a bloody business was enacted there. It is a huge dark room in the Schloss Ahlden in Hanover. Here the hideous

THE TROJAN ASSEMBLAGE ASCENDING THE GRAND STAIRCASE.
TROJA PALACE, PRAGUE.

old Countess von Platen plotted the crime to castrate Philipp von Königs-
mark on the night of his planned elopement with the gay and lovely
Electoral Princess of Hanover. The Elector, attracted to the black lacquer
room by tortured screams, discovered the whole plot. Later the Elector
became George I of England, but he kept his wife shut up in this room,
a prisoner, incommunicado, for thirty-five years, for her part in the in-
fidelity. It is told that when at last the Princess was let out, she had
scratched the walls of the room that had been her entire world, until not
a single gilt scroll or monkey remained. Only black lacquer walls.

No stranger pleasure house ever rose simpering from Mother Earth
than the one caused by Ferdinand IV to be built in the gardens of his
sumptuous Villa Favorita in Palermo. With the army of the French Revo-
lution at the gates of Naples, Ferdinand and his family fled, rather ig-
nominiously, to Palermo, on board Lord Nelson's flagship, *Vanguard*.
After a time, Palermo bored Queen Marie Caroline, who was forced to
rest for her approaching twelfth child; but something to build would
amuse her. It has amused many persons since. By Andrea Palladio,
through Sir William Chambers (his *Designs for Chinese Buildings* were
followed), Giuseppe Patricola evolved a *Palazzina Chinese* that hit the
bull's-eye for sheer unbridled fantasy. Actually the Palladian central
block, crowned by a rotunda and approached by a long flight of steps to
a high semicircular portico, is followed. But all resemblance ends here.
Thousands of tiny glass bells of every known color tinkle to distraction in
a latent breeze. A lacy pagoda tops the rotunda, and Chinese fretwork
colonnades and balustrades abound. Inside is a room where life-size paintings, crude beyond belief, depict Lady Hamilton in her "Attitudes."

Sicilian society was enlivened during this enforced rest from the
political imbroglios of Naples by the Royal Family. Many of the English
colony lived in pseudo-Palladian villas or outrageously frescoed rococo
palazzi. These overdecorated barracks were drafty and uncomfortable for
living but roomy and romantic for constant entertaining.

Among letters received by Mrs. Lock, wife of the British Consul at
Naples, from an Irish cousin, Mrs. Farley, one is given a vivaciously written series of pen-pictures of the gay doings that transpired in Palermo in
the frantic days when it became—much against the inhabitants' will—the
terrified court of King Ferdinand and Queen Caroline and their vast pen-
niless entourage, on their flight from Naples. It was a sojourn of problem-
atic duration. One letter reads:

At first the Hamiltons [Sir William and Emma] were lodged in the tomb-like Villa Bastioni next to the lovely gardens of Flora Reale. But the dampness of all the rooms reduced Sir William to such bouts of lung fever that a change, immeasureably for the better, has been arranged. Last night Lady Hamilton again reigned as Queen of Hostesses, although you, dear cousin, do not agree to my regard for her. Her *soirée* was given at Hamilton's new residence, the agreeably spacious Palazzo Palagoni, standing in gardens of its own. The suites of painted rooms are fine in color and riotous in subject. Were ever the roisterers on Olympus so lewdly exposed? One's eyes are dim with mirth and one's cheeks rouge at the sight. An inspired setting for lyrical Emma's parties, where her attitudinizing will carry full import.

My own small villa near the Colli Gate is a Palladian jewel. For you know the "Garden Casino" was very dear to the heart of the great Venetian architect. . . . The breakfasts at my pink and violet establishment are unending, for the pleasure of dalliance is very sweet. To describe a few of the joys of my attractive surroundings seems necessary for you to fully realize how pleasurable life can be in Palermo, constant complaining from their Neapolitan Majesties to the contrary.

The dining room is plastered in hyacinth blue and white, with a black and white terrazzo floor. My boudoir is all lilac and pale green. A small music room on the garden side is coral, silver, and puce. From this I descend a few steps to alleys of tubbed oranges, sweet Sicilian lemons, and tall variegated oleanders. The house actually reminds me of Ireland, for Lucan-on-the-Liffey, Sarsfield's charming Palladian house, is very like.

In another letter to her cousin, Mrs. Farley says:

I would fain transplant this house, entire, to Ireland and our demesne beside the River Nor. My bed, hung in caramine silk, embroidered in yellow pansies and mimosa is too charming to live without. I constantly tell Farley I shall never sleep so well in any other.

Far flung are the houses owing their place in the sun to the influence, however remote or thinned by time, of Palladio. Each has that touch of distinction, hovering about arched colonnades, fanlighted doors, or deeply carved pediment moldings, that arrests the eye of a chance visitor or daily passer-by. Nassau in the Bahamas has some fine galleried or porticoed houses, but one stands out far above its neighbors. Dundas House, named for the first Royal Governor of the Bahamas, has a singularly dignified yet welcoming aspect, lying as it does in pale smoky-blue radiance behind a screen of brilliant scarlet hibiscus bushes. The two-story oblong has great character, due to one of the finest double staircases one will see in a long journey. The balustrades rise in a richly sweeping curve to a door straight out of one of Palladio's houses in the hills near Caldogno. Pointed up by coinstones and window trim of gleaming white, the house has a dark plum-blue roof and shutters of soft mauve gray. If ever entrance steps rising to the *piano nobile* made a house sing architecturally, then it is here at Dundas House.

Poland once had marvelous Palladian country houses and town palaces. The richly carved classic pediment and dignified portico reached architectural importance when handled by the intelligent and imaginative Poles. Now nearly all the buildings have disappeared. Hungary, curiously, adopted in 1620 the pure Palladian farmhouse type for town and village buildings. The richest farmer in the province always stood under a low pediment, supported by thickly whitewashed clay columns, to survey his Puszta acres of a sunny morning. Tremendous castles and hunting-lodges were in the eighteenth century copied from the buildings of French Mansard. But some landowners with estates comprising seventy-five thousand

A Palladian Banqueting House in Poland.

275

acres, like that of Prince George Festetics, built Palladian houses, as did his warrior ancestor in 1650. Vitruvian in plan, of a central oblong and wings projecting at right angles and again jutting parallel to the main block—like Seaton Delaval, though ten times as big—Castle Készthély stands in gardens rivaling those of Le Nôtre at Versailles. A Mansard roof and French Renaissance decorations were added to this house in the eighteenth century. Count Andrássy has a great Palladian hunting-lodge in the far reaches of the Puszta, like a forgotten palace of frost and ice.

The Electors of Brandenburg, the Hereditary Grand Dukes of Württemberg and they of the Palatine Rhine all erected ornate, unwieldy hunting-lodges that staffed two thousand servants, and had stables boxing five hundred horses in the utmost luxury. Great paintings of the chase in all its fascinating aspects adorned the walls of the high-ceilinged rooms where banquets to celebrate a hunt were still in flow when the sun of another approaching day shot javelins of light across drunken faces and oceans of spilled wine. Windows were curtained with crimson, green, yellow, and plum, the colors of the chase. Stags' antlers were tipped in pure gold and hung with jeweled bridles used in the hunt. Women were kept in these lodges to pleasure the men after a hunt. They often appeared in gorgeous costumes of goddesses to welcome the hunt on its blood-spattered return. In bizarre costumes Dianas of the Chase fell over Aphrodites and Clios. And all under Vitruvian porticos.

Holland has, since the days of the Spanish invaders in 1587, shown a preference for white houses, I expect for the same reason that the Swedish housewife likes her white house. Big, rather rambling white country houses lie in beautifully wooded parks all about The Hague, Amsterdam, and in Friesland, Groningen, and Haarlem. The Royal Palace is a long white building with Palladian overtones. When Alessandro Farnese, Duke of Parma, entered the Netherlands as conqueror in the Spanish forces, he brought Italian artisans to erect for him "a proper palace, of stone and gilded bosses, not a pile of cheeses," as he is purported to have told his architect. It was a conceit of the Dutch to mold big Edam cheeses in the semblance of step-roofed houses and windmills. These were displayed in windows at night with candles behind them, a gay and simple pastime, probably a shade fatuous to the arrogant Duke. Whatever influence from Italian architecture there is in Holland today (mostly in the country) is of the best. Low white porticos, porthole windows, winged keystones, and long flights of curving steps and terraced garden paths.

BOOK V

AMERICA

THOMAS JEFFERSON:
VITRUVIUS AMERICANUS

Dawn came early on this fresh morning in May, 1789. As the sailing ship *Tunbridge* warped into the Norfolk dock, a long finger of clear yellow light slit the gray sky to the east; sun flickered upon the water of the quiet harbor, a warm sunlit day was spreading over Virginia.

To the tall man standing in the prow of the ship the sight of drifts of white dogwood edging the woods along the bay was like a draught of wine, early morning wine, to cool his eagerness to be ashore, to drive with all possible haste to his high-riding house set in rolling box alleys and dogwood, both pink and white. Dogwood trees brought from Shadwell to Monticello before fire had destroyed his birthplace. The gangway screeched ashore. Thomas Jefferson was home.

A light coach with two horses chosen for speed and staying power waited at the end of the pier. Wrapping his long black cape, circular cut and collared in the French taste, about him, against the sharp waterfront breeze, Jefferson hurried down the gangway, greeted his coachman and footboys, and sprang into the maroon coach. Voices shouted, ladder steps were folded into place by a grinning black footman, the horses settled into their collars. The long drive to Charlottesville had begun.

As the horses dashed along the red dirt roads towards the valley of the Piedmont, Jefferson continually leaned out the window of the coach to drink in the cool spring air, almost like mountain spring water, he felt. Removing his cocked black beaver, he let the sunlight warm his face and strike bright red lights in his unpowdered hair, drawn smartly back and clubbed in black silk.

Green rolling fields were crossed and recrossed by creeper-hung snake fences, some built long before any houses but log cabins had showed above ground. Stone walls, dry laid, marked boundaries of wide-spreading land grants, owned by his friends. Long rides, cut through the oak, poplar, and sycamore woods, showed knolls, peculiarly noticeable in this richly grassed countryside because of the way the mounds rose suddenly from level fields, for no apparent reason. Some said they were old Indian burial grounds or a kind of turf dais used for powwows when tribes met. Whatever the origin, Thomas Jefferson thought they would make wonderful rises upon which to build houses in the Palladian taste. He could visualize—none better than he—long driveways of arching trees planted at the base with mountain laurel, glorious in early summer blossom, rhododendron regal and warmly crimson, box bushes the very insignia of Virginia, and dark wine-red, blue-berried creepers. At the end of this long vista would rise white Doric columns crowned with pediments like the stone and stucco villas drowsing along the Brenta Canal.

What he wanted most of all was the use of warm red brick, rose red, made by the thousands of Negro slaves who would, as he well knew, take great pride in making the bricks personal, by pressing into the wet mud blocks, spread turkey claws, fluted shells, oak leaves, and acorns. He knew that when the bricks were dry and laid one upon another in walls, the texture of incised design would catch the last rays of a setting sun in rippling waves. The effect was like watered silk.

Yes, he would dot the landscape with white-porticoed, red brick houses. A classic air would ride the valley. For he had brought back shoals of ideas from France and Italy. Mereworth Castle, so stunningly Palladian, had thrilled him to the core. Chiswick had been spoiled by Wyatt's added wings, but was still the Villa Capra-Rotonda in miniature, in the main block. All this he would translate into his valley. First he had great plans for enriching Monticello, to bring it from a sort of mountain pavilion retreat to architectural importance. He would build a house in Palladio's finest manner, domed and pillared, gilded and touched with empyrean blue. There would be one room a firmament strewn with stars, as

Serpentine Wall, Monticello.

in Villa Norelli, Palladio's one villa in Turin, where the ceilings of every room seem not to exist, but one walks always—no matter what weather lashes outside—beneath a starry sky. All must go forward with haste, for so much there was to do, so many ideas crowded one upon another in the inventive mind of Thomas Jefferson.

Few men in any age have experienced the supreme content, the thrilling satisfaction of seeing their dreams come true, as did Thomas Jefferson. During his lifetime he saw his "Temple of Learning rise in my beloved Valley," as he wrote to Prince San Faustino in Italy, when the hugely circular, domed, and pillared University of Virginia materialized. Monticello became, under his sensitive hand, one of the most warmly beautiful of all existing country houses in any land: dignified, immensely elegant, European in design, but completely comfortable in the American country house tradition. A letter from the Marquis de Lafayette to Jefferson reads:

> Never was so pleasurable a house built for country living. Palatial yet convenient to every mood. Felicitous to health, appetite and relaxation.

More than that I challenge any house to offer.

When Jefferson was in France, he met Clérisseau, a French architect, who was as firm an admirer of the classic taste in architecture as Jefferson. Together these two devotees visited the shrines of classic architecture still left in France, at that time, from the Romans. Maison Carrée bewitched Jefferson, and the Vitruvian temple façade of the antique Roman money exchange at windy, gypsy-haunted Arles prompted him to fill a sketchbook with the little, freely drawn sketches for which he is so well known. Jefferson drew all sorts of hurried ideas on anything within reach at the moment of inspiration. There are small sketches for curtains, valances, bed-hangings, chair cushions, and even for a most stylish linen, tassel-hung "marquee for Martha's [his daughter's] birthday fete." Inspired by the striped canopies used in Venice to cover the state chairs in the gilded gondolas of the Doge, Jefferson noted on the margin of the sketch for the marquee, rather scratchily (apparently his goose-quill pen needed trimming): "Cut the scallops deep, and fringe heavily. Stripes to be ten inches wide, either red or green on a white ground."

Two books of architectural plates, which it would seem were constantly on the collapsible bedtable—especially designed for journeys—in Jefferson's bedroom at Monticello, and afterwards when he spent so much time at Poplar Forest, are Gibbs' *Book of Architecture* and Leoni's *The Architecture of A. Palladio.* The latter book came to his notice in 1770. The country villas of Andrea Palladio, particularly the long pavilion type that I mention in the chapter, Houses in the Hills, completely won Jefferson. It is said that whenever he dined with friends at their manorhouses, he held forth on the delights to be enjoyed from country villas with such power and eloquence that his hosts "shooed him home," laughing that his persuasion had almost convinced them that come the morrow they must tear down the ancestral roof over their heads and build a Vitruvian country villa designed by him.

Many of these joking friends did ask him to design a "country retreat," as he termed his houses. It was not always easy, it appears, to inveigle Jefferson into the designing of other men's houses. For one reason, he considered himself, and was, an amateur, in the same manner that Lord Burlington, the High Priest of the Palladians in England, was an amateur. Both built houses, laid out gardens, and suggested, as did Burlington, or actually designed furniture, as we know Jefferson did, because they loved to see a style of living that was dear to them appropriately housed. Both were brilliant, indefatigable men of wide intelligence. Both had style to the fingertips. Jefferson was the more creative of the two. He never took any kind of remuneration for his work. It is told that after Jefferson had designed Oak Hill at Aldie, Virginia, for James Monroe, he received a pair of French luster candelabra, sent as a token of appreciation for the beautiful, warm yellow house in its grove of oaks. At first Jefferson considered sending the present back to Monroe, lest people would hear of it and wonder. He finally sent a most entertaining letter to Monroe, saying in part:

> I am, of course, greatly pleased, but I shall put them under cover, taking them out at Christmas as a gift from you, forgetting I had a part in bringing Oak Hill to life.

When Jefferson set about, after his return from Europe, remodeling and greatly enlarging Monticello, he turned to Andrea Palladio for guidance. Before Shadwell burned, Jefferson had added the book on Palladian teaching, *Select Architecture,* by Robert Morris, whose most outstanding contribution to architecture had been the incomparable Palladian bridge at Wilton Park. This bridge had been built in conjunction with still another aristocratic and enthusiastic amateur, the Earl of Pembroke. For the first version of Monticello, Jefferson had resorted to the Morris plates. The house was built as a cube with two attached wings and a pediment. When later Monticello was redone, Jefferson was swayed by a plate in Gibbs' *Book of Architecture* of a pavilion with rotunda and east and west porticos. From then on Jefferson compiled his designs from his own observations and sketches of Palladian villas in Italy and England, most of which were either based upon the Villa Malcontenta—called by its name, Villa Foscari, in architectural books of the period—or Villa Capra-Rotonda. Jefferson introduced many interesting and unique features to embellish his house during the years he lived there. For example, the railings are in *chinoiserie* or Chippendale taste, a kind of geometrical fretwork, painted white, that, when handled with taste and imagination, is handsome. Jefferson set a style in America for this "Chinese Chippendale," as it is called, when he added the window grilles and balustrades to Monticello. The elevation at the head of the chapter is the first plan.

The idea of "painted papers from Pekin" swept the country about this time, via France and England. Jefferson was the first to use this engaging wall decoration to any extent. But it had become the accepted thing, among the landowners of the Tidewater and the valleys of the Piedmont and Shenandoah, to install in their big brick and stone houses any new idea fostered by Thomas Jefferson. In very truth he had become *arbiter elegantorum* on all facets of fine living in the countryside. His fame spread, and it was not long before half the houses in Virginia, Maryland, the two Carolinas, even into Delaware, were said to have been "designed by Jefferson." Of many houses it was said, "Jefferson added that portico to an old house." In some places it is true. Nine out of ten times it is not. But in the last analysis this does not signify, for one planter copied another, who had copied from Thomas Jefferson, who had been inspired by Andrea Palladio.

Whether Jefferson knew the great wave of Palladiana he was launching when he built Monticello, the University of Virginia, and Poplar Forest, one wonders. At any rate, we living today are unconditionally grateful to him. Certainly no lovelier architecture can be imagined to grace the "templed hills" of the American scene than white porticos, shimmering against soft red brick; or white houses, green-shuttered, with tall Palladian windows and colonnaded galleries. Whether these houses are backed by the mauve-blue mountains of Virginia, or veiled by Spanish moss along the bayous of Louisiana, they are right. Natchez holds annual festivals in her columned houses so that visitors may view them. The Carolinas are proud of their pillared manorhouses in which the woodwork is among the finest in the country. In South Carolina, Boone Hall lies long and beautifully expressed; the portico is splendid, in the finest Jeffersonian manner. Anne Arundel County in Maryland treasures Tulip Hill, as well she may, for the plan of this wide-spreading house is pure Palladian: a center oblong, with connecting galleries of one story, hinging two-story wings. The old slave-made brick is pale orange-pink.

A visiting Englishman, John Rowley, was entertained by Thomas Jefferson at Monticello. He was taken on a tour of the University of Virginia. On a "sweet summer day we set out," he says, to ride horseback to Poplar Forest. A week he stayed there, wandering among the box-bordered gardens, inspecting the surprising sheds where silkworms spun their tenuous threads, woven later into soft white silk for family use and for wedding presents to lucky Virginia brides who were friends of Jefferson and his wife. All the herbs, and grain seeds such as millet, that Jefferson had brought back from Italy, were husbanded here and grew as well as in native soil. A thorough, self-contained gentleman's estate, a demi-Paradise, is what John Rowley saw. He wrote in his letter of thanks to Jefferson, "Forget, I cannot, the hospitality of your houses. You live in plenty and in grace. Your white pillared rooms magnify your friendliness. Your friends call you genius. If Inigo Jones was called Vitruvius Britannicus, most meetly are you to be handed the laurels as Vitruvius Americanus." And so he stands to this day. Vitruvius Americanus.

Whatever else the mind, the heart, the statesmanship of Thomas Jefferson may mean to present-day Americans, his imagination and prowess in furthering the art of graceful living still holds. His generosity in giving so much of himself to foster a style of architecture he so deeply believed in and bequeathed as a shining heritage to his countrymen stands out in bold relief.

VIRGINIA—
BIG HOUSE
ON THE HILL
CABIN IN THE VALLEY

PALLADIAN INFLUENCE IN THE VALLEY OF THE PIEDMONT

For me to attempt to catalogue the hundreds of houses scattered about the Southern states, as well as those in the North, that are either definitely Palladian or show marked Palladian influence, would be impossible. It

286

would take an entire book, and a big one. It is a feat of major proportions, because until one has penetrated into the back roads—many nothing
more than cart tracks—of Virginia, the Carolinas, Maryland, Tennessee,
Mississippi, Georgia, and the bayou country of Louisiana, one has no
notion of how many houses in this category still exist. Some are falling
to pieces, practically before one's eyes. Some are silent, derelict, the
haunt of small field animals, and even more destructive animals that walk
on two legs and carry a bottle of "corn" on either hip. Some are sort of
"picnicked" in, the rather dispirited owners waiting, year in, year out,
for fortune to smile on them again, that everlasting "somethin' bound t'
turn up" attitude toward life. Many houses are as beautifully lived in today as the time when candles were first lighted in the gilt or crystal
candelabra for the housewarming.

I have ridden horseback across country to visit many of these
remote houses. Sometimes I have been rowed or poled in a flatboat to a
house not on any passable road. "Never was on no road," I've been told
often enough. When the house was built on the edge of the Rapidan, the
Shenandoah, the Rappahannock, or the Hazel rivers, the only means of
approach was by water. One house near North Cliff, Rixeyville, Virginia,
is called Windsor Lodge. Some old inhabitants say it was known, when
first built in 1790, as Windsor Castle, because the chatelaine had grand
ideas. It was certainly once a huge house with magnificent arched chimneys. The frontage, mostly fallen into the rank grass now, was immense.
Many houses in the back country are never photographed, never exploited
in any way, because the owners live so quiet a life that the world of maga-
zines and Kodachrome articles does not exist for them. One house I know
is pure Palladian. The carpets, quilted satin hangings, Chippendale furniture and "painted paper from Pekin" are all the original, 1782. Time
out of mind reporters have been turned away. The woman who owns this
house and has not stirred beyond its pineapple-topped gateway for fifteen
years will not allow any mention of the house to appear, in any form.
When this extremely gifted and charming woman is asked why she is so
antisocial, she replies, "But I'm not. I just don't like people."

Bremo Bluffs (there are three Bremos, like the three Crichels),
Bremo Recess, and Lower Bremo are on the banks of the James River.
Bremo Bluffs, the main house, was designed by Jefferson for his friend
General Cocke. In almost every particular the house follows the plan of

Villa Rotonda. The long galleries, which extend for two hundred feet on either side of the main block, have a wooden balustrade painted white. Along this walk it is possible to see many miles both up and down the James River. The stone cowbarns at Bremo, built before the house, were used by Jefferson to try out some of his ideas, such as lunettes over high windows or "arched apertures," as Jefferson writes on the margin of a sketch. To my mind, this barn is one of the great architectural gestures in America today. The stone columns supporting a white-painted wooden pediment are dressed in the round, but unpainted. The warm brown and gray of local stone, now wreathed with burnished ivy, is an unusual and extremely appropriate way to construct a country portico. The wide ramp under the portico is wonderfully convenient for approaching a doorway. The idea should be more generally used.

Menokin, in Richmond County, is a small, nearly square house but has tremendous style. Built of stone, it has been heavily stuccoed and whitewashed. A double stringpiece forms a sort of frieze between the first and second stories. Rusticated trim around the large windows, coinstones, stringpiece frieze, and the wide cornice are of warm red brick. An especially pleasant aspect is this façade as one approaches Menokin up a long driveway. Square, rose-brick schoolroom and smokehouses flank the entrance.

Gunston Hall in Fairfax County is the long, low, dormer-window style of early house. What makes this house one of the most noteworthy in the country is the superb Palladian room. No other house within my knowledge has a room to compare with this for imagination in the placing of cupboards on either side of the fireplace, and the mounting of window trim full to the cornice to carry the undulating line up, thereby leading the eye to the glorious broken pediments over all the doors and recessed cupboards. This display of wonderful carving is now painted oyster white. The walls are waxed pine, but show old handmade nails around the edge of the panels, attesting to the fact that deep rose-colored satin damask once covered these walls. I think, architecturally, this room has for its size more elegance and stature than any other in Virginia.

Running Gunston Hall a close second in outstandingly beautiful rooms is the Hammond-Harewood house in one of the main thoroughfares of Annapolis. The plan of this red brick "Georgian" house is the usual Palladian one of pedimented central oblong, with one-story galleries connecting two-story wings. It is the dining room that is so singularly fine. The justly celebrated William Buckland, who came from London to Virginia in 1755, worked first upon the aforementioned Palladian room at Gunston Hall. Later, after carving architraves and pediments in Dumfries, and Ballendine, he carved the sensational bed canopy for Mount Airy—later sent to England—which incorporated a cornice of clouds, stars, and flying swans, all revolving around a center appliqué showing Europa and the Bull being assisted across waves by mermaids. His dining-room windowcases at the Hammond-Harewood house show a more mature and infinitely sophisticated knowledge of the use of the coffered rosette and the console style of enriched window pediment.

The loveliest house in Maryland, in the simple pavilion style employed so successfully by Palladio and later Thomas Jefferson, is Whitehall, near Annapolis. The articulation of the long façade in three levels of roofs is perfection. Bricks made on the manorial grant are narrow and delicately colored, all shades of rose, violet-brown, and pale orange. In sunlight or shadow the walls are muted in color like a Medieval French tapestry. Against these walls the portico shows as if of white jade, so luminous are the four Corinthian columns. The shafts are fluted in wide striations, and stand upon important bases, richly molded. Indented deeply to catch powerful shadows, the pediment is a masterpiece of carving by an unknown craftsman. Many coats of whitewash down the years have imparted to this portico a patina rarely seen. Whitehall was built in 1765. The portico of Corinthian order is probably the oldest in America. It may, as well, be the most perfectly proportioned. A page torn from a notebook was found in a crevice of a wall in Anne Arundel Parish. Dated 1795, part of the torn page read: "Left Whitehall to board my ship. My hostess was very distressed she could not call her coach to bear me hither; the truth of the matter is, her husband is entertaining some cronies this evening and using her coach as a cock-pit. May the saints preserve the upholstery." There is no signature.

If Andrea Palladio could walk into Virginia today, I believe he would make straight for Stratford in Westmoreland County. I believe he has thought for two centuries that Stratford has more character to the square inch than almost any other house in Virginia. And the house is very far from being pure Palladian. The chimneys are like rampant guardhouses, worthy of Blenheim. The entrance steps suggest Chiswick and Mereworth. Easton Neston, Northamptonshire, and Shantyle in Ireland can be traced, as well as the casino in the gardens of the Palazzo del Strà. All Brenta certainly contributed to Stratford, *via* Palladio and Vanbrugh. Yet the house of Stratford has no confusion of design. The two squares built around a parterre are in effect twin houses. The piercing of the mass with windowlike arches between the chimney columns, grouped in fours, is amazingly entertaining. One seems never to tire looking; there is always something new in detail to be found. Yet I have heard Stratford called a "big, plain brute of a house." To me it isn't. When one comes from afar off across the fields, the house in late autumn sunlight is warmly inviting. For I know the pleasures to be had in the great paneled hall: buttered rum and corn twists before the applewood fire. Outwardly Stratford is disarming. It is huge but gentle.

One other house, little known by chroniclers it appears, that would delight Palladio if he could see it, is Belo House in Winston-Salem, North Carolina, built in 1849. What amazing character and sweep this house has! Eminently Italian in feeling, the big gaunt pile embraces three or four of Palladio's pet theories. For one thing, there are four porticos to catch the breezes and disperse them about the house. There are eight pediments, for no reason except that the builder, Colonel Belo, had a pediment complex. Brick built, stuccoed over and washed white, it has lots of lacy ironwork galleries and a flagrantly impressive entrance guarded by iron mastiffs. For all its gauntness, Belo has a convincing air of great doings having happened behind its carved doors.

On the outskirts of Warrenton, Virginia, topping a long gradual rise, stands a pavilion-style house called Leeton Forest. Red brick pointed with white trim it is, and gains in distinction on two counts. The long, green-shuttered windows are beautifully proportioned and spaced, and the situation of the house could not be bettered. The house is backed by immense old oaks, and the panorama of Virginia countryside rolling away to the misted Blue Ridge Mountains is spread out in front of the portico of Leeton Forest, as great a picture as ever I beheld.

In the main street of Warrenton is a big old whitewashed building, five tall stories high. I expect it is just an ordinary sort of dwelling house made into flats. It has great manner, big doors, wide, tall windows, and massive chimneys. Built before the Revolutionary War, this old building is a winner. Real Virginia town architecture, high, dormered, unspoiled.

A big brick house in the backlands of Rappahannock River country is called Presque Isle, and it is very nearly an island because rivers converge at its very gates. Big brick barns are a unique feature. Not many of these remain intact on Virginia farms today, for most of them have long since been dismantled.

Sabine Hall, Richmond County; Brandon, Prince George County; Raseby Hill, Chesterfield County, all are built on the plan of the long central block, galleries, and flanking wings. A wide hall or dog-trot slices through the main house, with two or four (depending on the size) reception rooms on either side.

Mount Vernon, Fairfax County, is known architecturally as Colonial Palladian. Certainly the house has all the units prescribed by Palladio at Villa Trissino and Villa Emo at Fanzolo. There is an oblong center house as well as colonnaded demilunes, swinging in a wide curve to attach wings and outbuildings, so pleasantly described by John Langley Fortnum, Baltimore builder, as "gentlemen's out-huts." These were evidently the very last and least of the many smokehouses, springhouses, corn-cribs, and the like, which made up the legion appendages so necessary to early colonial living.

One might say of Mount Vernon that it was the first house to be built in America stemming in inspiration from an already built Scottish mansion. It is intensely interesting that Virginia gentlemen—many of them from well-known English landed families with huge country houses—should go to Scotland to find architectural stimulation. If one can rely on old documents, it appears that Balveny House, Banffshire, loomed large in the picture when Mount Vernon was designed. Certainly the mock rustication of grooved wood, laid off in blocks in place of stone, suggests Balveny House. In 1757, alterations took place at Mount Vernon. The house was given another story, and a dormered attic. Later a pediment was added, with a porthole window, and the frontage was increased to nine windows across.

The finest feature at Mount Vernon is the beautiful Palladian window at either end of the main block. No finer window exists, in detail of keystoned center and broken pediments over the wing windows.

John Ariss, gentleman architect out of England, had, apparently,

*Gaunt Hill, County Galway. Prototype of Virginia Farmhouse,
with Palladian Detail.*

a great fondness for the dignified Scottish ducal seat, built in the Palladian style.

Mount Airy, Richmond County, derives almost directly from Haddo House, Aberdeenshire. Main house oblong. Curved demilunes and two-story wings. Drum House appears in the Virginia scene as Blandfield, Essex County. Not stone, however, but brick, pointed with white.

Two houses built in Virginia in the 1700's that quicken my pulse, that really lead me "far off and away by the hand," are Rosewell, in Gloucester County, and Elmwood, Essex County. Both houses are derelict. Rosewell was burnt out, gutted, in 1916. Elmwood decays in splendor, slowly, falling gradually to ruin. Both houses have, in their wretched state, more panache than any others in the country. Or so it seems to me. Often, old houses that are lived in and well preserved—Chatham, Stafford County, for example—and have every possible advantage to give style to the proceedings, fall flat on acquaintance. No allure seems to surround the house. It is just well-tailored stone, brick, and plaster. Not so with Rosewell and Elmwood. Both fairly throb, even depressed as the houses stand now, with great doings that have happened behind their walls. Terrible sorrows. Wild disappointments leading to murder. Extravagant happiness that has sprayed the walls with pure gold. Yes, all these things have happened in both houses.

Rosewell was built in the high central block style. There are three stories above a deep basement. John Prince, who signed the elevations, was the architect. Little is known of him, but he was a man of immense taste, surely, for the distinction of mass and detail at Rosewell arrests the eye. Everything about the riven walls of Rosewell is big, smashing in scale, and elegant in conception. If I were offered any house in America tomorrow, to reconstruct and live in, it would unhesitatingly be Rosewell.

Elmwood is tremendous in frontage. Eleven tall windows, widely spaced, lend sweep to the oblong, which stands two stories and a high basement. Four great arched chimneys at one time flanked the pediment. In William Adam's *Vitruvius Scoticus*, he shows the elevations for a "Mansion of Alexander Murray of Broughton, in Galloway, Scotland." It is very evident that John Ariss, the architect of Elmwood, found inspiration in this Scottish house. The brickwork is exceptionally fine, and has withstood the battling elements in an amazing manner. It is within, not without, that the years of neglect show ruin. The drawing room has Palladian detail of very high order. Great scrolls over doors, windows, and chimney-breast form broken pediments, supported by fluted Doric pilasters. This room was originally painted hyacinth blue, white, and silver. Now a rime of ancient dust covers all in a transparent veil of gray. In an upstairs bedroom hangs a long-skirted riding habit, such as women wore in 1850. A green glove lies on a chair. A comb on a table still harbors a few long brown hairs. A low-crowned riding hat with torn veil hugs the baseboard. All this lay untouched through the years, because a woman from the North had to flee in haste after her morning ride, to a gunboat lying in the Rappahannock. The gunboat bore Miss Stevens to Castle Point near Hoboken. She never again returned to Elmwood.

Until three years ago, Poplar Forest, a few miles from Lynchburg, Virginia, was owned by Mr. Hutter. One day his son Christian Hutter drove me from Charlottesville to Poplar Forest to show me the house. A "retreat in a poplar forest" it is, to the hilt. When Thomas Jefferson and his family lived there in its full flower, it was as near Utopia as will ever be seen in this world, according to his letters to his wife when he was forced to be in Washington. The circular room in the center corresponds to the rotunda room at Villa Capra or Malcontenta. Sitting in the middle of this room on a hot summer day, one could feel a *courant de l'air* from the north, south, east, and west porticos. The house is completely deceiving as to its size. From the entrance drive it looks almost small, smaller than Monticello. It is as large, and far more spacious. The series of rooms for dining, and those for kitchens and airy bedrooms in the high-ceilinged basement are wonderfully pleasant. Mr. Hutter told me that a traveling bag of oxhide had been found, fully packed for a night's visit, stuffed under the eaves in the attic at Poplar Forest, very evidently hidden with care. A silk nightshirt, the silk from his own looms, was one of the articles that had been carefully packed by Jefferson. Some time after I had visited Poplar Forest, I was telling a friend in Newmarket, Virginia, about the house. He said, "The food at Poplar Forest was considered the best in Virginia. Let me show you a menu from a birthday dinner at Poplar Forest. My great-great-grandfather ate himself into a coma at Jefferson's table."

I present the menu. The year is 1787.

First Course	Second Course
Tender ducks (wild and tame)	Partridge, crust potatoes
Boiled neck of mutton, currant sauce	Sweetbreads, sour cream
Venison pasty	Collared pig, claret puff
Ox-tails in mustard	Fricassee of eggs
Roast loin of veal	Scalded crabs, tart sauce
Mushrooms creamed	Pigeons, greens
Plum pudding	Root salad

Black and red cherry tart
Honey cream

The result of this dinner, even if one only sampled each dish, would be the hospital, I should think.

In Georgetown and Alexandria, Virginia, there are extremely beautiful and representative houses of the Georgian period in American Colonial architecture. All are influenced to greater or lesser degree by the Palladian style. For Sir Christopher Wren first built the type of house that appeared in Virginia as Byrd's Westover, and the Governor's Palace at Williamsburg. Tudor Place in Georgetown is more nearly the Palladian idea in plan than any other there, the semicircular portico lending a lovely lightness to the garden front.

In Alexandria, the same Georgian atmosphere, as against very little of the Palladian, prevails. The Carlyle House built by a Scotsman from Dumfries has the most Palladian air. This house is built of the constantly used "Georgian" red brick, with white stone trim, rusticated. There is a three-story central cube, five windows across, with detached two-story dependencies. The Blue Room in the Carlyle House has the Palladian quality of powerful elegance. The scroll and pineapple finials in broken pediments over the doors are very handsome. A wealth of Palladian detail in doorways, window pediments, and carved finials is everywhere evident in both Alexandria and Georgetown.

And so the Virginia houses drowse behind their porticos. In Natchez, Mississippi, there is an embarrassment of riches as far as fine houses are concerned. The most Palladian in style is Monteigne. Built later than most of the galleried houses of Natchez, about 1840, it nevertheless embodies many of Palladio's country pavilion details. The roof sloping to a squared-off "widow's walk" might easily support a dome or rotunda. The house is a cube of pale rose brick. The impact of almost black shutters and a superb Ionic portico, white as alabaster against the brick, is exciting. The high-arched entrance door of Monteigne is copied from Palladian drawings.

In Tennessee there is great grandeur in architecture. Much of it derives from Palladian style. We have this vista splendidly opened before us in a book called *Grandeur in Tennessee* by Gifford Cochran and F. Burrall Hoffman. I will not dwell on these houses, except to pick out three that I am particularly fond of.

Rattle and Snap is one. A more engaging name for a house I have never heard. And a mighty handsome affair it is. A curiously designed portico, full of style, has eight Corinthian columns, fluted, and flat, Corinthian-capped pilasters flush with the corners of the house. Rattle and Snap was built by George Polk in 1845.

Severely handsome is the Major Franklin house, in Leadvale, Jefferson County. This four-square cube has a stark, triumphant air of standing for no nonsense from man or the elements. Five flat pilasters, molding-capped, divide each side of the house into ascending panels in a curiously charming way. The house is brick. The pilasters are stucco, whitewashed. Date of building is unknown.

Cragfont has terrific style: whitewashed brick with porthole windows, as a Palladian touch, though it is an early Virginia farmhouse type. These Tennessee houses combine the classical idea with pioneer forthrightness in a most satisfying manner.

There is a strange resemblance between the immortal Gibbes house in Charleston, South Carolina, and Dundas House, Nassau. Perhaps it is not so much architectural resemblance—though many details are similar —as it is affinity of the spirit. Both houses have led charmed lives, yet today there is a look of the raised chin, the proud but wary eye, the detachment from wars, riots, pillage, mankind in all his phases, even time itself, in the calm brow of each house.

The Gibbes house suffered a very hail of bombardment in 1776 and 1861. But not a shot fell closer than an areaway. Dundas House was the center of race-riots in 1800, and twice since has been set on fire, but quickly restored. That is one reason the pale blue paint seems so fresh on its walls today.

GARDEN PORTICO AT OAK HILL. DESIGNED BY THOMAS JEFFERSON
FOR JAMES MONROE.

OLD WARD MANSION, CHARLESTON, SOUTH CAROLINA.
PURE PALLADIAN PORTICO.

The Gibbes house is raised, as is Dundas, on a rusticated stone basement, one story from street level. A tremendously effective double staircase ascends straight up from the sidewalk for ten steps, then turns at right angles and rises to the wide balcony in front of the superbly pedimented doorway. Many will call this house Adam–Georgian, but to me it seems far more related to the Palladian villas along the Brenta and in the hills near Padova. Certainly the sweeping pediment supported by console brackets and indented by an oval porthole window, rusticated and terminated by a flange keystone, is in the true Palladian taste.

In Charleston is another house that takes the frosted cake for sheer *brio*. It is called the Ward Mansion. Dingy in color, lacking paint for no one can remember how many years (indeed, I feel the house never had a lick of paint), it still has the grand air as few other houses have, anywhere. The soaring portico is unique, for it is in effect more like that of the Villa Malcontenta at Brenta than any other in America today. This is largely because the terrace of the portico is set fifteen feet above the street on massive stone arches. A wooden banister, rather spindly, lines the curving steps and the terrace between the columns. Bedraggled, grimed from the near-by railroad smoke, neglected to a point of disaster, the house rises among warehouses and garages like an imperial prisoner among slaves in the marketplace. Conceived in the grand manner, not even filthy lace curtains blowing from an open window can blur the outline or harm the stature of the façade.

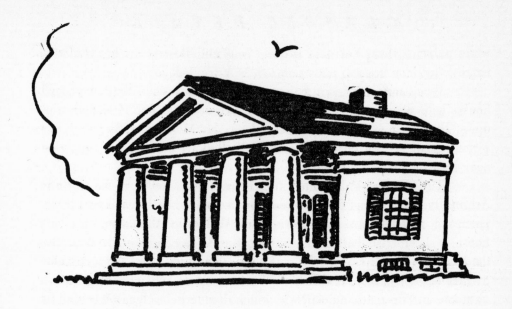

CLASSIC DETAIL
NORTH OF THE
MASON-DIXON LINE

In cities, towns, villages, and the wide countryside of nearly every state in the Union, houses showing Palladian and late Georgian influence crowd the picture. A great deal of this detail is unimportant, some definitely bad, but there it is. The Greek Revival and the plain, square pilastered houses with a screaming eagle launching forth from the pediment are known as Federal Architecture. Many people have told me they thought the White House in Washington was Federal. It is not, of course. Palladian it is, taken from plates in *Vitruvius Britannicus* and Gibbs' *Book of Architecture*. This was before fire destroyed the original building.

New England is exceedingly proud of her Georgian architecture, which New Englanders keep in the very shining pink of condition. Fresh white paint is always evident in New England. Boston has her diffident, narrow Bulfinch houses, putty colored, bow fronted.

Woodstock, Vermont, has at least thirty spacious white clapboard houses with pedimented fronts, without columns, with fine Palladian windows. The Green at Woodstock is a sight to see. Montpelier, Vermont, has a number of stately porticoed houses, both stone and marble, quarried near by.

The one real Palladian house, from start to finish, in the North is Ashintully, a sweeping, fifty-two-room white stucco house rearing its three-porticoed façade above the Tyringham Valley in Massachusetts. This house is sheer Irish Palladian. It has a Gaelic name as well: Ashintully, the House on the Hill. The long building is two rooms deep and a corridor divides the house from end to end. White it stands, and gleaming, in sun or moon, and dramatic no end, with black thunderheads massed behind its widow's walk and lashing rain half obliterating the massive columns. The fifty-foot dining room is the finest room in the house with beautifully carved cornice and fireplace detail. Ashintully is owned by John McLennan.

Reflected in a primula-fringed lake at Syosset, Long Island, stands a long white house of the pavilion style, which I consider one of the finest, anywhere. Little Ipswich, it is called. Mrs. Chalmers Wood is the owner and it was designed by Mrs. Wood and William Adams Delano. One time when Mrs. Wood was traveling in England she passed the gatelodge to Kimbolton Castle in Huntingdonshire. While Kimbolton is a vast impressive building designed by Sir John Vanbrugh, the gatelodge is said to be by Robert Adam. Most surely his fluid, lightly balanced touch is evident. At Little Ipswich, Mrs. Wood has substituted the drive-through arch of the Kimbolton gatelodge for a circular entrance hall. A beautifully proportioned dome surmounts a small pediment. A gilded swan, almost the insignia of the house, surmounts the dome. The house is built around three sides of a stone-paved court. Wide steps lead down to a lawn that slopes greenly to the water's edge. There are many enchanting moments in this house. Indigo and white brocade curtains hang in the white dining room. Huge paintings, showing two aspects of an eighteenth century hunt, glow upon one wall in the long drawing room. Swans being favorite with Mrs. Wood, I slept in a bed with small gilt swans about to take off from the four posts. Outdoors there is always green in sight, for in the drearest winter the ivy gardens all about the house glow like green enamel. This is a most personal house. Everywhere one sees great taste.

In 1936, I was in Udaipur in the early autumn when the most exciting event in this teeming old city (called "city of princes and prince of cities") was the return of the Maharajah's huntsmen with young eagles and falcons, some destined to be trained for the sport of falconry and some to decorate the ornate aviary attached to the Maharajah's palace.

Huge pomegranate trees are placed in the aviaries, for Himalayan birds of all kinds are monstrously fond of the brilliant juicy fruit. I witnessed a veritable "Rape of the Pomegranates" by these hungry birds. There and then I resolved to paint this vivid scene on a ceiling some day. Some day, yes. But where? So few houses in America offer an opportunity of this magnitude to a painter. In Europe I have painted a dozen or more great ceilings in the Italian *bravura* manner, but even in Europe, today, the chances for decoration such as described are few and far between.

Suddenly, like all good things in my life, a chance conversation with a friend from California brought this dream of painting a ceiling of falcons and pomegranates instantly into focus. In the house of Richard Hanna, in Burlingame, California, it is now an accomplished fact, and most surely the most exciting decoration I have ever painted. In a magnificently proportioned room of sweeping length and height, lighted by five tall, wide windows, over seventy eagles and falcons found in the Himalayas and the Vale of Kashmir rip and tear pomegranates to shreds. The design keeps its place, however, so that the finished room is as restful as a glade in the Gardens of Srinagar. Brocade curtains, as fluid as waterfalls and deep emerald in color, cascade from cornice to dark sepia floor. Furniture from the Venice of Longhi and Guardi, in gray-white and gilt, mellows the room. In this room are the three things I find most important to live with: sweeping scale, great elegance, unbridled comfort.

A room in a New York house which I always like to enter is decorated in gray, soft ivory-beige, and many tones of white: the drawing room of Mrs. Thomas Kelly. The room is high, the wall spaces deep, and only important pictures appear. A full-length portrait of General, Count Rochambeau, by Geille, gives a note of singing color to the room, for he wears a uniform of rich blue and scarlet, laced in gold. Touches of dark green leaves give accent to the muted color in upholstery. It is a room expressing the finest taste of the eighteenth century, for the furniture is notable of its epoch. Exquisitely French in feeling, this room would fit perfectly into an English house or an Italian house or an Irish house.

Taste, and knowledge of how to wield it, is the great thing. The old orders change. A great deal of the new must be accepted with as good grace as possible by the die-hards. But as long as the beautiful architecture of the world survives, architecture which has magnificently stood the test of changing tastes, I feel we have great treasure. Palladio knew he was going to build houses for many changing generations to live in when he measured Vitruvian monuments in Rome as a young man. Young men studying architecture still measure Roman monuments; many are the same monuments Palladio saw. If anything in this world is lasting, given any kind of chance, it is architecture.

One of the greatest reasons that the Palladian pavilion style of house has been so deservedly popular with all types of persons down the years is its size. Since the colonists walked out of smoke-filled log cabins into more roomy quarters, with fireplaces that drew, and small-paned casement windows that opened, the small or medium-size house with all rooms on one floor has been much admired. If one wants a house with high rooms and large windows, rooms with elegance in which to display antique treasures, the Palladian pavilion is the ticket. No house could be more comfortable or splendid in detail than Stratford. No house has higher ceilings or more charmingly arranged rooms than Little Ipswich. Leeton Forest is easy to run and satisfies all creature comforts. All three are Palladian pavilions.

THE END

Author's Note

A great many of the Italian, the Irish, and the English houses, gardens and interiors, mentioned in the preceding pages, even a few in Virginia such as the Governor's palace at Williamsburg, have been illustrated in the magazine, *English Country Life*, over a period of the last ten years. Bound copies of this magazine are available in most large public libraries.

APPENDIX

APPENDIX

The following are various houses in the American scene where architectural importance is gained by complete or partial Palladian influence.

Rose Hill, *Port Tobacco, Maryland*
A tall old house of rose brick, once whitewashed. Five cube and oblong units strung together give the house character. Four immensely high chimneys spring from the gable ends of the central block. The boxwood garden, planted in widely curving crescents, was laid out in 1731. The bushes are now ten feet high and of a remarkable thickness of leaf.

Mount Pleasant, *Maryland*
A white house particularly distinguished by its pedimented entrance door and the richly carved cornices and architraves in the first-floor rooms. The box gardens are noteworthy and very old.

Gore Place, *Waltham, Massachusetts*
A fine example of Georgian brick country mansion in the rather formal style. Five units comprise the whole: a three-story central block, and two one-story galleries linking pavilion wings of one story and a half. The pavilions have large Palladian windows beneath a pediment.

Hope, *near Easton, Maryland*
The one surviving house of three built about 1790 by the brothers Starr. Faith and Charity have both been burned. The interior woodwork at Hope is considered as fine in detail as any other in Maryland.

Carrollton Manor, *Frederick County, Maryland*
After spending seventeen years abroad, Charles Carroll (1737–1832) returned to Annapolis to take possession of the tract of ten thousand acres of land presented to him by his father. He forthwith built a long-frontaged brick house, which he called Carrollton Manor. A house noted for its lavish hospitality, the rooms at Carrollton are large and spaciously planned for huge entertainments. White columns and window trim gleam against the soft texture of dark red brick.

APPENDIX

MANTUA, *Northumberland County, Virginia*
This brick house has a distinctly Palladian air, a sense of strength and considered massivity, because of the great scaled portico rising on columns of the Doric order for three stories. This portico forms a room in itself. The builder of Mantua was James Smith, an Irishman from the County of Derry. The date of this house is about 1770.

BOSCOBEL MANOR, *Peekskill, New York State*
The façade of Boscobel is copied from one of Palladio's finest houses, Villa Pisani at Montagnana. A serene Italianate air prevails here; even the name derives from *bosco bello,* "fair woods." A detail seldom seen is the carved swags of drapery hanging from the pediment cornice of the upper cut-under porch. The arched and pillared hall is very fine, with its sweeping stairway branching off from a landing to right and left. Staats Dyckman built the house in 1792.

SAMSONDALE, *Garnersville, New York State*
A house of splendid proportions, said to be copied from the Bishop's Palace at Winchester, England. English workmen were brought over to this Hudson River estate of Theodore Peck to build the house, for the heavy stuccoing of stone was not understood in America at the beginning of the nineteenth century. Samsondale commands the crest of a hill with a far-flung view of the Hudson River.

MOUNT PLEASANT, *Fairmount Park, Philadelphia*
In 1761, Mount Pleasant was built by John Macpherson, who was known as the most lavish dispenser of money in the entire state of Pennsylvania. Breasting a rise of ground, almost a bluff, above the lordly amber Schuylkill, this perfectly proportioned house of moderate size is so richly designed and so simple and direct in considered detail and careful placing of doors, windows, cornice, dormers, and pediment that its legion admirers place it very high on the roster of existing houses of pure Palladian influence.

Three dominant features make Mount Pleasant noteworthy in architectural design: First, the center panel of the façade, supporting a deeply incised and corniced pediment at roof level, is pierced by a remarkably designed doorway, which appears to support on the apex of its pediment a Palladian window comparable to the splendid ones at Mount Vernon.

Second, the coins and stringpiece dividing the first story from the second story are old plum-colored brick, pointing up the whitewashed stucco that covers the stone walls. This impact of dark color against the luminous white imparts singular style to the whole structure. Third, there are two brick chimneys so skillfully placed that they have the same relation to the four-square block of the house as those at Stratford. A keystoned arch pierces each side of the massive brickwork of the chimneys, giving lightness and the effect of twin gazebos.

Woodford, *Fairmount Park, Philadelphia*

This symmetrical house was first built as a pavilion with decided Palladian overtones. Later a second story was added. A wide white wooden cornice accents the place where the joining of pale wheat-colored brick was added. Memorable features of Woodford, which was built in 1756, are the elegantly proportioned entrance door supporting a Palladian window, and the balustrade of the "widow's walk," in the Chinese taste.

Llangollen, *Upperville, Virginia*

The long main block with flanking wings that one sees at Llangollen is much older than the handsome columned portico. This was erected—some say by Thomas Jefferson—about 1790. A federal eagle is carved in high relief in the center of the pediment. Great ragged boxbushes drift about the portico, giving the house a romantic quality.

The Jumel Mansion, *Harlem Heights (Mount Morris), New York State*

In 1750, Colonel Morris, a Royalist of rigid convictions, built a house on a rise of ground which he called Mount Morris. Later when Stephen Jumel bought the house and installed the notorious woman known as Madame Jumel within its walls, the place took its name from her. The most noteworthy feature of the house is the superb octagonal drawing room, of rousing dimensions. The dining room has some fine carving around the fireplace and over the doors.

Buxton Hill, *Williamstown, Massachusetts*

Situated upon a hill, this big square house is extremely impressive. The placing of the windows in the walls is very much in the Irish Palladian manner. Tall, well-placed for scale, the façade of Buxton is architecturally early Georgian with Palladian detail.

APPENDIX

HAIL AND FAREWELL, *near Covington, Kentucky*

Hail and Farewell in the grassy meadowlands of Kentucky is very like in appearance Rattle and Snap, in Tennessee. Four square, the house has flat pilasters dividing the seven windows across the front. A richly carved pediment embraces a porthole window with a band of carved bay leaves as a border. The whole house has consummate style.

EDGEHILL, *near Keswick, Virginia*

Edgehill was built by Thomas Jefferson for his daughter Martha. The house suffered a disastrous fire early in the nineteenth century, and when alterations were made, the pavilion character of the original was altered. Today the house has the grand air because of the perfection of proportion seen in all the windows, doors, and chimneys. A white pillared porch is reached by a flight of extremely graceful steps. A pediment, but no portico, crosses the main block. In effect, though it is not actually a copy, Edgehill reminds one of Monticello. Jefferson seldom varied his main theme.

THE RYNNE HOUSE, *near the Hudson River, New York State*

On a lonely back road near the river stands a really surprising fawn-colored brick house. Everything about this commanding structure is grand and spreading in scale. Four stories high, at least 100 feet across the frontage, the house is built of hand-made bricks nearly as large as dressed stone usually is. Tall pedimented windows and a very handsome fan-lighted doorway add great elegance to the façade. Four massive chimneys lend character to the gable ends. In every respect this house has tremendous stature. In my opinion, it is the finest Georgian house in the state, with outstanding Palladian detail.

BIBLIOGRAPHY

BIBLIOGRAPHY

Over a period of twenty years or more, I have had access to many diaries, letters, and notes written by persons of the sixteenth, seventeenth, eighteenth, and nineteenth centuries. Many are in the possession of my own family. Others have been shown me by friends, from private collections, or by persons who were eager to help me compile this book on the life of Andrea Palladio. To all of them I extend my grateful thanks.

The following reference books have been consulted:

ADAM, WILLIAM. *Vitruvius Scoticus*. Edinburgh: 1726.

BARRINGTON, SIR J. *Beauchamp Bagenal, Eccentric Extraordinary*. Dublin: 1833.

BELLI, RANERI. *Caterina Cornaro di Villa a Castello*. Venezia: 1645.

BENNASSUTI, GIUSEPPE. *Teatro Olimpico di Vicenza*. Verona: 1824.

BERTI, GIUSEPPE. *Sul Monumento a Palladio*. Lonigo: 1818.

BLAKE, S. *The Francini in Ireland*. Waterford: 1821.

BOITO, CAMILLO. *Terzo Centinario di Andrea Palladio*. Vicenza: 1880.

BOLTON, T. *Architecture of Robert and James Adam*. London: 1785.

CALIARI, PIETRO. *Paolo Veronese, sua Vita e sua Opera*. Rome: 1888.

CAMPBELL, COLIN. *Vitruvius Britannicus*. London: 1717–25.

CHAMBERS, SIR WILLIAM. *Treatise of Civil Architecture*. London: 1759.

CHIPPENDALE, THOMAS. *The Gentleman and Cabinet Makers' Director*. London: 1754.

CICOGNARA, LEOPOLDO. *Dell' Architettura in Vicenza*. Padova: 1845.

———. *Elogio di A. Palladio*. Venezia: 1830.

CLARK, MRS. M., EDITOR. *Gleanings from an Irish Gentleman's Portfolio*. Dublin: 1895.

Conversazione del Contessa Ricaffo della Lanzia. Turin: 1728.

Country Life Magazine. London: Dec. 19, 1936; Nov. 25, 1939; Dec. 15, 1944; Apr. 18, 1947.

Country Life Magazine. "Henry Keen and John Sanderson in Dublin." London: May 11, 1945.

DARANNI, FILIPPO. *Vita de Capitano* [Colleoni]. Bologna: 1676.

DELANY, MARY GRANVILLE. *Correspondence and Flittings*. Dublin: 1760.

DE MIKLOS, E. *Hungaria, ā Baroque í Rococo*. Budapest: 1934.

Diaries from the Noble House of Schönberg of Meissen, 1754.

DOLFI, LORENZO. *Della Rotonda*. Rome: 1820.

DORSEY, STEPHEN, AND OTHERS. *Alexandria Houses, 1750–1830.*

————. *Georgetown Houses of the Federal Period, 1780–1830.* Washington, D.C.: 1944.

EDGEWORTH, MARIA. *Mrs. Middleton, Gossip*. Dublin: 1797.

EDWIN, RALPH. *Edwin's Pills to Purge Melancholy*. Dublin: 1788.

FERRARI, LUIGI. *Palladio e Venezia a di Brenta*. Venezia: 1860.

FLETCHER, B. *Palladio, His Life and Works*. London: 1902.

GAUTHIER, MAXIMILIEN. *Palladio, L'Art Vivant*. Paris: 1926.

Georgian Society Records. Vols. III, IV, V. Dublin: 1913.

GIGI, LUIGI. *Nobile Antonio Barbaro*. Genoa: 1799.

GUALDO, PAOLO. *Vita di Andrea Palladio*. Venice: 1749.

HARDY, F. *Memoirs of the Earl of Charlemont*. Dublin: 1810.

HÉNARD, ROBERT. *La Villa Emo*. Paris: 1911.

Hibernian Magazine. Dublin: 1777.

JEFFERSON, THOMAS. *Autobiography*. Virginia (Monticello): 1821.

————. *Memoranda on Travel*. Collection of Hutter Family of Poplar Forest, Virginia.

————. *Notes on Virginia*. Paris: 1782.

JONES, INIGO. *Architecture of A. Palladio in Four Volumes*. London: 1640.

LANGLEY, BATTY. *Treasury of Designs*. London: 1759.

LEASK–COLLINSON–BUTLER. *Thomas Cooley, Dublin Architect*. Dublin: 1932.

LEONI, GIOVANNI. *A. Palladio: Dell' Architettura*. London: 1765.

LITTLE, BRYAN. *Building of Bath.* London: 1947.

LOUKOMSKI, GEORGES. *Andrea Palladio.* Paris: 1924.

———. *Les Palais et les Villas d'Andrea Palladio.* Paris: 1923.

———. *Palladio un Architette Classico o Barocco.* Vicenza: 1910.

LUCCELO, CARLO. *Doge Grimani.* Venezia: 1670.

MAUREL, ANTON. *Petites Villes près Padua.* Paris: 1920.

MAXWELL, CONSTANTIA. *Dublin Under the Georges.* Dublin: 1946.

MONCK, MRS. *Virginia Papers.* Fredericksburg: 1802.

MOON, PAUL. *William Kent: Furniture and Architecture.* Plymouth: 1831.

MORSOLIN, L. *Giangorgio Trissino, Memorie.* Vicenza: 1878.

PALLADIO, ANDREA. *I Quattro Libri dell' Architettura.* Venezia: 1570.

———. *L'Anticchita di Roma, Miravigliose di Roma.* Rome: 1575.

SCORO, D. *Villa della Brenta. Teatro Olimpico a Palazzi di A. Palladio.* Venezia: 1676.

SCRIBBEN, F. *London Squares.* London: 1811.

SITWELL, SACHEVERELL. *British Architects and Craftsmen.* London: 1946.

UNIVERSITY OF VIRGINIA FOLIO. *Thomas Jefferson.* Charlottesville: 1920.

Vasari Lives. London: 1852.

VON CHLEDOWSKI, CASIMIR. *Die Menschen des Barock.* Munich: 1919.

VON KLARWILL, VICTOR, AND DE CHARY, PAULINE. *The Fugger News-Letters.* New York: 1925.

WATERMAN, THOMAS. *The Mansions of Virginia.* North Carolina: 1945.

WHISTLER, LAURENCE. *Sir John Vanbrugh.* London: 1938.

WHITE, W. H. *The Burlington–Devonshire Collection of Drawings.* London: 1892.

WOOLF, VIRGINIA, EDITOR. "Laetitia Pilkington, Memoirs of an Adventuress," in *The Common Reader.* London: 1925.

ZORZI, GIANGIORGIO. *La Véritable Origine de Palladio* (en Italien). Paris: 1924.

INDEX

INDEX

INDEX

THIS VOLUME IS SET IN TWELVE-POINT LINO-
TYPE BODONI BOOK. THE INITIAL LETTERS ARE
BERNHARD MODERN ROMAN, DESIGNED BY LU-
CIAN BERNHARD. THE PAPER, WHICH WAS SUP-
PLIED BY PERKINS AND SQUIER, IS GLATFELTER
LAID STOCK WITH TITANIUM. THE CLOTH FOR THE
BINDING IS CULVER SCOTCH LINEN. THE TYPOG-
RAPHY IS BY FLORA FINN AND THE BOOK WAS
PRINTED AND BOUND IN THE UNITED STATES BY
AMERICAN BOOK—STRATFORD PRESS, NEW YORK.

'RUSSBOROUGH'
COUNTY WICKLOW.